The Dilemmas of
American Conservatism

The Dilemmas of American Conservatism

★ ★ ★

Edited by
Kenneth L. Deutsch
and Ethan Fishman

★ ★ ★

THE UNIVERSITY PRESS OF KENTUCKY

Copyright © 2010 by The University Press of Kentucky

Scholarly publisher for the Commonwealth,
serving Bellarmine University, Berea College, Centre College of Kentucky,
Eastern Kentucky University, The Filson Historical Society, Georgetown
College, Kentucky Historical Society, Kentucky State University,
Morehead State University, Murray State University, Northern Kentucky
University, Transylvania University, University of Kentucky, University of
Louisville, and Western Kentucky University.
All rights reserved.

Editorial and Sales Offices: The University Press of Kentucky
663 South Limestone Street, Lexington, Kentucky 40508-4008
www.kentuckypress.com

14 13 12 11 10   5 4 3 2 1

Library of Congress Cataloging-in-Publication Data

The dilemmas of American conservatism / edited by Kenneth L. Deutsch and
Ethan Fishman.
    p. cm.
  Includes bibliographical references and index.
  ISBN 978-0-8131-2596-1 (hardcover : alk. paper)
  1. Conservatism—United States. 2. Conservatism—United States—Philosophy.
3. United States—Politics and government. I. Deutsch, Kenneth L. II. Fishman,
Ethan M.
  JC573.2.U6D55 2010
  320.520973—dc22   2010020649

This book is printed on acid-free recycled paper meeting
the requirements of the American National Standard
for Permanence in Paper for Printed Library Materials.

Manufactured in the United States of America.

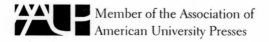 Member of the Association of
American University Presses

Contents

Preface

Since the Second World War, there has appeared an extraordinary renaissance in American conservative political philosophy and public discourse. Such putative conservative thinkers of the first rank include John H. Hallowell, Eric Voegelin, Leo Strauss, Richard Weaver, Robert Nisbet, John Courtney Murray, Russell Kirk, F. A. Hayek, and Willmoore Kendall. Whether or not these philosophers would accept the title "conservative," each of them has made a profound contribution to the fundamental themes of conservative dialogue: virtue, liberty, the rule of law, the parameters of state power, and the roles education and religion should play in the creation of public order and national purpose. We offer a comprehensive analysis of their diverse approaches to these themes in order to both illuminate the creative intellectual tension that their thought produces and reveal the most serious political dilemmas that derive from their philosophical differences.

We wish to thank Stephen Wrinn and his outstanding staff at the University Press of Kentucky for all their help in developing this project. We also wish to thank our copy editor, Linda Lotz, for her consummate professionalism. Finally, we acknowledge the willingness of the contributors to this volume to work within our framework.

We dedicate this volume to our intellectual mentors John H. Hallowell (Fishman) and William C. Havard (Deutsch) and to our own students.

Introduction

ETHAN FISHMAN AND KENNETH L. DEUTSCH

This volume explores the thought of those intellectuals commonly credited with having the greatest philosophical influence on the resurgence of American conservatism during the second half of the twentieth century, when the movement emerged from the shadow of the New Deal and began reasserting its power over the formulation and execution of public policy in the United States. The nine thinkers examined are John H. Hallowell, Eric Voegelin, Leo Strauss, Richard Weaver, Robert Nisbet, John Courtney Murray, Russell Kirk, F. A. Hayek, and Willmoore Kendall. Although Voegelin, Strauss, and Hayek were not born in the United States, their ideas had at least as much impact here as in their native countries.

In general terms, the meaning of conservatism is straightforward. It refers to the reality of a flawed humanity and a hierarchy in which human abilities are unequally distributed. It teaches that political positions should be prudently considered in the context of historical precedent. It opposes radical ideologies based solely on perfectionist ideals and is skeptical of a rationalist politics of abstract theoretical principles that produces fanaticism and an all-or-nothing approach to public life. The institutions of society—political, religious, educational, family, and so forth—are understood to develop slowly with much trial and error and must be viewed as containing considerable wisdom, especially when defending ordered liberty, the rule of law, and rewards based on merit.

As this volume demonstrates, however, in the United States conservatism is a much more complicated concept beset by several contradictions. Supreme Court Justice Samuel Alito revealed the core of the problem when, in his application for a position in the Reagan administration, he claimed that he believed very strongly in limited government, federalism, free enterprise, the supremacy of the elected branches of government, the need for a strong defense and effective law enforcement, and the legitimacy of a governmental role in protecting traditional values. The Alito statement reveals at least two basic tensions in American conservatism — namely, limited government versus government protection of traditional values, and free enterprise versus the supremacy of the elected branches of government.

A battle is being waged in the United States for the soul of conservatism. Its combatants are the three major variants of the contemporary American conservative movement: traditional conservatism, laissez-faire conservatism, and neoconservatism.

Traditional Conservatism

This variant of conservatism, based on the political philosophies of Aristotle and Edmund Burke, is concerned with the hyperindividualism regnant in American culture. To traditionalists, the American view of freedom as morally self-fulfilling is a distorted and burdensome freedom. They criticize American society for failing to recognize the fragile bonds of social order and for neglecting to defend the authority of ancestral institutions. Traditional conservatives also emphasize the role of the rule of law in securing liberty and the role of one's betters in limiting individual desires and in fostering by example rational choices. In effect, liberty and the individual must be understood in a social context, finding meaning through social relations with others. Ultimately, the traditional conservative argues with Russell Kirk that there exists a transcendent moral order, manifested in certain natural laws, to which the ways of society ought to conform in a prudent manner. We need "ordered liberty." Among the thinkers discussed in this volume, Kirk, John H. Hallowell, and Richard Weaver stand within the ranks of traditional conservatives whose views regarding moral transcendence and natural law are held by only a minority of American conservatives.

Laissez-Faire Conservatism

There are two types of laissez-faire conservatism in the United States: economic liberalism, which applies natural law standards to social issues such as speech, press, sex, and marriage, but not to economics; and libertarianism, which applies laissez-faire across the board to all aspects of human behavior. Economic liberalism is the most popular variant of American conservatism. As a whole, laissez-faire conservatives fear the threat posed by weak and envious people to risk-taking entrepreneurs who seek to produce wealth both for themselves and for society. F. A. Hayek's approach to freedom, for example, takes the view that liberty or freedom begins with a simple dichotomy: liberty versus coercion. These terms are linked together by definition: liberty or freedom is the state in which a person is not subject to coercion by the arbitrary will of another or others. The supreme good emerges for Hayek when there is the absence of external restraints. Social justice or equality is a delusion; they only serve to diminish freedom. A free society is self-adjusting, leading toward greater productivity and public order, and this means inequality. Such a robust view of freedom makes the claim that the freedom to pursue one's* private vices, such as greed, will somehow produce public benefits. Traditional conservatives and laissez-faire conservatives inevitably find themselves in conflict over the issue of amoral capitalism.

Neoconservatism

This variant of American conservatism rose to prominence during the administration of George W. Bush. Best described as a persuasion or a perspective rather than a movement, it represents a reaction against the advocates of the liberal welfare state, radical liberationist values, idealist foreign policies, and affirmative action. As the "godfather" of neoconservatives, Irving Kristol, put it more than thirty years ago, they were "mugged by reality" (the reality of the welfare state and what they perceived to be a weak foreign policy). In positive terms, Kristol claims that patriotism is a natural and healthy sentiment and should be encouraged by both private and public institutions. Precisely because we are a nation of immigrants, this must be a powerful American sentiment. Neoconservatives are suspicious of international organizations that could lead to world government and, they anticipate, world tyranny. For Kristol, a statesman should above all have the ability to distinguish friends from enemies. Barring crisis situations, the United States should always feel obliged to defend, if possible, a democratic nation under attack from nondemocratic forces, external or internal. With power comes responsibilities, whether sought or not, whether welcome or not. Kristol claims that if a country has the kind of power the United States possesses, either it will find opportunities to use it or the world will discover such opportunities for it. Neoconservatives such as Kristol claim to have been influenced by the thought of Leo Strauss. Traditionalists consider the neoconservative perspective to be imprudent. Laissez-faire conservatives view it as a form of militarism.

Fusion or Confusion: The Possibilities of Dialogue

These traditional, laissez-faire, and neoconservative variations express significant differences in their ultimate principles. Can these positions be reconciled? Are they simply emphasizing different aspects of the inchoate status of contemporary conservatism? Can we discern a "true" conservatism worthy of evaluating the present state of American liberal democracy?

William F. Buckley's *National Review* served as a galvanizing force for the American conservative movement during the post–World War II era. Buckley's colleagues at the *Review* included Willmoore Kendall and Frank Meyer. Kendall defies classification as a conservative thinker. Meyer is a conservative fusionist who thinks that the traditional and laissez-faire positions can be reconciled. He maintains that they share common assumptions about the dignity or innate importance of the individual person and the importance of value, virtue, and order. Both positions, he observes, are concerned with the need to place limits on state power; however, they both sometimes fail to recognize that both the rulers and the ruled are subject to the effects of original sin. What Meyer does not recognize is that, given their different ultimate principles, they will collide on whether to emphasize freedom over the need for justice and order in society. Despite his best efforts, the question of whether "statecraft is soulcraft" will not go away.

A more recent effort to unify the diverse variants of American conservatism is offered by the editors of *American Conservatism: An Encyclopedia*. What all conservatives share, the editors argue, is opposition to the emergence in the twentieth century of atomized and deracinated individuals, or "mass men," who lack the support of strong families and communal organizations. Without the political filtering function traditionally performed by these institutions, conservatives such as Robert Nisbet warn, "mass men" become increasingly vulnerable to the direct assault of governments and demagogues seeking their unconditional allegiance. The problem with the editors' unification approach is that other groups, including the decidedly nonconservative counterculture movement of the 1960s and 1970s, also fear the advent of social atomization.

Within the American conservative movement, reactions to the significant contradictions among the traditional, laissez-faire, and neoconservative variants, as well as to the apparent failure of the unifiers, have been mixed. Some conservatives remain curiously indifferent to the contradictions. After recognizing that American conservatism is "a complex, multifaceted phenomenon" for which there probably can be no "single, satisfactory, all-encompassing definition," George Nash, author of the highly regarded and thoroughly researched *The Conservative Intellectual Movement in America,* confesses:

> At some point . . . an insistent reader may still object to my use of the word "conservative." How, it may be asked, can you label someone a conservative when he was "actually" a nineteenth-century liberal? How can you discuss individuals who deny that they are conservatives, or even intellectuals? To these questions one answer, I hope will suffice: I have designated various people as conservative either because they called themselves conservatives or because others (who did call themselves conservatives) regarded them as part of their conservative intellectual movement. I have counted diverse people within the conservative fold because study shows that, existentially, they belonged to the American conservative ranks in the postwar period. Whatever our sense (or their sense) of the propriety of these alignments may be, that was the way it was.[1]

Any list of the most influential American conservative thinkers of the twentieth century must include Voegelin, Strauss, Hayek, and Hallowell. Yet, as Nash suggests, they reacted to the contradictions that beset American conservatism by refusing to affiliate with the movement. Voegelin judged it to be a political ideology supplying superficial answers to profound philosophical questions. Strauss preferred to be known as an academic conservative who sought to foster students' ability to think critically and act responsibly through the careful study of the great books of the great political philosophers. Hayek chose the label "Old Whig" to characterize his defense of individual freedom against policies, supported by liberals as well as conservatives, that he deemed statist. Hallowell proudly called himself a conservative but declined to be linked with the movement because he considered its beliefs to be essentially incoherent.

According to such scholars as Louis Hartz, Arthur Schlesinger Jr., Lionel Trilling, and Clinton Rossiter, the cause of the incoherence identified by Hallowell can be traced to the origins of American colonial history. The conservatism that Aristotle developed in the third century BC and that remained relatively unchanged for millennia in Western history was shaped by a balanced, realistic view of human nature; an emphasis on moral responsibilities to the community, defined by transcendent natural law standards; and respect for custom and tradition. When the Pilgrims first set foot on Plymouth Rock in 1620, however, they introduced a way of life for Americans emphasizing optimism, individualism, and dynamic change that was antithetical to Aristotelian prudence.

How were conservatives supposed to react to the contradictions thrust on them by the New World? They could either rebel against American culture entirely or find a way to graft traditional conservative views onto it. As it turned out, a majority of them chose the latter alternative and devised an indigenous form of conservatism in the United States that sought to combine both pessimism and optimism, community and individualism, tradition and dynamism. The result was that, instead of following Aristotle's lead and applying natural law moderately to all human activities, most American conservatives began limiting moral standards to social issues and leaving business matters to individual initiative — without providing an intellectually satisfying explanation to justify the discrepancy.

The United States has "never had a real conservative tradition," Hartz contends. "One of the enduring secrets of the American character," he writes, is "a capacity to combine rock-ribbed traditionalism with high inventiveness, ancestor worship with ardent optimism. Most critics have seized upon one or the other of these aspects of the American mind, finding it impossible to conceive how both can go together. That is why the insight of Gunnar Myrdal is a very distinguished one when he writes: 'America is . . . conservative. . . . But the principles conserved are liberal and some, indeed, are radical.' Radicalism and conservatism have been twisted entirely out of shape by the liberal flow of American history."[2]

Hartz's thesis that traditional Western conservative views did not play a central role in the development of American culture was challenged by Jesuit theologian John Courtney Murray. For Murray, the inalienable rights celebrated in the Declaration of Independence have their roots in such ancient Christian precepts as the fundamental equality of all human beings and the absolute integrity of the individual person created in the image of God. His views were resisted by liberals, libertarians, and most of the Catholic hierarchy.

The editors of this volume confess to being traditionalists who take the meaning of words seriously and reject moral relativism. When people describe themselves as conservative, we want to know both what they mean by the term and whether their definition makes sense logically and historically. Simply asserting that one is somehow affiliated with conservatism is not enough. And if the adherents of a political belief system find it impossible to agree on a logical and historically accurate definition of what they purport to believe, then we must consider the possibility that their views lack substantive meaning.

There can be no doubt that politicians calling themselves conservative have had a significant impact on American politics. But they have been unable to define and practice their beliefs with a tolerable degree of cohesive logic. Without a consistent set of philosophical principles to replace the traditional natural law standards that American culture distrusts, conservatives have often approached public policy in a haphazard fashion. The administrations of Ronald Reagan and George W. Bush illustrate this disconnectedness all too well. Reagan and Bush claimed to harbor deep suspicions of public indebtedness and centralized government. Yet both administrations proceeded to amass unprecedented national debt and arbitrarily abused executive power—most notably by violating congressional directives in the Iran-Contra affair and by illegally tapping private email and telephone transmissions. Their abuses were not merely a product of hypocrisy but failures of both rational clarity and intellectual probity.

We recognize that, in a society where liberals and most conservatives oppose traditional conservative positions, we will be relegated to the role of gadfly, warning citizens of the dangers of choosing instant gratification over long-term goals, license over liberty, literal equality over equality of opportunity, unregulated economic activity over fair business practices, and blind patriotism over a critical assessment of our country's willingness to pursue its highest ideals. Few Americans will heed these warnings. Fortunately, authentic gadflies have never required large audiences.

We are confident that the ideas of the nine political philosophers examined in this volume will serve as profound resources for rethinking the issue of conservatism in the United States. We have not shied away from staking out a set of concerns we would like readers to consider. But our primary concern is to enlarge the debate about what is worth conserving in American public life. We hope you will join the debate.

Notes

1. George H. Nash, *The Conservative Intellectual Movement in America: Since 1945* (New York: Basic Books, 1979), x, xiv, xv–xvi.

2. Louis Hartz, *The Liberal Tradition in America* (New York: Harcourt, Brace and World, 1955), 57, 50.

Bibliography

Frohnen, Bruce, Jeremy Beer, and Jeffrey O. Nelson, eds. 2006. *American Conservatism: An Encyclopedia*. Wilmington, Del.: ISI Books.

Harbour, William R. 1982. *The Foundations of Conservative Thought: An Anglo American Tradition in Perspective*. Notre Dame, Ind.: University of Notre Dame Press.

Hartz, Louis. 1955. *The Liberal Tradition in America*. New York: Harcourt, Brace and World.

Nash, George H. 1979. *The Conservative Intellectual Movement in America: Since 1945*. New York: Basic Books.

Thorne, Melvin J. 1990. *American Conservative Thought since World War Two*. New York: Greenwood Press.

The Classical Realism of John H. Hallowell

Ethan Fishman

When I entered Duke University as a graduate student forty years ago, my political affiliations were confused. I considered myself a conservative with moderate political views but felt uncomfortable identifying with the advocates of a bellicose foreign policy, supporters of a laissez-faire economic program, and defenders of the Jim Crow status quo in the South, who then dominated the American conservative movement. John H. Hallowell (1913–1991) opened my eyes to a more cautious and thoughtful version of conservatism known as classical realism. Today a similar group of right-wing ideologues continues to portray itself as the authentic voice of conservatism in the United States. Thanks to Hallowell, however, I now possess a developed set of principles that I introduce to my own students to help them distinguish between mainstream American conservatism and its classical Western counterpart.

The classical realism Hallowell offered as an alternative to the conservative American mainstream borrows heavily from the political philosophies of Aristotle, St. Thomas Aquinas, and Edmund Burke. It contains elements of the thought of Plato, St. Augustine, Alexis de Tocqueville, Eric Voegelin, and Reinhold Niebuhr as well. Included in its intellectual design are a distinctive view of human nature; an adherence to the traditional Western theories of natural law and prudence; discussions of the benefits of family life, private property, and religion; and an attempt to balance individual rights with communal responsibilities. Among its aversions are relativism in general and positivism in particular, revolutionary change, ideological thinking, egalitarian democracy, and the realpolitik school of international relations.

At the heart of Hallowell's politics lies the view that all conclusions about government are based on certain assumptions about human nature. "More often than not, this idea of man is implicit rather than explicit," he explained in his seminal work, *The Moral Foundation of Democracy*. "But if not always explicit, it is always fundamental. For what we think government can and ought to do will depend in large part upon what we think about the capacities of men and the purpose of human existence."[1] Hallowell adopted the classical Western position that, alone among living organisms, humans possess the ability to make freely willed decisions, that these decisions have a profound effect on our lives, and that we are responsible for their consequences.

Hallowell often cited the Old and New Testaments to illustrate his realistic assessment of the quality of our freely willed decisions. From Genesis 18:32 he retold the story of Abraham urging God not to destroy the cities of Sodom and Gomorrah and their inhabitants. After some haggling, God finally agrees that if Abraham can discover ten good people in these cities, their destruction will be averted. Even that number proves elusive. And from Romans 7:19 Hallowell repeated Paul's famous lament concerning human frailty: "For the good that I would, I do not; but the evil which I would not, that I do."

Hallowell clearly did not have an optimistic view of human beings. But neither was he a cynic. He embraced instead a more balanced approach by expecting neither too much nor too little from himself and others. "A view of man that regards him as totally depraved is as one-sided and distorted as is the view which regards him as completely well-intentioned," he wrote. "A balanced view of man will emphasize both his propensity to do evil and his capacity to do good; it will not overestimate his motives, but it will not underestimate his potentialities."[2]

To provide the guidance necessary for frequently immoral and irrational people to coexist with an acceptable degree of common decency, Hallowell turned to traditional Western natural law theory. Thinkers such as Aristotle, the Stoics, Cicero, and St. Thomas Aquinas interpreted natural laws to be transcendent moral principles that are accessible to human reason. "The rational creature is subject to Divine providence in the most excellent way, in so far as it partakes of a share of providence, by being provident both for itself and for others," Aquinas wrote. "Wherefore it has a share of the Eternal Reason, whereby it has a natural inclination to its proper act and end: and this participation of the eternal law in the rational creature is called the natural law."[3]

Although these principles apply to all people everywhere and to all aspects of human existence, including government, no person, group, or government has the authority to define them. Their meaning must derive from ongoing communal dialogues. Although Hallowell recognized that fallible people are incapable of fully comprehending infallible natural law concepts such as love, justice, and honor, he insisted that when communities provide a cultural milieu that encourages citizens to come to grips with these concepts, their lives will become more loving, just, and honorable in the process.

Hallowell used the following diagram to illustrate the relationships he perceived among individuals, government, and natural law.[4] The points being made are that natural law transcends individuals and government, and when individuals and government reject natural law, what inevitably results is either chaos (total sovereignty of the individual) or dictatorship (total control by the government).

Figure 1

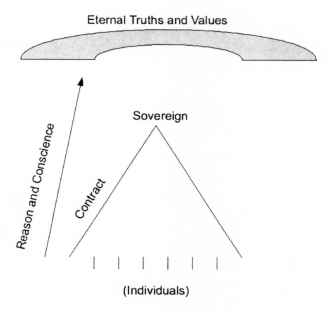

Eternal Truths and Values

Sovereign

Reason and Conscience

Contract

(Individuals)

Natural law is eternal. What about the here and now? Hallowell located the nexus between abstract natural laws, which are transcendent in character, and concrete political issues, which vary from place to place and from time to time, in Aristotle, Aquinas, and Burke's concept of prudence. In Book VI of his *Nicomachean Ethics,* Aristotle explained how theoretical reason and the intellectual virtues or faculties it employs differ from practical reason and the moral faculties. Theoretical reason and the intellectual virtues are used to study subjects such as mathematics and metaphysics, which are learned for their own sake and produce universal truths that cannot be affected by human volition. Practical reason and the moral virtues involve subjects such as political science and economics, which people can influence, are learned for the sake of action, and admit of exceptions. Aristotle described prudence as the master moral virtue because of its power to realize abstract goals through concrete means so that we can do the right thing to the right person at the right time "for the right motive and in the right way."[5] In this fashion, he observed, prudence is able to translate morally preferable ideals into politically feasible laws and policies.

To illustrate the unique ability of prudence to integrate abstract principles and practical experience, Hallowell compared professors of anatomy to skilled surgeons. When we need an operation, he explained, we do not go to a professor of anatomy, who possesses knowledge of where human body parts are located in theory but not where they can be found in a specific patient; who understands the rules for conducting a successful operation but has never performed one. "Surgical practice is, indeed, dependent upon theoretical knowledge," Hallowell wrote, "but it is wider in scope. The surgeon has to apply theoretical knowledge to patients who are suffering from particular diseases or defects and must be able to recognize anatomical abnormalities. The surgeon is engaged not in the theoretical study of the human body but in practice. The knowledge possessed by the surgeon is real knowledge, but it is a knowledge learned less from textbooks than from experience. The surgeon learns by watching more experienced surgeons perform operations and then, in fact, by operating."[6]

Among the leaders in American history that Hallowell rated as prudent were Abraham Lincoln and Franklin Delano Roosevelt. Hallowell generally preferred less government to more. He realized that government officials are usually just as immoral and irrational as the citizens they govern. Nevertheless, he learned from the examples of Lincoln and FDR that unprecedented circumstances often create unprecedented problems that may require increases in political power. To preserve the Union during the Civil War and help citizens cope with the severe economic deprivations of the Great Depression — two of the most serious crises this country has ever confronted — Lincoln and Roosevelt had no choice but to resort to levels of government intervention previously unmatched in our history. Citizens, Lincoln and FDR recognized, should be permitted to rely on as much government as necessary under the circumstances to help them deal with problems they cannot reasonably be expected to solve on their own.

In addition to a balance between good and evil, Hallowell found rooted in human nature the impulses to possess our own property, live with our own families, and worship God. Private property serves as an effective means for both the development and the expression of our individuality, he maintained. Without private property, he added, generosity would be largely an empty virtue. The daily interactions between parents and their sons and daughters and between siblings teach children how to get along in society with superiors and peers, he observed. Watching how their fathers and mothers relate, moreover, teaches boys and girls how to treat each other. Hallowell was especially concerned that the contemporary dissolution of the two-parent family would prove dangerous for the future of American society by making it more difficult for citizens to master these critical social skills. And though he considered property and family to be fundamentally private matters, like Aristotle, he realized that even they are not immune from natural law constraints.

The role that religion played in Hallowell's personal life and politics was profound. Be it God, power, money, sex, or drugs, people feel a need to worship something, he believed, and God is the most noble among the alternatives. Worshipping God also secured for Hallowell the balanced view of humanity he both admired and sought. When we confront God's omnipotence and omniscience, he taught, we are simultaneously humbled by God's power and exalted by the sound moral direction it offers us. In God, theologian Keith Ward wrote (echoing Hallowell), "we can discover the changeless good in the changing ambiguities of time. We can hope to move beyond time itself to the contemplation of the timeless and eternal, and that is the beatitude which validates creation and seals it as incomparably good."[7]

Hallowell's own Christian faith was heavily influenced by St. Augustine, who helped him come to terms with sin and the function of will in how we choose to live our lives. Augustine famously divided human beings into two groups: the City of Man, composed of self-seeking people whose sinful pride leads them to love themselves over God, and the City of God, composed of individuals who dedicate their lives to humbly obeying God's commandments. Augustine concluded that human institutions, including government, tend to be dominated by self-seeking people who are primarily interested in gaining and maintaining power. Government may be necessary to prevent societal chaos, he taught, but the hunger for power that characterizes politics renders it incapable of attaining justice.

Hallowell was not as pessimistic about government as Augustine was. He considered the attainment of political justice improbable, but his prudent approach to politics required that he continue to strive for it. At best, parties and administrations create policies that represent prudent compromises between ethical principles and power politics. At worst, they create policies that are patently unethical. When certain churches become identified with certain parties and specific policies, Hallowell observed, they risk either compromising their theologies or violating them outright.

A similar view on the relationship between church and state was expressed more recently by Josef Ratzinger, Pope Benedict XVI: "Again and again, faith has risked being suffocated in the embrace of power," the pope said. "The struggle . . . to avoid identifying Jesus' Kingdom with any political structure is one that has to be fought century after century. For the fusion of faith and political power always comes at a price: faith becomes the servant of power and must bend to its criteria."[8]

Hallowell valued democratic government because he considered it the necessary political correlate to his belief in personal free will. His pessimistic view of human nature, however, led him to conclude that, for even a semblance of political justice to be achieved, moral responsibilities to the community must take precedence over individual democratic rights. Rights may be deduced logically and follow practically from obligations, he maintained, but the converse does not necessarily hold true. When owners pay workers a fair wage, provide them with safe working conditions, and treat the environment with respect, for example, their behavior can justify private ownership of business. Yet the right to own a business cannot ensure that owners will deal honestly with their workers and respect the environment.

As Hallowell explained: "Men have rights because they have responsibilities which transcend the demands of the natural world. Because we have a destiny that transcends time and, as a consequence, responsibilities that transcend the demands of the particular time and society in which we live, we must have the freedom proportionate to those responsibilities and the rights that are derived from those obligations. Because rights are correlative to responsibilities, they are . . . relative to the way in which such responsibilities are conceived and carried out. Our rights are derived from our obligations."[9]

Hallowell's emphasis on moral responsibilities to the community applied not just to a majority of citizens, nor even to all citizens living in a particular community at a particular time, but, in Burke's words, to "those who are living, those who are dead, and those who are to be born."[10] Just as the present is informed by the past, Burke taught, it must be morally bound to the future. Hallowell interpreted Burke's admonition to mean, in part, that authentic conservatives must be conservationists. We are commanded in Genesis 1:28 to assume dominion over nature. Among our communal obligations is to pass the earth down to our children and our children's children in at least as good a shape as we received it. Hallowell thus commended Theodore Roosevelt's effort to prudently reconcile Americans' right to make a profit through the mastery of nature today with the moral responsibility to preserve the environment for generations to come.

Hallowell's defenses of natural law and religion led him to oppose relativists who rejected the possibility of discovering the transcendent meaning of such concepts as love, justice, and honor. "It has become increasingly fashionable . . . to insist that moral judgments are nothing more than expressions of individual taste or preference, that law is simply what certain men arbitrarily declare it to be," he observed. The harm caused by this kind of approach, he maintained, is that when communities cease trying to ascertain a rational basis for settling differences of opinion, "then we have no alternative but to submit (those differences) by default to the arena of force. In that sense it is not the best reason that will prevail, but the mightiest fist."[11]

The modern form of moral relativism Hallowell found most pernicious was positivism, which he linked to the thought of Auguste Comte in the first half of the nineteenth century. In Hallowell's widely acclaimed *Main Currents in Modern Political Thought*, he defined positivism as the "attempt to transfer to the study of social and human phenomena the methods and concepts of the natural sciences in the belief that human phenomena, like physical phenomena, obey certain laws of nature which can be inductively discovered by the empirical examination of successive events."[12] It represented to him a "cult of objectivity" in which words such as "truth, wisdom, beauty, goodness or justice" are not encountered; we "find only 'facts' and 'values.'" We do not ask "what is true, but what are the facts?" We do not "pronounce actions to be just or unjust, good or bad, nor objects to be beautiful or ugly, instead we speak of 'value judgments.'"[13]

There are two fundamental problems with positivism, Hallowell taught. First, positivism makes the fatal mistake of seeking to conform reality to the scientific method. Rather than tailoring its methodology to the specific issue being investigated, it insists that one method alone is relevant for investigating every issue. Second, positivism's promise of objectivity is illusory. Facts do not come prelabeled in nature. Observers, applying their own preconceptions, do the labeling themselves. The result, Hallowell concluded, is that "instead of eliminating metaphysical speculation and ethical evaluation, the positivist simply removes them from the scrutiny of reason by obscuring even from himself the speculation and evaluation that must, of necessity, enter into his descriptive endeavors. Surreptitious speculation and evaluation are then often proclaimed as the latest discovery of 'science.' Thus science is used, or rather misused, to lend prestige to ideas whose origin is not in nature or in science but in the uncritical mind of the person promulgating them."[14]

Associated with positivism is the belief, promulgated by such thinkers as the Marquis de Condorcet at the end of the eighteenth century, that, through the use of science, humans will be able to create perfect societies over time. This belief, known as the modern Western concept of progress, represents a secular version of the traditional Judeo-Christian teaching that God alone will bring about heaven on earth at the end of time. As Hallowell maintained, one need only consider contemporary weapons of mass destruction as well as the gas chambers and crematoria of the Holocaust to recognize the fallacy of ascribing divinity to human beings and the danger of transferring faith from God to the scientific method.

Hallowell traced the movement away from universal moral principles in the history of Western political philosophy back to the publication of Machiavelli's *The Prince* in 1532. By "divorcing politics from its foundation in metaphysics and ethics," Hallowell noted, Machiavelli played pivotal roles in anticipating "the attempts of the nineteenth century positivists to found a natural science of politics" and in replacing classical realism with a realpolitik approach that declares the state "to be an autonomous entity" quite apart from any "considerations of justice or injustice."[15]

Hallowell's adherence to the classical theory of prudence, as a reconciliation of politics and ethics, also led him to oppose the role of ideologues in politics. To prudent leaders, reality represents a complex, fluid combination of immutable ideals and constantly changing circumstances. In his *Reflections on the Revolution in France*, Burke wrote: "Circumstances (which with some gentlemen pass for nothing) give in reality to every political principle its distinguishing color and discriminating effect. The circumstances are what render every civil and political scheme beneficial or noxious to mankind."[16] By offering virtually the same explanation for every issue and rigid solutions to every problem regardless of the circumstances, an ideologue seeks to reduce reality to a static, one-dimensional activity. The ideologues with whom Hallowell found fault included laissez-faire capitalists, with their inflexible free-market economic policies; communists, who rely solely on the theory of economic determinism to explain the entire course of human existence; feminists, who argue that social, political, and economic institutions invariably reflect the exploitation of women by men; and positivists, who reject the significance of issues that do not lend themselves to investigation by the scientific method.

Among his contemporaries, Hallowell found Eric Voegelin's analysis of ideology most persuasive. Hallowell played a significant role in introducing Voegelin's thought to Americans after World War II and edited *From Enlightenment to Revolution*, a compilation of Voegelin's writings. Voegelin rejected what he considered to be ideologues' attempt to simplify human existence by providing complete and final resolutions to the tensions that he regarded as intrinsic to human existence. He viewed this endeavor as a foolish conceit and warned of its serious consequences. "Existence has the structure of the In-Between, of the Platonic *metaxy*, and if anything is constant in the history of mankind it is the language of tension between life and death, immortality and mortality, perfection and imperfection, time and timelessness, between order and disorder, truth and untruth, sense and senselessness of existence," Voegelin wrote.

If we split these pairs of symbols, and hypostatize the poles of tension as independent entities, we destroy the reality of existence as it has been experienced by the creators of the tensional symbolisms; we lose consciousness and intellect; we deform our humanity and reduce ourselves to a state of quiet despair or activist conformity to the "age," of drug addiction or television watching, of hedonistic stupor or murderous possession of truth, of suffering from the absurdity of existence or indulgence in any divertissement (in Pascal's sense) that promises to substitute as a "value" for reality lost. In the language of Heraclitus and Plato: Dream life usurps the place of wake life.[17]

To Voegelin and Hallowell, indeed, tension is not a dilemma to be resolved but a permanent feature of human existence to be respected. They therefore urged students to resist the temptation to gain a monopoly on truth and seek contentment in discovering partial and temporary solutions to ultimately insolvable problems. This is the same frame of mind that the poet John Keats identified in Shakespeare: "*Negative Capability*, that is when a man is capable of being in uncertainties, Mysteries, doubts, without any irritable reaching after fact and reason."[18]

After graduating from Harvard College with a bachelor's degree in 1935, Hallowell spent a year studying in Nazi Germany, where he witnessed the dangers of positivism and ideology firsthand. How could a nation as civilized as Germany produce a movement dedicated to the death of civilization? How could a culture that nourished artists such as Bach, Beethoven, Brahms, and Goethe degenerate into book burning? In his doctoral dissertation, published in 1943 as *The Decline of Liberalism as an Ideology*, Hallowell identified positivistic liberalism as the culprit. According to Hallowell's analysis, the Enlightenment had imparted a heavy liberal influence on modern German culture. Since liberalism emphasizes the individual over the community, he claimed, it became necessary for Germans to rely on the limitations of metaphysical natural law to prevent the licentious abuse of individual freedoms. When positivism came to Germany in the second half of the nineteenth century, however, these limitations, being inaccessible to the scientific method, lost their relevance. The result, Hallowell argued, was a morally vacuous and socially unstable environment that proved incapable of withstanding the brutal onslaught of Nazi ideology. "How can you condemn a tyrant as unjust when you have purged the word justice from your vocabulary?" he wrote. "How, indeed, can you recognize tyranny when it arises?"[19]

Like Aristotle and Burke before him, Hallowell recognized that societal change is inevitable. They were not reactionaries. For change to be constructive, however, Aristotle and Burke advised that it should proceed through evolution, rather than revolution, and be integrated into a society's history. Aristotle had no illusions about our ancestors. He understood that they were at least as irrational and immoral, if not more so, than his own generation. Yet he cautioned about overturning ancestral laws too often and too quickly for fear that it would inculcate in citizens a disrespect for the rule of law that leads to the rise of ideologies that endanger civilization. Burke opposed the French Revolution not because he disparaged the ideals of "liberty, equality and fraternity" but because the French were trying to bring these ideals into full bloom overnight in a society that had only limited prior experience with them. The results of this imprudence, Burke predicted correctly, would be a level of death and destruction far beyond anything the French had ever before witnessed.

Hallowell put it this way: "When we stand upon the shoulders of those who have gone before us we increase our vision. It is presumptuous as well as foolish to think that our reason and our experience are the only things that matter. If each generation literally insisted upon the 'right' to make over the social order in its own image we should have chaos instead of community. The newest is not necessarily the best nor the latest necessarily the truest."[20]

In the 1960s and 1970s Hallowell was critical of what he judged to be the imprudence of American foreign policy that tried to bring about radical changes in Southeast Asia similar to those the revolutionaries had sought in France. In its attempt to force free government on South Vietnam, he argued, the United States neglected the fact that never in their history had the Vietnamese people demonstrated a willingness to fight and die for democratic liberties. In its quest to contain communism throughout the world, the United States also erroneously considered all Marxist states to be part of an international monolith and ignored thousands of years of antipathy among the peoples of Vietnam, China, and the Soviet Union. Were he alive today, he would have opposed the American invasion and occupation of Iraq for similar reasons. Once again, all Muslim opponents of American foreign policy have been characterized as existing within a so-called Islamofascist bloc, and the United States has acted like a social engineer, seeking to create democracy in Iraq even though Iraqis lack anything remotely resembling a democratic tradition.

Just as misguided as the attempt to impose democracy on unready states is the exaggeration of equality in democracies. Egalitarian democracies have a dangerous propensity to develop into totalitarian dictatorships. From his study of Tocqueville's and Plato's thought, as well as from his experiences in Nazi Germany, Hallowell learned how easily egalitarianism can lead to relativism and, eventually, to totalitarian control.

Tocqueville considered equality to be the main feature of democratic societies. In contrast to feudalism, democracies are supposed to follow the principle of equality of opportunity and judge people on the basis of what they do, not who they are. The principle of equality of opportunity does not deny that human beings differ in terms of their abilities, ambitions, and work ethics. The practice of equality of opportunity, however, refuses to prejudge people and insists that they be evaluated on their own merits.

Problems arise when citizens begin to grow frustrated by the intense competition engendered by equality of opportunity. There is tremendous pressure on people who are judged on their own merits. When failure inevitably occurs, they have no one to blame but themselves. To escape this pressure, democracies may seek to replace equality of opportunity with equality of results or egalitarianism, whereby all people and all ideas are accorded the same value. But egalitarianism raises serious problems for free government. With no individuals and no ideas to turn to for guidance, a condition of cultural anomie or aimlessness may set in. If this void becomes intolerable, citizens may choose to "escape from freedom" by forsaking democracy for a totalitarian government that is eager to supply them with the direction egalitarianism has denied them. In a totalitarian dictatorship, competition between individuals and between ideas comes to an abrupt halt. Everyone is equally constrained. Only one set of opinions is tolerated.

According to Tocqueville:

> I think democratic peoples have a natural taste for liberty; left to themselves, they will seek it. . . . But their passion for equality is ardent, insatiable. . . . They want equality in freedom, and if they cannot have that, they still want equality in slavery. They will put up with poverty, servitude, and barbarism, but they will not endure aristocracy. This is true at all times, but especially in our own. All men and all powers who try to stand up against this irresistible passion will be overthrown and destroyed by it. In our

day freedom cannot be established without it, and despotism itself cannot reign without its support.[21]

Another eloquent warning about the dangers posed by egalitarian democracy, to which Hallowell often referred, is found in Book VIII of Plato's *Republic*. There Plato described a situation in which families are falling apart because parents have no authority over children; schools are failing because teachers have lost the respect of students; and self-control has given way to crass materialism, sexual promiscuity, and drug dependence. Into this confusion steps a charismatic figure who promises to raise society to unprecedented levels of stability, wealth, and power in return for total acquiescence. Totalitarian rule is consolidated through constant warring, "so that the people will be in need" of the dictator; through heavy taxation, so that citizens "will be compelled to stick to their daily business and be less inclined to plot against him"; and through "purg[ing] the city" of free thinkers. Through this process, Plato observed, the evil of despotism emerges from egalitarianism: "Too much freedom seems to change into nothing but too much slavery, both for private man and city, the greatest and most savage slavery out of the extreme of freedom."[22]

Hallowell also distinguished classical realism from what is called the realpolitik or realist school of international politics. As we have seen, Machiavelli was one of the founders of this school. Others who played significant roles in its development were Thucydides, Prince Klemens von Metternich, and political scientist Hans Morgenthau. The realist school defends the proposition that self-interest, power, and domination are the paramount motives in foreign affairs. It considers moral ideals to be essentially irrelevant for understanding relations between nations. Hallowell, in contrast, argued that it is not impossible to reconcile ideals with national egotism. When countries violate these ideals, he maintained, their interests suffer as well. The Bush administration's widespread use of torture in the war on terror, for example, tended to reduce both the moral authority and the practical influence of the United States around the world.

This, then, is the classical realism that John H. Hallowell taught generations of students at Duke University and a number of other institutions of higher learning. Throughout classical realism are found the ideas of limits, restraint, and caution that traditionally have characterized conservatism in the West. Humans are viewed as beings with great potential but limited capacity to act ethically and think rationally. Individual freedom and governmental power are answerable to natural law and religious restraints. Leaders should be prepared to accept prudent limitations on what they hope to achieve in politics. Cautious evolutionary changes are preferable to revolution. There are moral and practical restraints on how we should treat the environment. Churches should limit their appetites for political power. The relativism that characterizes egalitarian democracy leads inevitably to totalitarian dictatorship, which, in its quest for unlimited control over citizens, represents the epitome of political evil. In foreign policy, moral restraints and power politics are not mutually exclusive.

The main problem Hallowell had with mainstream American conservatism is that, for the most part, it lacks the pessimistic view of human nature that leads classical realists to favor limits and restraints on human behavior and take a cautious approach to politics. What stands for mainstream conservatism in the United States, Hallowell would describe as a curious hodgepodge of economic liberalism, social Darwinism, populism, neoconservatism, libertarianism, and other schools of thought. For each of these schools, natural law is disavowed, and the rights of individuals take precedence over moral responsibilities to the community.

Economic liberalism arose in Europe in the eighteenth century as a reaction to mercantilism, a system that used state intervention to serve the financial interests of the feudal aristocracy. In contrast to mercantilism, economic liberals such as Adam Smith sought a reduction of taxes and an end to all restraints placed on economic activity. Benefiting from this unlimited economic freedom was the emerging class of capitalist entrepreneurs. F. A. Hayek and Ronald Reagan were economic liberals. In the post–Civil War United States, a new theory was disseminated that posited a scientific justification for capitalists' newfound wealth and power. Applying Darwin's biological concept of natural selection to society, social Darwinists such as Herbert Spencer and William Graham Sumner extolled laissez-faire as the key to human progress.

Populism arose in the second half of the nineteenth century as an egalitarian political movement led by small farmers from the American South and West against those they accused of exploiting them in the northeastern business establishment. In order to become a majority party, the farmers sought to forge an alliance with industrial workers. Cloaking their demagogic appeals to the emotions and prejudices of voters in the rhetoric of evangelical Protestantism, populists such as Tom

Watson of Georgia opposed laissez-faire and lashed out at Wall Street, racial minorities, intellectuals, and immigrants. Joseph McCarthy and George Wallace were populists, as are Sarah Palin and Rush Limbaugh.

Lately, a group of people known as neoconservatives has added an aggressive foreign policy to the mainstream American conservative hodgepodge. Their theory, promulgated by such authors as Irving Kristol and Norman Podhoretz, is that there should be no restraints on the United States' power to export its form of government to the rest of the world.

Libertarians share the same allegiance to laissez-faire as economic liberals and social Darwinists but extend their belief in inalienable individual rights to a wider range of activities, including abortion, prostitution, drugs, and immigration. They oppose the aggressive foreign policies of the neoconservatives. Notable American libertarians were Barry Goldwater and novelist Ayn Rand. The Tea Party movement in American politics was first organized by supporters of libertarian presidential candidate Ron Paul in 2008 to protest the federal bailout of financial institutions. Members of the movement today express a confusing array of libertarian and populist viewpoints.

Despite the significant differences among these schools of thought, they share a sanguine spirit that sets them apart from classical realism. Their confidence is a reflection of American history. According to Niebuhr, whose neo-Augustinian thought Hallowell admired, the history of the United States was "ushered in on a wave of boundless social optimism"[23] when, against all odds, the Puritans established what they considered to be a divinely inspired "shining city upon a hill" in Massachusetts at the beginning of the seventeenth century. Since then, Americans have frequently behaved, in Niebuhr's ironic phrase, like "harmless egotists"[24] who believe that, with God on their side, nothing they do will have deleterious consequences: markets will self-regulate; nature is self-healing; churches will escape political manipulation; totalitarianism cannot happen here; and, when Americans invade and occupy foreign countries, they will be accepted as saviors.

Rarely have we Americans subscribed to the humble "philosophy of imperfection, committed to the idea of limits" that, according to political theorist Noel O'Sullivan, characterizes traditional Western conservatism. Seldom have we viewed ourselves, in O'Sullivan's words, as "imperfect, dependent" creatures who are "doomed to make the best of things by the more modest policies of compromise and accommodation."[25]

Hallowell well understood that a nation's history and culture play significant roles in shaping its politics. Given the uniqueness of this country's experience, he was not surprised that differences would exist between American and traditional Western conservatism. What did concern him was how significant these differences turned out to be. At heart, conservatism places great stock in tradition and is predisposed to accept evolutionary change. To Hallowell, the issue was that the tradition of Aristotle, Aquinas, and Burke has undergone nothing less than revolutionary changes on American soil.

Another problem Hallowell had with mainstream conservatism in the United States was its tendency to extol the Southeast as the region most opposed to relativism and most compatible with the values of tradition, stability, community, religion, and family. While appreciating these aspects of southern life, Hallowell, who made his home in North Carolina for forty years, repeated Aristotle's and Burke's lessons about blind obedience to tradition. At various times, slavery, Jim Crow, and racial intolerance have been notable features of southern culture. Since all these features violate the moral imperatives of natural law, Hallowell argued, none is defensible. For example, in his review of Russell Kirk's 1953 volume *The Conservative Mind*—a book that many mainstream American conservatives still venerate—Hallowell found Kirk's "predilection for the arguments of Southern states rightists" to be disturbingly evasive on the subjects of slavery and racism.[26]

The differences between mainstream American conservatism and Hallowell's traditional alternative were brought to a head by one historical event: McCarthyism. Hallowell ranked Joseph McCarthy as one of the most odious figures in American history. A fervent opponent of communist ideology himself, Hallowell watched in disgust as McCarthy manipulated the "Red Scare" in the United States after World War II to his own advantage while others, calling themselves conservative, either passively or actively encouraged his demagoguery. For classical realists, ends and means must be ethically commensurate. McCarthy claimed he was trying to protect American democracy from Russian totalitarian aggression. Yet, in Hallowell's opinion, the damage he did to democratic freedoms through his politics of fear and bullying tactics often exceeded the Soviet threat. Those individuals McCarthy identified as traitors and spies were usually nothing more than critics of his unsavory politics. With his friend Will Herberg, Hallowell viewed McCarthyism as a form of egalitarian "government by rabble-rousing."[27]

While he was alive, Hallowell was mistrusted by mainstream conservatives because they considered him an undemocratic elitist whose constant references to ideals and moral responsibilities to the community asked too much of people and put Americans' inalienable rights at risk. Some of the charges they leveled against him were truly bizarre. Frank Meyer, for example, accused Hallowell and other more traditional conservatives such as Peter Viereck and Robert Nisbet of divesting individuals of their integrity by using government to force ideals on them and by seeking to make them appendages of the state.

Hallowell responded that his critics were wrong on at least two counts. First, natural law principles apply as much to governments as they do to individuals. Second, far from being undemocratic, these principles are essential for democracy to exist. Ideals such as "the absolute moral worth of the individual . . . the spiritual equality of individuals, and . . . the essential rationality of man," he wrote, make it possible to "understand the words in the Declaration of Independence that 'all men are created equal' and strive toward the attainment of equality of opportunity for all men." As he explained, "The phrase derived originally from the belief that all men are created equal in the sight of God, that the souls of men are equally precious to God, and that all individuals should be treated with the respect due to a creature made in the image and likeness of God. . . . God's image in man is reflected in the capacity of human beings to reason, and the disparagement of that capacity can lead only to the denial of man's uniqueness."[28]

Invoking the teachings of Tocqueville and Plato, as well as his own experiences in Nazi Germany in 1935, Hallowell noted that just as the possession of natural law principles ennobles democracy, the lack of such principles emboldens totalitarianism. Hitler, he reminded critics, put forth Nazism as an irrational "triumph of the will" in which every idea and moral standard was subverted by hatred and murder and every question of legitimacy was decided by force alone. Through their concepts of economic determinism and historical materialism, Marxist-Leninist commissars taught that truth is always relative to the economic conditions prevailing at any particular time.

Similar points were made by Walter Lippmann. Democratic institutions, Lippmann argued, are unable to succeed in relativistic societies that reject universal ideals. When "there is no public criterion of the true and the false, of the right and the wrong, beyond that which the preponderant mass of voters, consumers, readers and listeners happen at the moment to be supposed to want," he claimed, "it is impossible to reach intelligible and workable conceptions of popular election, majority rule, representative assemblies, free speech, loyalty, property, corporations, and voluntary associations."[29]

Meyer, Hallowell's vocal critic on the Right, was the founder of a movement known as fusionism, an attempt to organize the assorted groups that constituted the American conservative hodgepodge. Hallowell, for his part, would have none of it. The practical differences among the economic liberals, social Darwinists, populists, neoconservatives, and libertarians were too great; the intellectual contradictions between them and the classical realists too profound. American culture disconnected conservative political philosophy from its traditional natural law and prudential roots, Hallowell believed. Deprived of its intellectual foundations, he concluded that mainstream conservatism in the United States had been relegated to a largely incoherent right-wing ideology incapable of offering realistic solutions to the pressing issues confronting American politics.

Notes

1. John H. Hallowell, *The Moral Foundation of Democracy* (Chicago: University of Chicago Press, 1954), 89.

2. Ibid., 127.

3. Dino Bigongiari, ed., *The Political Ideas of St. Thomas Aquinas* (New York: Hafner Press, 1974), 13.

4. John H. Hallowell, *The Decline of Liberalism as an Ideology* (Berkeley: University of California Press, 1943), 11.

5. Aristotle, *The Nicomachean Ethics*, ed. J. A. K. Thomson (Baltimore: Penguin Books, 1966), 65.

6. John H. Hallowell and Jene M. Porter, *Political Philosophy: The Search for Humanity and Order* (Scarborough, Ontario: Prentice Hall Canada, 1997), 68.

7. Keith Ward, *God: A Guide for the Perplexed* (Oxford: Oneworld, 2005), 136.

8. George Weigel, "A Jesus beyond Politics," *Newsweek*, May 21, 2007, 49.

9. Hallowell, *The Moral Foundation*, 84.

10. Edmund Burke, *Reflections on the Revolution in France*, ed. Thomas Mahoney (Indianapolis: Bobbs-Merrill, 1955), 110.

11. Hallowell, *The Moral Foundation*, 23.

12. John H. Hallowell, *Main Currents in Modern Political Thought* (New York: Holt, Rinehart and Winston, 1950), 289–90.

13. John H. Hallowell, "The Christian in the University," *Motive* 23 (March 1963): 40.

14. Hallowell, *The Moral Foundation*, 76.

15. Hallowell, *Main Currents*, 53, 58.

16. Burke, *Reflections*, 8.

17. Eric Voegelin, *From Enlightenment to Revolution*, ed. John H. Hallowell (Durham, N.C.: Duke University Press, 1975), viii.

18. Quoted in David Donald, *Lincoln Reconsidered* (New York: Vintage Books, 1961), 143.

19. John H. Hallowell, "Modern Liberalism: An Invitation to Suicide," *South Atlantic Quarterly* 46 (October 1947): 459.

20. Hallowell, *Main Currents*, 195–96.

21. Alexis de Tocqueville, *Democracy in America*, ed. J. P. Mayer, trans. George Lawrence (New York: Anchor Books, 1969), 506.

22. Plato, *Republic*, trans. Allan Bloom (New York: Basic Books, 1968), 246, 242.

23. Reinhold Niebuhr, *The Children of Light and the Children of Darkness* (New York: Charles Scribner's Sons, 1944), 16.

24. Ibid., 18.

25. Noel O'Sullivan, *Conservatism* (New York: St. Martin's Press, 1976), 22.

26. John H. Hallowell, Review of Russell Kirk's *The Conservative Mind*, *Journal of Politics* 16 (February 1954): 151.

27. Will Herberg, "Government by Rabble-Rousing," *New Leader* 37 (January 18, 1954): 15.

28. Hallowell, *The Moral Foundation*, 80–81.

29. Walter Lippmann, *Essays in the Public Philosophy* (Boston: Little, Brown, 1955), 114, 80.

Bibliography

Aristotle. 1966. *The Nicomachean Ethics*. Edited by J. A. K. Thomson. Baltimore: Penguin Books.

Bigongiari, Dino, ed. 1974. *The Political Ideas of St. Thomas Aquinas*. New York: Hafner Press.

Burke, Edmund. 1955. *Reflections on the Revolution in France*. Edited by Thomas Mahoney. Indianapolis: Bobbs-Merrill.

Donald, David. 1961. *Lincoln Reconsidered*. New York: Vintage Books.

Hallowell, John H. 1943. *The Decline of Liberalism as an Ideology*. Berkeley: University of California Press.

———. 1947. "Modern Liberalism: An Invitation to Suicide." *South Atlantic Quarterly* 46 (October): 453–56.

———. 1950. *Main Currents in Modern Political Thought*. New York: Holt, Rinehart and Winston.

———. 1954. *The Moral Foundation of Democracy*. Chicago: University of Chicago Press.

———. 1954. Review of Russell Kirk's *The Conservative Mind*. *Journal of Politics* 16 (February): 150–52.

———. 1963. "The Christian in the University." *Motive* 23 (March): 36–43.

Hallowell, John H., and Jene M. Porter. 1997. *Political Philosophy: The Search for Humanity and Order*. Scarborough, Ontario: Prentice Hall Canada.

Herberg, Will. 1954. "Government by Rabble-Rousing." *New Leader* 37 (January 18): 3–16.

Lippmann, Walter. 1955. *Essays in the Public Philosophy*. Boston: Little, Brown.

Niebuhr, Reinhold. 1944. *The Children of Light and the Children of Darkness*. New York: Charles Scribner's Sons.

O'Sullivan, Noel. 1976. *Conservatism*. New York: St. Martin's Press.

Plato. 1968. *Republic*. Translated by Allan Bloom. New York: Basic Books.

Tocqueville, Alexis de. 1969. *Democracy in America*. Edited by J. P. Mayer. Translated by George Lawrence. New York: Anchor Books.

Voegelin, Eric. 1975. *From Enlightenment to Revolution*. Edited by John H. Hallowell. Durham, N.C.: Duke University Press.

Ward, Keith. 2005. *God: A Guide for the Perplexed*. Oxford: Oneworld.

Weigel, George. 2007. "A Jesus beyond Politics." *Newsweek*, May 21, 49.

Eric Voegelin and American Conservatism

JAMES L. WISER

In reacting to numerous efforts by others to classify his thinking according to the terms of a particular school of thought or intellectual tradition, Eric Voegelin (1901–1985) wrote: "Because of this attitude I have
been called every conceivable name by partisans of this or that ideology. I have in my files documents labeling me a Communist, a Fascist,
a National Socialist, an old Liberal, a new Liberal, a Jew, a Catholic,
a Protestant, a Platonist, a new-Augustinian, a Thomist, and of course
a Hegelian—not to forget that I was supposedly influenced by Huey
Long. . . . Understandably I have never answered such criticisms; critics
of this type can become objects of inquiry, but they cannot be partners
in a discussion."[1] It is interesting to note that among the labels listed,
Voegelin did not include the one that is perhaps most commonly attributed to him: conservative. Although he himself never claimed to be a
conservative thinker, others have frequently classified him as such. Why
is this the case? I think there may be two types of "evidence" generally
available to support this attribution: the indirect or associational, and the
direct or thematic.

As examples of indirect or associational evidence I offer the following:

- Voegelin's work has often been described and favorably commented on in such conservative publications as *National
  Review, Intercollegiate Review, Modern Age,* and *American Spec-
  tator.* Although Voegelin declined an offer by William Buckley
  to write a monthly one-page essay for *National Review,* he did
  publish articles in both *Modern Age* and *Intercollegiate Review.*

- Voegelin's work has been highly praised by such conservative intellectuals as William Buckley, Russell Kirk, Frank Meyer, Brent Bozell, and Henry Regnery.
- Within the North American academy, those who were most interested in introducing their students to Voegelin's work were often scholars who understood themselves to be working within an essentially European conservative intellectual tradition. Examples would be Gerhart Niemeyer at Notre Dame, John Hallowell at Duke, Willmoore Kendall at Yale, and George Grant at McMaster.
- Throughout his career, Voegelin sought and received funding for his scholarly work from a variety of private foundations. Several that were particularly supportive of his research program were often associated with conservative causes, including the Earhart Foundation, the Relm Foundation, and the Volker Fund.
- In 1958 Voegelin left Louisiana State University, where he had taught since 1942, to establish a new institute for political science at the University of Munich. Voegelin was one of several émigrés who returned to Germany after the war to introduce students there to the principles of Western political science, anticipating that these ideas would prove helpful in the construction of a new postwar, democratic European society. Theodor Adorno and Max Horkheimer went to Frankfurt; Arnold Bergstraesser went to Freiberg; and Voegelin went to Munich.[2] Voegelin's appointment to the university was highly contested, and he had to be vetted and approved by the Bavarian Ministry of Culture. He was not the first choice, but his candidacy was championed by Catholic philosopher Aleis Demof, who held a distinguished professorship at the university. Voegelin's appointment was eventually made possible only because of the support of a group of conservative Catholics who knew of him primarily through his 1952 publication *The New Science of Politics.*[3]
- After leaving Munich in 1969 Voegelin joined the Hoover Institution on War, Revolution, and Peace at Stanford University. He was the Henry Salvatori Distinguished Scholar from 1969 to 1974 and remained as a senior research fellow until his death in 1985. The Hoover Institute is a prominent conservative think tank, and Voegelin's major sponsors at Hoover were two impor-

tant conservative Republican political leaders. Glenn Camp-
bell, director of the institute from 1960 to 1989, was a senior
adviser in Barry Goldwater's 1964 presidential campaign and
was later appointed by President Ronald Reagan as chairman of
the President's Intelligence Oversight Board. Richard Allen, one
of the few American students to study with Voegelin in Munich,
later served as Reagan's assistant for national security affairs.

This listing of Voegelin's association with conservative individuals
and institutions does not establish that Voegelin himself was a conservative or that he wished to be thought of as such. It does, however,
explain why the popular perception of Voegelin as a conservative is so
widespread—especially among those who may be familiar with only a
portion of his writings. At the same time, this listing raises a larger set
of questions. What was there in Voegelin's writings that so many conservatives found appealing? Why did they draw attention to his work,
and why were they interested in financially supporting his research
program? What themes in Voegelin's writings did they regard either
as conservative in nature or as helpful to the conservative position in
general? Given the constraints of this chapter, I examine only three of
these themes.

Critique of Marxism

American conservatism is a complex entity. The term captures a variety of political movements and ideologies that often exist in tension
with one another. For example, there are social and cultural conservatives, libertarian conservatives, neoconservatives, and free-market conservatives. In many cases their policies differ, as do their priorities and
principles. Yet in spite of such differences they appear to have cohered
sufficiently to be regarded as a "position," "attitude," or "perspective" in
today's political discourse. In writing about post–World War II American
conservatism, Gerhart Niemeyer acknowledged a lack of "cement holding the whole together as a 'deliberate consensus' from which policies
would emerge."[4] Yet at the same time he mentioned three concerns that
broadly engaged the conservatives of the postwar era: a strong sense of
the communist threat, a concern about America's military strength, and
the desire to return the country to a classical liberal economic program.
If Niemeyer was correct, Voegelin's repeated and powerful critique of

Marxist communism would have had an obvious appeal for the conservatives of his day.

Obviously, the fear of communism was not a uniquely conservative issue. Indeed, many liberals and socialists strongly opposed Soviet totalitarianism. But what made Voegelin's critique appealing to conservative thinkers in particular was his emphasis on those important qualities shared by both the liberal and Marxist traditions. On its surface, liberalism's emphasis on individual autonomy and personal freedom seemed to stand in sharp contrast to communism's "new socialist man" and its communitarian implications; however, according to Voegelin's analysis, these differences simply masked a more important and substantive similarity.

In *The New Science of Politics* Voegelin analyzed the nature of political modernity and sought to differentiate its conception of political order from the classical Greek and Judeo-Christian understanding of the good society. He argued that, in essence, political modernity is an attempt to actualize in history a modern version of the dreamworld found in traditional Gnostic speculations.[5] Gnosticism's goal was to transform human nature by overcoming the difficult and, in many cases, debilitating existential tensions that arise from the fact that, given God's radical transcendence, men and women can neither possess nor fully know the ground of their being. To achieve a release from this tension, Gnosticism denied the necessarily unfulfilled or "fallen" quality of the human condition and posited instead humankind's future perfection in time as the inevitable result of a historical project. The fulfillment of the human person, which Christianity understood as a salvific event occurring after the end of time (*eschaton*), was transformed by Gnosticism into a historical possibility—the realization of which is dependent on human resolve and effort. For Voegelin, this project must necessarily fail because it ignores or denies the actual structure of reality and is, in fact, nothing more than "a fallacious immanentization of the Christian eschaton."[6]

The arguments presented in *The New Science of Politics* are complex, historically wide ranging, and philosophically challenging. For our purposes, however, a key point is Voegelin's contention that, rather than being a unique philosophical system, Marxism is only a more recent and radicalized form of the Gnostic project that has appeared in various manifestations throughout Western history. Earlier forms of Gnosticism can be found in the High Middle Ages, the Renaissance, and the Reformation. In Marxism, Gnosticism has assumed a particularly powerful and widely persuasive form of expression, yet its fundamental principles and assumptions remain unchanged. By arguing that the essential feature of all Gnostic systems is their common immanentist eschatology, Voegelin saw a fundamental similarity among different intellectual traditions that others perceived as distinct or, in some cases, actually in conflict with one another. A prime example of this reordering of the traditional perspective was Voegelin's likening of the traditions of Marxism and liberalism: "A clear understanding of these experiences as the active core of immanentist eschatology is necessary, because otherwise the inner logic of Western political development from medieval immanenticism through humanism, enlightenment, progressivism, liberalism, positivism, into Marxism will be obscured."[7]

Voegelin did not simply equate liberalism with Marxist totalitarianism, for there are important distinctions that need to be acknowledged. Liberalism's immanentist character may be apparent in the political philosophy of John Locke, but Voegelin admitted that Locke's theory is a caricature of bourgeois society and that it would "be ridiculous to take Locke's theory as an adequate description of bourgeois reality."[8] The liberal regime—especially as it evolved in the United States and Great Britain—is a much more complex affair. In addition to its Lockean elements, it is characterized, at least in Voegelin's understanding, by the desirable and pervasive influence of the tradition of "commonsense philosophy," as represented in the works of Thomas Reid, William Hamilton, and John Dewey, and by the notable influence of Protestantism on Anglo-American popular and political culture. Nonetheless, Voegelin's analysis of liberalism's and Marxism's shared Gnostic character was meant to correct a more common interpretation that posits liberalism and totalitarianism as being at opposite poles of the modern political spectrum. Such an interpretation is found in Hannah Arendt's *The Origins of Totalitarianism.* In his review of her study Voegelin wrote: "And this attitude is, indeed, of general importance because it reveals how much ground liberals and totalitarians have in common; the essential immanentism that unites them overrides the differences of those that separate them. The true dividing line in the contemporary crisis does not run between liberals and totalitarians but between the religious and transcendentalists on the one side and the liberal and totalitarian immanentist sectarians on the other side."[9]

Given this line of demarcation, it is not difficult to see why conservatives rather than liberals found much to admire in Voegelin's critique of Marxism.

Appreciation of the Western Tradition

By most accounts, Voegelin's greatest work is his five-volume study *Order and History.* The first three volumes were published during 1956–1957, volume 4 was published seventeen years later in 1974, and the final volume appeared posthumously in 1987. With volume 4 Voegelin announced a "break in the program" that had been the original organizing principle for the entire project. This break did not negate the analyses offered in the first three volumes, which dealt with the ancient Near East, Israel, and classical Greece, but it did necessitate a reconsideration of how to deal with the historical materials from the Hellenistic age forward. The argument of *Order and History* is that, although human nature itself does not change, our understanding of that nature has emerged historically. Over time we have gained greater insight into our place in the order of being. As our self-understanding becomes more highly differentiated during this process, we perceive a "before" and an "after," demarcated by those events in consciousness that produced the differentiating insight. This experience of a "before" and "after" imparts a historical structure to our experience of time, and it was Voegelin's intent to explore that structure and understand its meaning for the creation of human and social order.

In volume 4 Voegelin's analysis assumed a truly universalistic character. He not only returned to an examination of the major Greek and Israeli figures he had discussed in earlier volumes but also expanded the scope of his analysis to include Mani, Muhammad, and the Chinese ecumene. It was this expansion of his interests to encompass non-Western and even prehistoric sources,[10] along with the explosion of materials this expansion produced, that led Voegelin to break from the schematic order of his original project.

Nonetheless, in Voegelin's work, the Western intellectual tradition — especially its classical Greek and Judeo-Christian elements — holds a privileged place. Its special status is due to the fact that universally valid insights into the order and structure of being have been expressed with particular clarity in the dominant traditions of Western culture. According to Voegelin, the historical record shows that humankind has always experienced the presence of the divine and has attempted to express and communicate this experience through a variety of artistic and linguistic symbols. These efforts at symbolic expression can be loosely grouped according to the various rules that govern their proper usage and by the nature of the underlying experience they are attempting to articulate. For instance, when reality was experienced cosmologically, it found its proper expression in such mythopoeic symbols as the Homeric epic. The pneumatic experience of reality found its expression in those stories associated with the history of ancient Israel. The noetic experience of order found its proper expression in the symbols of classical Greek philosophy, and the soteriological experience of reality formed the existential basis for the symbols of Christian revelation.[11]

These symbolic systems are not strictly equivalent, however. Mythopoeic symbolism is relatively compact and fails, at least from the perspective of philosophy and revelation, to adequately characterize the transcendent nature of God's being. In the myth, the sacred and the profane coexist within a single cosmological reality, whereas in Platonic and Aristotelian philosophy and Christian revelation, the good or God is experienced as radically transcendent and thus as existing apart from and beyond the events of profane history. In Voegelin's terminology, philosophy's and theology's experience of the sacred is more "differentiated" than the "compact" experience expressed within the myth. However, it is not as if, during the cosmological era, one experienced God as transcendent and simply failed to find the proper symbols to express this. On the contrary, the symbols of the myth are entirely adequate, inasmuch as they accurately express the engendering cosmological experiences that serve as their sources. The sacred was experienced as present within the cosmos; history was experienced as containing both a sacred and a profane dimension; and humankind understood itself as simply one cosmological element among the many that are moved by the sacred forces that structure the whole.

The move from mythology to philosophy that occurred in classical Greek philosophy was not simply a move to experiment with new or different literary or symbolic genres. Rather, this symbolic adjustment was, in fact, necessitated by a concrete spiritual event at a particular time and place within Western history. In the Platonic quest for meaning, the experience of the philosopher's rational participation in the transcendent ground of being shattered the unity of the cosmological order and thereby exposed the inadequacy of those myths that were its appropriate expressions

Similarly, according to Voegelin, the creation of new symbols describing the Christian experience of God's love and grace was required by the fact that the symbols of Greek philosophy were incapable of expressing this newest revelation. In Greek philosophy the defining human action was the rational effort to encounter reality even unto its divine ground. Plato's allegory of the cave is perhaps the best expression of this understanding. Individuals are most fully human when, becoming philosophers, they seek to order their lives by undertaking the never-ending pursuit of wisdom. This search to encounter the "divine beyond" by opening one's self to the transcendent and attuning one's soul to its order defines the fully rational, and therefore fully human, life.

This human effort to encounter the divine ground of being is also central to the Christian experience; however, it is secondary to an even more important search: God's original effort to encounter the individual person. The Christian experience of the incarnation and of grace places a priority on God's own desire to engage his creation. Indeed, from the Christian perspective, we seek God essentially as a response to our experience of God seeking us. Being loved, we seek to love. And being unworthy of this original love, we can receive it only as a gift or in grace.

Here again, as in the move from myth to philosophy, the judgment that philosophical symbols are no longer adequate and thus need to be replaced by those of Christian theology is the result of a specific event in Western history: the radically new Christian experience of the dual, reciprocal, and soteriological nature of the divine-human relationship.

Voegelin's *Order and History* is a detailed analysis of the most important moments in the Western movement from myth, through philosophy, to the Judeo-Christian tradition and its eventual rejection by European modernity. This movement is important not simply because it establishes an interesting historical pattern that ties seemingly disparate events together in a single story but because, according to Voegelin, it depicts humankind's historical advance to and eventual retreat from an adequate understanding of reality and therefore of the conditions for human and social order. The experiences that initiated this movement were "spiritual outbursts" that occurred as events in the consciousnesses of concrete individuals at specific times and places. This specificity, which locates them within Western civilization, does not, however, negate the universality of their importance.

For Voegelin, this changing articulation of the historical experience of the human-divine "in-between" is the actual order of history. In other words, whatever substantive meaning has emerged within history has become apparent in and through the historical evolution of Western consciousness. For Voegelin, the Western movement through mytho-

poeic, pneumatic, noetic, and soteriological forms of human consciousness is not just a story of change but the story of "the tortuous ways in
which man moves historically closer to the true order of being."[12]

Statements such as these obviously privilege Western civilization in
a manner that affirms the arguments of American social and cultural
conservatives who seek to preserve and enhance the authority of the
"great tradition." They, like Voegelin, urge us not to forget the insights
of the past, and they see "remembering" rather than "creating" as the
beginning of true human wisdom.

Critique of Progressivism

One set of criticisms that arose in reaction to Voegelin's study of the
historically evolving forms of Western consciousness was that his work
represented a new variant of philosophical historicism. Some saw it as
similar to Hegel's philosophy of history, wherein history was understood
as the story of the divine spirit's progression toward its own perfection
in absolute consciousness. This, however, was not Voegelin's argument.
For him, the development of human consciousness is the story of an
increasingly differentiated insight into the order of being; the order of
being itself, however, does not change. Similarly, although humankind's
conscious participation in the order of being has become increasingly
intelligible, this increasing luminosity does not constitute a change in
human nature itself, inasmuch as the human person always remains in
the "in-between"—simultaneously attracted to and pulled by both the
transcendental and the mundane poles of existence. Finally, the historical movement from compactness to differentiation is not understood by
Voegelin to be the result of the historical "working out" of an inevitable
logic. It is and will remain a mystery why the spiritual irruptions that
produced these transformations in consciousness occurred as they did.
Inasmuch as individuals experience being as the comprehending reality within which they self-consciously exist as participants, they cannot
achieve the external or disengaged perspective that is necessary for a scientific understanding of objective phenomena. For humankind, being
is, at its core, mysterious; as an element or participant within being, so
too is the human person. Whereas for Hegel, history had overcome ignorance, for Voegelin, history could only affirm reality's fundamentally
mysterious character: "Hence, the symbols can illuminate the mysterious structure of existential reality as a tension tending toward an order

beyond itself and they can articulate the mysterious experience of an ordering Beyond irrupting into experienced presence; but the illuminating articulation cannot make the mystery of the Beyond and its Parousia less mysterious."[13]

Voegelin's insistence on the constant reality of the mystery of being is at the root of his critique of progressivism. In his classic study, J. B. Bury described the idea of progress as follows:

> The idea of human Progress then is a theory which involves a synthesis of the past and a prophecy of the future. It is based on an interpretation of history which regards men as slowly advancing . . . in a definite and desirable direction, and infers that this progress will continue indefinitely. And it implies that . . . a condition of general happiness will ultimately be enjoyed which will justify the whole process of civilization. . . . There is also a further implication. The process must be the necessary outcome of the psychical and social nature of man; it must not be at the mercy of any external will.[14]

In his examination of the concept of progress, Bury discusses, among others, Locke, Voltaire, Helvetius, Turgot, the Encyclopedists, and Marx. These and several others also became the focus of Voegelin's own sustained critique of progressivism as developed in his book *From Enlightenment to Revolution*.

For Voegelin, the progressivist thinkers of the eighteenth and nineteenth centuries, be they positivists, Enlightenment rationalists, or utopian socialists, shared a common trait: they sought to create a "second reality" as a replacement for the true reality of human existence. In introducing Voegelin's study, John Hallowell summarized its major argument in the following manner: "Dream life usurping the place of wake life is the theme of this volume when reason torn loose from its moorings in the ground of being seeks to create man-made constructions of reality in place of the mysterious reality of God's creation."[15]

According to Voegelin, the progressivist belief that humankind is capable of creating a substantively superior human and social order is based on a fundamental—and perhaps willful—misunderstanding of the established character of human nature and its proper place within the order of being. This misunderstanding leads to two potentially disastrous consequences.

First, by positing that the present is necessarily superior to the past, progressivism devalues the traditional insights of the past and reclassifies them as early or immature attempts to formulate truths that have only fully emerged in the present. Thus, what Voegelin understood to be the universally valid insights of the pneumatic (Judaic), noetic (classical Greek), and soteriological (Christian) forms of consciousness become in the progressivist system of Auguste Comte the primitive results of the mind's historical evolution through its "theological" and "metaphysical" forms of infancy. According to Comte, it is only during the modern era that the mind has achieved its "positive" or mature form, and therefore only *its* discoveries can rightfully and exclusively claim the status of scientific truth. In this view, philosophy and theology are exploratory systems consisting of earlier erroneous attempts to achieve that which has now been made possible by the development of the modern scientific method. In a similar manner, Comte's contemporary, Henri de Saint-Simon, posited the mind's progressive development through polytheistic, monotheistic, and scientific stages. In his political writings he was quite consistent, therefore, in advocating the expulsion of theologians and metaphysicians from contemporary society. Representing the errors of the past, they could only interfere with the rightful rule of those modern scientists of human behavior who had for the first time grasped the actual laws of social existence.

Second, just as the logic of progressivism favors the present over the past, it favors the future over the present. If history is seen as the stage for humankind's movement toward a more perfect future, every moment is in some sense simply a preparation for the next. As this movement assumes the form of a particular and concrete social order, this order not only embodies what has been achieved vis-à-vis the past but also serves as an institutionalized impediment to further progress. For those who are impatient with the pace of change or sensitive to the lingering inadequacies of the present, the political temptation is to aid the historical process by destroying those structures that serve to maintain the present and thereby better position humankind for the future. According to Voegelin, this activist attitude can be found in such disparate political movements as German fascism, the anarchism of Bakunin, and the communism of Marx and Lenin. In each case the promise of the future overrides the substantive integrity of the present. Given this logic, it is hard to imagine a viewpoint more antithetical to the traditional conservative perspective as described by Michael Oakeshott: "To be conservative, then, is to prefer the familiar to the unknown, to prefer the tried to the untried, fact to mystery, the actual to the possible, the limited to the unbounded, the near to the distant, the sufficient to the superabundant, the convenient to the perfect, present laughter to utopian bliss . . . [The] grief of loss will be more acute than the excitement of novelty or promise."[16]

Voegelin's Own Understanding

In suggesting those elements of Voegelin's work that were attractive to various conservative thinkers, I focused on just three that I think are particularly important. But I could have included additional items: Voegelin's critique of the fact-value dichotomy, his emphasis on the role of prudential judgment, his critique of ideological fanaticism, his appreciation of both the fragility and the necessity of order, his understanding of the centrality of religion, and his insistence on the important yet limited nature of political action. In spite of such affinities, however, it is quite clear that Voegelin did not consider himself to be a conservative thinker. In a letter to Gerhart Niemeyer in 1964 he wrote: "Any move undertaken by whomsoever, apt to associate my work as a scholar with any political party, group, or movement whatsoever, but especially with Goldwater, conservatism, or rightist groups, is made not only without my permission or tacit consent, but against my declared intention. I consider any such attempt at association as an attack on the intellectual integrity of my work."[17]

Similarly, in 1978 he wrote to John East: "After all, I have not spent the time of my life and done my work, in order to amuse and comfort American Conservatives. . . . In order to make it [East's article about the reception of Voegelin's work among conservatives] complete, you would have to confront the actual content and purpose of my work which has nothing to do with conservative predilections."[18]

There are at least two reasons for Voegelin's insistence on distancing himself, at least privately, from modern conservatism: his understanding of the nature of political conservatism, and his understanding of the nature of his own work as a political scientist in the twentieth century. According to Voegelin, both modern conservatism and modern liberalism were examples of ideological responses that generated "positions," "attitudes," or "perspectives" rather than offering timelessly valid scientific propositions about political reality. Instead of developing a truly scientific understanding of contemporary politics, which would have required an explicit philosophical anthropology grounded in a metaphysics adequate for the age, both liberalism and conservatism were primarily engaged in establishing their positions vis-à-vis the other. By debating each other rather than confronting the truly substantive issues of the day, each offered at best a second-level analysis of political reality. The ephemeral nature of the conservative-liberal debate is evidenced by the fact that the terms have changed their meaning over time. Today's "conservative" is the "old-style liberal" of the nineteenth century, and today's "liberal" has become "conservative," to the extent that "the movement of liberalism has been overtaken by new, more radical views of revolution, in opposition to which it plays the role of conservatism; just as formerly, in the decade from 1810 to 1820 conservatism was conservative in opposition to revolution and to liberalism."[19] To the extent that "conservatism" is "old liberalism" protesting the radicalization of the liberal movement, neither conservatism nor liberalism moves beyond the level of mere ideology. Voegelin, however, was insistent that the crisis of modernity required a scientific response. To simply operate at the ideological level would have been a waste of his time and energy.[20] More important, from Voegelin's perspective, his engagement with such issues could undermine the perception of his own work as a legitimate scientific undertaking. Voegelin expressed this concern in a letter to Henry Regnery: "The science which I represent is in a delicate situation today and I don't want to expose myself to attacks from either 'liberals' or 'conservatives' because of formal affiliation in the one or the other direction."[21]

At the core of Voegelin's rejection of political conservatism was his understanding of the modern crisis and of society's need for that therapeutic alternative available only in a new science of politics. For Voegelin, the essential task of political science had not changed since its founding by Plato and Aristotle in Athens. "Political society . . . is as a whole a little world, a cosmion, illuminated with meaning from within by the human beings who continuously create and bear it as the mode and condition of their self-realization."[22] Central to every political *cosmion* is an understanding of the right way of living and the right ordering of society. It is apparent, however, that especially in times of crisis or change, opinions vary as to what these understandings should be. Individuals and groups offer different answers to such questions as: Whose understanding of the "good life" or the "just society" should predominate? Who establishes the priority among the many goods that individuals pursue and is thereby allowed to set the public agenda? Who determines what the common good requires in a specific concrete situation and thereby establishes authoritative public policy? Given the variety of opinions regarding such matters, another question naturally arises: Is it possible to determine which of the opinions put forward, if any, are true? According to Voegelin, Platonic and Aristotelian political science originally arose as a response to this challenge. It emerged as an effort to transcend the realm of opinion (*doxa*) and, in so doing, acquire a scientific understanding (*politike episteme*) of human and social order. This effort achieved success with the spiritual outburst Voegelin associated with the transition from cosmological to noetic consciousness, as described earlier in this chapter: "The decisive event in the establishment of 'politike episteme' was the specifically philosophical realization that the levels of being discernible within the world are surmounted by a transcendent source of being and its order. . . . Only when the order of being as a whole unto its origin in transcendent being comes into view . . . only then can current opinions about right order be examined as to their agreement with the order of being."[23]

If the establishment of a true political science had already occurred in the fourth century BC, why did Voegelin feel the need to establish a "new science of politics" for his own day? The answer to this question is found in his analysis of what he termed the "pneumopathological" condition of modernity. Those who lived in the cosmological era were unaware of the pneumatic and noetic experiences that would eventually find their symbolic expression in Judaism and Greek philosophy. Similarly, the prophets of Israel and Plato and Aristotle were unaware of the soteriological experience that found its expression in the symbols of Christianity. In both cases, the more highly differentiated experience of being that characterized the subsequent period was not yet available to the people of the earlier period. In this sense, their "ignorance" of the more highly differentiated experience is understandable. However, according to Voegelin, the modern situation is quite different. In his analysis, modernity—precisely because of its Gnostic character—does not offer a vision of human and social order that expresses a new and more highly differentiated experience of being. Instead, it is an experiment in rejection that seeks to build its order by denying the truth that was already established by previous differentiations. As such, it does not represent a move toward a greater openness to the order of being; rather, it reflects a prior decision to construct society on a willful act of closure. According to Voegelin, those thinkers who best represent the modern age, Nietzsche and Marx, fully understood what had been achieved during the previous centuries. These achievements, however, were inconvenient because they called into question the rationality of the modern Gnostic project. To attempt to answer these questions would undermine the project itself because the mere act of engaging these questions put the project's certain success at risk. It was better that such questions be forgotten or, if not forgotten, then eventually forbidden. Because of the ultimately mysterious nature of being, all ages are characterized by a degree of ignorance. However, the age of modern Gnosticism—based on a forgetting or, in its more radical form, a forbidding of questions—was the first age to be characterized by the willful quality of its ignorance. For Voegelin, the task at hand was to explain why humankind would willfully turn away from a historically achieved truth in order to base its understanding of human and social order on what it knew to be nothing more than a self-imposed deception.

What is "new" today that requires a "new political science" is that, for the first time, it is willful ignorance rather than natural ignorance that resists the effort of science to advance beyond opinion to truth. Inasmuch as neither conservatism nor liberalism understands this dimension of the problem, neither is able to provide an appropriate response.

Notes

1. Eric Voegelin, *Autobiographical Reflections* (Baton Rouge: Louisiana State University Press, 1989), 46.

2. In assessing the success of this effort years later, Voegelin wrote: "On the whole, however, I believe that the idea of injecting an element of international consciousness, and of democratic attitudes, into German political science has not been much of a success beyond the immediate circle of young people that I could train personally. . . . The damage of National Socialism has been enormous." Ibid., 91.

3. The support of Voegelin by conservative politicians, educators, and church officials would eventually diminish. In 1964 he delivered a series of lectures attended by hundreds of students entitled "Hitler und die Deutschen." The general topic of the lectures concerned the German people's complicity with Nazi rule, and in a section entitled "Descent into the Ecclesiastical Abyss," Voegelin offered a detailed criticism of the behavior of both the Lutheran and

Roman Catholic churches during Hitler's regime. Two years later Voegelin published an essay, "The German University and the Order of German Society: A Reconsideration of the Nazi Era," in which he extended his critique of "Germany's spiritual disorientation" to include its dominant academic, intellectual, and cultural elites. The reaction among his former supporters was as one would anticipate. On January 1, 1969, somewhat embittered by his inability to exercise significant influence within the German academy, Voegelin resigned from the institute he had founded ten years earlier.

4. Gerhart Niemeyer, "Eric Voegelin, 1952," *Modern Age* 26, no. 3–4 (summer/fall 1982): 265.

5. Voegelin would later modify the analysis of modernity he offered in *The New Science of Politics*. Modernity is more complex than originally presented, and although Gnostic consciousness is a major determinant of modernity, it is not its "essence." In 1973 Voegelin remarked: "Gnosticism is certainly not the only trend. One has to include . . . apocalyptic strands, the neo-Platonic restoration at the end of the fifteenth-century, and the hermetic component which resulted in the conscious operation of sorcery and in Hegel's determinology." "An Interview," *New Orleans Review* 2 (1973): 136.

6. Eric Voegelin, *The New Science of Politics* (Chicago: University of Chicago Press, 1952), 166.

7. Ibid., 125.

8. Eric Voegelin, *History of Political Ideas: The New Order and Lost Orientation* (Columbia: University of Missouri Press, 1999), 152.

9. Eric Voegelin, "The Origins of Totalitarianism," in *Collected Works*, vol. 11, ed. Ellis Sandoz (Columbia: University of Missouri Press, 2000), 22.

10. During his years at the Hoover Institute, Voegelin became increasingly interested in Paleolithic and Neolithic drawings, and he visited sites in Ireland, Malta, Iran, Turkey, and the caves of Ile-de-France.

11. Voegelin's emphasis on the underlying experience (cosmological, pneumatic, noetic, soteriological) as opposed to the symbols created to express such experience (myth, the stories of ancient Israel, classical Greek philosophy, Christian theology) explains his focus on human consciousness rather than on dogma or doctrine. His analysis sought to elucidate the existential experiences of real persons. In doing so, he read their writings as efforts to portray or illuminate their experiences of order and reality rather than as dispassionate statements about external objects. When these creative symbols are treated as "definitions," "doctrines," or "systems," they become opaque to their underlying experiences and thus lose their true meaning. This temptation to turn symbolic elucidations that "point to" experiences into dogmatic systems that deduce conclusions from principles is a constant threat to true reason. Voegelin saw examples of this occurring in Aristotle's treatment of Plato and repeatedly arising within the traditions of Christian theology.

12. Eric Voegelin, *Israel and Revelation* (Baton Rouge: Louisiana State University Press, 1956), 11.

13. Eric Voegelin, *In Search of Order* (Baton Rouge: Louisiana State University Press, 1987), 97.

14. J. B. Bury, *The Idea of Progress* (New York: Dover Publications, 1955), 5.

15. John Hallowell, preface to *From Enlightenment to Revolution* by Eric Voegelin (Durham, N.C.: Duke University Press, 1975), ix.

16. Michael Oakeshott, *Rationalism in Politics and Other Essays* (New York: Basic Books, 1962), 169.

17. Eric Voegelin, *Selected Correspondence: 1950–1984*, ed. Thomas Hollweck (Columbia: University of Missouri Press, 2007), 472.

18. Ibid., 841.

19. Eric Voegelin, "Liberalism and Its History," in *Collected Works*, 11:86.

20. This was precisely Voegelin's concern regarding the efforts of Willmoore Kendall: "On the debit side must be set at least as far as I am concerned, his publicist activities for the cause of ideological conservatism. One could, of course, make a case for it by saying that in the economy of public opinion one foolishness should be balanced by another one, so that neither one will run to extremes. . . . Anyway I deeply regret that a man of Kendall's potential as a scholar should waste his time and energy on such activities." Eric Voegelin, "The Eric Voegelin–Willmoore Kendall Correspondence," ed. Steven D. Ealy and Gordon Lloyd, *Political Science Reviewer* 33 (2004): 383–84.

21. Voegelin, *Selected Correspondence*, 733.

22. Voegelin, *The New Science of Politics*, 1.

23. Eric Voegelin, *Science, Politics, and Gnosticism* (Washington, D.C.: Regnery Publishing, 1997), 12.

Bibliography

"An Interview." 1973. *New Orleans Review* 2: 136.

Bury, J. B. 1955. *The Idea of Progress*. New York: Dover Publications.

Hallowell, John, ed. 1975. Preface to *From Enlightenment to Revolution* by Eric Voegelin. Durham, N.C.: Duke University Press.

Niemeyer, Gerhart. 1982. "Eric Voegelin, 1952." *Modern Age* 26, no. 3–4 (summer/fall): 265.

Oakeshott, Michael. 1962. *Rationalism in Politics and Other Essays*. New York: Basic Books.

Voegelin, Eric. 1952. *The New Science of Politics*. Chicago: University of Chicago Press.

_____. 1956. *Israel and Revelation*. Baton Rouge: Louisiana State University Press.

_____. 1987. *In Search of Order*. Baton Rouge: Louisiana State University Press.

_____. 1989. *Autobiographical Reflections*. Baton Rouge: Louisiana State University Press.

_____. 1997. *Science, Politics, and Gnosticism*. Washington, D.C.: Regnery Publishing.

_____. 1999. *History of Political Ideas: The New Order and Lost Orientation*. Columbia: University of Missouri Press.

_____. 2000. "Liberalism and Its History." In *Collected Works*, vol. 11. Edited by Ellis Sandoz. Columbia: University of Missouri Press.

_____. 2000. "The Origins of Totalitarianism." In *Collected Works*, vol. 11. Edited by Ellis Sandoz. Columbia: University of Missouri Press.

_____. 2004. "The Eric Voegelin–Willmoore Kendall Correspondence." Edited by Steven D. Ealy and Gordon Lloyd. *Political Science Reviewer* 33: 383–84.

_____. 2007. *Selected Correspondence: 1950–1984*. Edited by Thomas Hollweck. Columbia: University of Missouri Press.

Leo Strauss's Friendly Criticism of American Liberal Democracy

Neoconservative or Aristocratic Liberal?

Kenneth L. Deutsch

Leo Strauss (1899–1973) remains one of the most revered and reviled political thinkers since World War II.[1] Both academically serious and politically bizarre controversies surrounding Strauss's legacy have intensified since his death. His alleged influence over contemporary neoconservatives and their Iraqi foreign policy objectives is only one of the many problematic aspects of his intellectual patrimony. Characterizations of Strauss's teachings concerning natural right and moral relativism have ranged from morally absolutist and authoritarian to morally nihilist and atheist. This chapter makes the claim that Strauss was both a sober friend of liberal democracy who refused to be one of its "flatterers" and a subtle and profound creator of a natural right rhetoric that would both defend and criticize liberal democracy in order to render it safe for the philosophic enterprise.

Strauss, to be sure, greatly challenged his students and disciples to recognize the pervasive "crisis" of liberal democracy and the need to come to its defense. His critique of the doctrine of moral relativism and the ideology of cultural relativism resonates strongly today in the neoconservative rejection of a liberal multiculturalism that views all cultures as equal in moral status and worthy of toleration. His critique of progressivism rejects any idealistic notions of inevitable human progress and raises serious questions about the neoconservative promotion of liberal democracy around the world. I suggest that Strauss's connection with contemporary neoconservatism is both substantial and tenuous. His teachings actually challenge us to conserve and balance features of both Aristotelian ancient liberalism and modern Lockean liberalism by supporting liberal education. Only in this way can the weaknesses of liberal democracy and its moral confusion be moderated by the wisdom of statesmen and the informed consent of the governed. Strauss, as I argue here, is an academic conservative.

Friendly Critic of Liberal Democracy

In what sense was Leo Strauss a friendly critic of liberal democracy? For Strauss, human beings can never create a perfect society that is free of contradictions. One can discern the tenor of his friendly criticism of modern liberal democracy's rather serious contradictions in the following statement:

> Liberal democracy claims to be responsible government, a political order in which the government is responsible to the governed. . . . [I]n order to be responsible, the government must have no secrets from the governed. Of course, liberal democracy also means limited government, the distinction between the public and the private. Not only must the private sphere be protected by the law, but it must also be understood to be impervious to the law . . . the true place of secrecy is not the home but the voting booth. We can say the voting booth is the home of homes, the seat of sovereignty, the seat of secrecy. The sovereign consists of individuals who are in no way responsible, who can in no way be held responsible: the irresponsible individual. This was not simply the original notion of liberal democracy. The original notion was that this sovereign individual was a conscientious individual, the individual limited and guided by his conscience. It is perfectly clear that the conscientious individual creates the same difficulty as Hobbes's enlightened despot. You cannot give a legal definition of the conscientious individual. You cannot limit voting rights to conscientious people as you can limit voting rights by property qualifications, literacy tests, and the like. Conscientious[ness] can only be fostered by non-

legal means, by moral education. For this no proper provision is made, and the change in this respect is well known to all. This change which has taken place and is still taking place may be called the decline of liberal democracy into permissive egalitarianism. Whereas the core of liberal democracy is the conscientious individual, the core of permissive egalitarianism is the individual with his urges. . . . The man who wants to indulge his urges does not have the slightest intention to sacrifice his life and hence also his urges, to the satisfaction of his urges. This is the moral decline which has taken place.[2]

Strauss also viewed liberal ethics as having contributed significantly to political principles that draw the line on government authority, but such ethics have not sufficiently recognized the connection between the exercise of private freedom in a limited state and the virtues the public (or the voter) must exercise to remain free from oppression. The decay of an earlier ethos of personal and social morality and moral education, along with the absence of statesmen capable of reviving a sense of public duty, has made it difficult for liberal democratic regimes to contend effectively with such problems as delimiting the role of technology in the public and private realms, distinguishing the problems of discrimination in the public and private realms, and countering the influence of perfectibility or progressive ideologies that threaten the conservation of liberal democratic-constitutionalist regimes.

The larger context for Strauss's analysis of liberal democracy is what he understood to be the crisis of modernity stemming from the rejection of Greek antiquity and biblical religion in the name of the new sciences of nature and politics. The goal of the modern project—improvement of the human condition through the technical mastery of nature—was formulated by modern political philosophy. What predominates today within liberal democracies is a morally neutral methodology in the form of the fact-value distinction of positivist social science, a historicist ideology, and dogmatic atheism. The dominance of positivism, historicism, and dogmatic atheism within contemporary social science and academic life is, according to Strauss, tantamount to the demise of political philosophy as traditionally understood—the search for the naturally best regime. Thus, there is no philosophical grounding or justification for the central principles of contemporary liberal democracy. Social scientists have failed to develop standards of political morality by which to judge and influence actions that affect the character and preservation of the regime itself. As Strauss says: "The crisis of liberalism [is] a crisis due to the fact that liberalism has abandoned its absolutist basis and is trying to become entirely relativistic."[3]

Contemporary liberal democracies, argues Strauss, need a viable notion of natural right. In the absence of a standard of natural right, the alternative confronting liberal democracy is nihilism: "The problem posed by the conflicting needs of society cannot be solved if we do not possess knowledge of natural right. . . . If our principles have no other support than our blind preferences, everything a man is willing to dare will be permissible. The contemporary rejection of natural right leads to nihilism—nay, it is identical with nihilism."[4]

In the face of such nihilism, Strauss would consider a reexamination of the principles of premodern political philosophy. The modern notions of nature and freedom have to be reexamined in light of the classical dependence of morality on purposive nature. The exaltation of human creativity, along with the concomitant despair of finding a rational source of ends to guide that creativity, is the "deepest" reason for the crisis of liberal democracy. The crisis of liberal democracy is thus a continuation of the quarrel between the ancients and the moderns. Strauss's "return" to ancient philosophy is neither nostalgic nor an exercise in intellectual history. It is required by the present crisis because the progression in the history of the West from nature to reason to history to will as the standard of thinking and acting has produced an intellectual and moral vacuum. Modern liberals celebrate tolerance as an ideal: "They appear to believe that our inability to acquire any genuine knowledge of what is intrinsically good or right compels us to be tolerant of every opinion about good or right or to recognize all preferences or all 'civilizations' as equally respectable. Only unlimited tolerance is in accordance with reason."[5]

Strauss argues that in order to rehabilitate natural right, the notion of the beneficence of nature or the primacy of the Good must be restored. This requires no less than a rethinking, through the tradition of political philosophy, of the fundamental experiences responsible for its emergence. To say that there are universal characteristics of human experience especially relevant for political philosophy is to say that there are experiences, intelligible at a pretheoretical level, that serve to demarcate politically significant from politically insignificant phenomena.

The fundamental experience of politics, whose perspective is that of the involved citizen rather than the scientific observer, is that of individuals who decide courses of action on the basis of competing claims. Such competing claims, when made explicit, serve as criteria or principles of justification. The implicit notion of the good in politics is made thematic when it is recognized that political action involves either preservation or change and therefore "must be guided by some thought of better or worse." In this way, political philosophy as a sustained reflection about the merits of completing claims emerges from the pretheoretical experience. The moral neutrality of contemporary political science renders such a genesis invisible by concealing the fact that the ever-present experience of political life at all times and in all places is an experience that involves unavoidable moral discriminations and judgments. In our age, it has become impossible to evaluate social action, for "if there is no standard higher than the ideal of our society, we are utterly unable to take a critical distance from that ideal."[6]

Strauss's dissatisfaction with both modern liberalism and traditional conservatism can be grasped indirectly through his extended exegetical interpretations of the fathers of modernity—Machiavelli, Hobbes, Spinoza, Locke, and Rousseau. In this chapter, Strauss's teachings on modern liberalism and moral relativism are approached directly through his papers and lectures in which he reveals his own position or speaks in his own name. He clearly speaks in his own name when he reveals his nuanced view of modern liberal democracy in these terms: "We are not permitted to be flatterers of democracy precisely because we are friends and allies of democracy. While we are not permitted to remain silent on the dangers to which democracy exposes itself as well as human excellence, we cannot forget the obvious fact that by giving freedom to all, democracy also gives freedom to those who care for human excellence."[7]

The modern academy faces a great dilemma. Although most of its members may wish to remain liberal, they do so despite the apparent inconsistency between their alleged value neutrality and their liberal convictions. Value neutrality implies "that before the tribunal of reason all values are equal," yet they assume that "the rational society will be egalitarian, or democratic and permissive or liberal: the rational doctrine regarding the difference between facts and values rationally justifies the preference for liberal democracy—contrary to what is indicated by the distinction itself."[8] The modern political scientist has no criterion for distinguishing specious from genuine claims on sympathy because the fact-value distinction subjects such persons to the kind of moral suasion that consists of little more than direct appeals to sympathetic emotions. Public morality is simply defined in terms of sympathetic emotions. Modern liberals are unable to say no or exercise restraint by appeal to high principles. Modern liberals have become feckless. When the sympathetic response becomes the organizing or dominant quality of conscientiousness, modern liberal political scientists can no longer appreciate that a political order must establish a hierarchy of values that represses some values so that others may flourish.

Strauss understood modern liberal political science and its fact-value distinction to be a replacement for the prescientific experience of traditional political philosophy. As a result, the old political universals—the various regimes and their respective notions of the human good and the common good—have given way to new empirical ones, such as freedom and coercion. Traditional political philosophy was a sustained reflection about the merits of competing claims that emerged from pretheoretical political experience. Politics is a world of value, not a compendium of morally neutral facts or theoretical constructs. In order to see the natural development of political philosophy from political opinion, our point of departure must be political opinion itself—that is, political disagreements concerning good and bad actions, types of people, and types of laws and governments. As Strauss points out, it is impossible to ground the empiricism of modern liberal political science empirically. This is the case because the only way to grasp the sense and utility of scientific discourse is to translate it back into the terms of prescientific experience, which is both its genesis and its arbiter. The effect of an ostensibly value-free conceptuality is to mask the differences of opinion from which controversy arises and thus to neutralize politics.

Strauss is especially critical of the modern liberals' invention of conceptions such as "lifestyle," which mask fundamental disagreements about right and wrong under the cosmetics of mere differences in "taste," which only the prejudiced and unenlightened world take seriously. This kind of value-free conceptuality neutralizes politics. For Strauss, contemporary liberal democracies are also dominated by a theory of progress that presses toward the continuous expansion of goods, services, and personal freedom. This value-free politics assumes that human beings' political nature—their natural need for the common good and the establishment of a hierarchy of values—can be replaced by new experiments in changing lifestyles, in which each creates his or her own lifestyle driven by greater technological progress, pushing back indefinitely the constraints of natural scarcity and the need for human temperance.

Strauss contends that in the absence of the primacy of the common good, the "good" of the society becomes the open society of radical individualism. Understanding that that which has no nature can have no meaningful goal, the modern liberal state claims to be the regime demanded by human nature. The fixity of radical individualism is taken to be the firm and lasting foundation of the modern liberal project. However, as Strauss observes: "The characteristic assertion of liberalism seems to be that man and hence also morality is not 'a fixed quantity'; that man's nature and therewith morality are essentially changing; that this change constitutes History."[9] Since the essentially changeable is the essentially malleable, we confront a major paradox of modern liberalism. Human nature is simultaneously the political norm and that which is to be altered and controlled by rulers and "proper" institutional and judicial arrangements. Strauss points out that this paradox of the fixity and changeability of human nature has persisted throughout the historical development of liberal democracies in the West. Gone is the conception of the soul as a natural hierarchy of parts. By teaching the equality of all values, by denying the distinction between the naturally high and intrinsically low, modern liberal academic culture, argues Strauss, unwittingly contributes to the victory of the low and its commensurate lifestyles, along with an irresponsible electorate and government.

Strauss considered the results of the modern liberal project to be the self-destruction of reason itself. His most stinging charge against modern political science was his claim that it "rests on dogmatic atheism."[10] Strauss presents his position as follows:

> The new science rests on a dogmatic atheism which presents itself as a merely methodological or hypothetical. For a few years, logical positivism tried with much noise and little thought to dispose of religion by asserting that religious assertions are "meaningless statements." This trick seems to have been abandoned without noise. Some adherents of the new political science might rejoin with some liveliness that their posture toward religion is imposed on them by intellectual honesty: not being able to believe they cannot accept belief as the basis of their science. . . . Yet just as our opponents refuse respect to unreasoned belief, we on our part, with at least equal right, might refuse

respect to unreasoned unbelief; honesty with oneself regarding one's unbelief is in itself not more than unreasoned unbelief, probably accompanied by a vague confidence that the issue of unbelief versus belief has long since been settled once and for all. It is hardly necessary to add that the dogmatic exclusion of religious awareness properly renders questionable all long-range predictions concern[ing] the future of society.[11]

Many modern political scientists such as John Schaar and Sheldon Wolin were stung by Strauss's charge. They claimed that Strauss was in no position to demonstrate the actual connection between a modern political scientist's religious beliefs and his work as a political scientist. "On what basis, then, can Professor Strauss confidently assert the dogmatic atheism which underlies the new science? What is the relevance or the propriety, of such a charge in a work which presents itself as an academic and professional work?"[12] Schaar and Wolin have simply misread Strauss's comments on dogmatic atheism. Strauss was rejecting the "refutation" of the biblical faith that pervades the profession of modern political science. Modern liberal political philosophers, such as Benedict Spinoza, rested their political teachings on a "dogmatic exclusion" of the possibilities of biblical faith. The disintegration of philosophy or the modern self-destruction of reason begins with the unwarranted belief that philosophy can "refute not the necessarily inadequate proofs of revelation but revelation itself. Modern science and historical criticism have not even refuted the most fundamentalistic orthodoxy."[13] For Strauss, "political atheism" is "a distinctly modern phenomenon. No premodern atheist doubted that social life required belief in, and worship of, God, or gods."[14] Modern atheists have become "active, designing, turbulent and seditious."[15] Modern political atheism has produced a grim record, providing "negative proof of the inadequacy of any non-believing position."[16]

Premodern philosophers such as Plato and Maimonides possessed the qualities of sobriety, respect, and moderation in dealing with the city and its God or gods. A thoughtful and respectful approach to the contributions and tensions of reason and revelation to the establishment of political order is required. For Strauss, the philosopher must be sober in deed in order to be liberated in thought. The goal of modern dogmatic atheism is nothing less than the relief of one's estate; it is an uncritical and immoderate faith in historical progress. As a progressive political doctrine, modern liberalism must constantly go forward toward new liberties, more democracy, greater equality, and greater enhancement of the material and social quality of life. The modern liberal's view of the transformational power of scientific technology has, in a sense, rendered the notion of a fixed boundary between reality and imagination obsolete. Both modern liberalism and modern liberal democracy are in crisis because both have lost a sense of the fixed boundary between reality and imagination. Modern liberal democracies and modern political thought must undergo revision or risk further political disintegration and deterioration into useless dogma.

Strauss's teachings express a deep concern for the health of American liberal democracy. He is concerned that the moral relativism of American cultural elites has led to a loss of conviction that the Declaration of Independence expresses true principles of natural right. He warns that the central problem of our age lies in the fact that the West has been losing faith in the modern project itself. The early modern political project should be defended against the teachings of late, nihilist radical modernity. Most important of all, it must be understood that the modern project of liberal democracy is fundamentally defective and should be tempered and bolstered by classical ancient liberalism, which emphasizes human excellence and the common good. Strauss called the United States of America "the only country in the world which was founded in explicit opposition to Machiavellian principles."[17] Although he favored the theoretical politics of the ancients, he was appreciative of the practical wisdom of the American framers. He wrote concerning America: "liberal or constitutional democracy comes closer to what the classics demanded than any other alternative that is viable in our age."[18] Strauss agreed with the ancients about the chance realization of the naturally best regime.[19] Modern liberal democracy, when it includes an aristocratic dimension that respects human excellence, becomes the best regime possible. Strauss's qualified praise of the Declaration of Independence is therefore praise for the foundations of the best practical contemporary political alternative. It is true that nowhere in Plato's or Aristotle's writings do we find unqualified acceptance of such self-evident truths as natural human equality and individual rights on a universal scale; the protection of life and liberty and the pursuit of idiosyncratic happiness as the purpose of the regime; guidance by the *is* rather than *ought* character of human nature; the overcoming of chance; the dominance of private interest in the form of property and commerce; and the use of political institutions rather than character development to promote political success.[20] For Strauss, contemporary political life demands an articulation and defense of the best regime possible given the circumstances and the available alternatives. Strauss deeply respected American liberal democracy. He persistently taught the distinction between the feasible or legitimate regime as opposed to the best regime. His respect for American liberal democracy was grounded in its stability and durability only when led by prudent statesmen and supported by liberal education. The great problem of preserving American liberal democracy is the loss of resolve concerning its mission. Strauss himself witnessed an increasing decline of such stability and durability due to the absence of such statesmen from public life and the decline of liberal education in the face of an academic world clinging to the fact-value distinction. Whether due to an allegiance to positivistic science or historicism, the political and educational elites teach the nonrational character of all value judgments, rejecting the superiority of a sound liberal democracy over its adversaries. A sound liberal democracy combines wisdom and consent. The informing of modern liberalism by classical political philosophy and the Hamiltonian perspective is the best possible way to establish the kind of public life in which statesmanship and liberal education permit the survival of the unfinished dialogue that is philosophy. This includes the nondogmatic grappling of the fundamental alternatives of ancient and modern liberalism. For Strauss, true liberals today must oppose the perverted liberalism that claims that living securely, happily, and unregulated is humanity's supreme goal and forgets about quality, excellence, wisdom, or virtue.

Conservatism, Statesmanship, and the Great Books

For Strauss, "true" liberalism requires the recognition of "essential differences in human beings" and an awareness "that the [political] whole consists of heterogeneous beings; that there is a heterogeneity of beings, this common sensible notion on which we fall back all the time, and this has in no way been refuted [by evolutionism]."[21] Human beings are naturally unequal in specific ways, especially in terms of their intellectual capabilities. Given this inequality, the wise are better suited to rule over others. The best regime depends on the chance appearance of rulers who are friendly to philosophy, and the best possible regime eliminates chance through the lowering of standards in which there is a compromise between wisdom and unwisdom, tyranny and consent. Such a regime includes the rule of law in which the political whole (the state) entrusts its administration to "gentlemen." A gentleman is independently wealthy, well bred, and public spirited, a person who reflects and imitates philosophical wisdom. The gentleman founder or statesman possesses practical wisdom that allows the proper ordering or synthesizing of the moral virtues. He seeks balance between the rule of law and the security of the national state and finds the hierarchy of goods in promoting the common good. There are no fixed rules in statesmanship. For Strauss and for Hamilton, statesmen are those who are most outstanding by merits and talents and by ability and virtue.

Although Strauss favored the theoretical politics of the ancients, he was very appreciative of the practical wisdom of the framers in trying to reconcile wisdom and consent—statesmanship and citizenship. His hope for the success of "true" liberalism in the context of contemporary liberal democracy was founded on the emergence of prudent statesmen among a well-educated citizenry—an endeavor supported by liberal education. Strauss was not a public intellectual. His role as a teacher through his courses and his books was the central activity of his vocation. As he put it quite directly, "I own that education is in a sense the subject matter of my teaching and my research."[22]

The goal of education, argues Strauss, is "education at its best or highest"—namely, the Socratic or philosophical way of life. The only valid art of education is the task of making practical judgments about how to draw intellectually capable people toward the philosophical way of life. He views liberal education classically—as liberation from the moral relativism, historicism, and dogmatic atheism that afflict contemporary liberal democracy. It is liberation from the vulgarity of our time— a vulgarity that is a lack of experience of things beautiful. For Strauss, "liberal education is the necessary endeavor to found an [intellectual] aristocracy within democratic mass society."[23] Liberal education must be available to the talented, among whom there will be a continuum of wisdom from gentleman to philosopher.

Both liberal education and religious education are necessary in facing the crisis of liberal democracy. For Strauss, permissive liberal democracy is "caused by the decay of religious education of the people and by the decay of liberal education of the representatives of the people."[24] Both forms of education are concerned with moral education and the virtues of justice, temperance, and prudence. They produce a "fruitful and enabling" tension, as is the case between the claims of revelation and reason. Neither side has been able to refute the other, producing this creative tension. Liberal education itself is the primary means of securing a true liberal democracy. It "is the ladder by which we ascend from mass democracy to democracy as originally meant."[25] Religious education for the people at one end of the continuum stresses responsibility for one's actions toward God and neighbor, whereas liberal education demands, from those capable of pursuing it, a "complete break with the noise, the rush, the thoughtlessness, the cheapness of the Vanity Fair intellectuals as well as their enemies."[26] Excellent teachers and talented and receptive learners need to be liberated from the dominant forces of mediocrity, vulgarity, and political correctness.

Liberal education for Strauss means "studying with proper care the great books which the greatest minds have left behind."[27] This method stresses the existence of "fundamental alternatives" in human thought and the important differences between great minds, thereby producing a dialogue as these differences are thought through. When serious liberal education is unavailable, Strauss calls for teachers to pursue "a modest, pertinent, practical" course to teach their subjects in a way that "broadens and deepens the understanding," as opposed to producing nothing more "than narrow and unprincipled efficiency."[28] Education that develops the critical faculties and personal responsibility cannot be restored easily. It requires prudent and persistent critics. It is only by fostering this kind of education that we as a society are enabled to search for a way "to reconcile order which is not oppression with freedom which is not license."[29] When liberal democracy permits liberal education to exist, then liberal democracy "gives freedom to those who care for human excellence."[30] This freedom to teach "liberally" and to persuade different kinds of citizens is what a flawed but corrigible Athens allowed for a time, and it is what a flawed but corrigible America must continue to allow.

Strauss was not a Burkean conservative with regard to divinizing historical traditions. He was not an advocate of dogmatic capitalism or xenophobic patriotism or the justness of majoritarian democracy. He was certainly uninterested in protecting the oligarchic conservatives of old families. He rejected the conservative positivists who have become constitutional literalists defending the Constitution's alleged support for states' rights, thereby rejecting the best part of the American liberal democratic tradition of the Declaration of Independence and the statesmanship of Lincoln. For Strauss, parts of our tradition were better and parts were worse. Thus, southern agrarian conservatism grounded in class and caste must likewise be rejected. It is important to note that Strauss was not an anti–welfare state advocate. Politics, for Strauss, requires a prudent balance between principles such as private property and welfare, merit and human need.

Strauss was an academic conservative who taught that good political judgment requires a moral reasonableness that accepts the irreducible ambiguities and tensions of the human condition, especially the tension between our bodies and our souls and between our own good and the common good. Only by keeping alive or "conserving" the dialogue of the great minds on issues such as classical and modern natural right versus liberalism, reason versus revelation, and the philosopher versus the state can we equip future generations with the intellectual capacity to make nuanced *moral distinctions* between the tyrant and the statesman, rights and duties, and the constitutional form and political exigencies or emergencies. Whether or not there is cosmic support for natural right principles, Strauss taught that certain actions or decisions are likely to be destructive to those individuals or nations that indulge in them. Strauss provided no "philosophical kit" that can easily resolve these issues. The Straussians themselves have been divided on how to resolve them. Strauss's academic conservatism, which advocates liberal education and religious education, preserves human intellectual greatness in society and allows for the founding of an aristocracy within democratic mass society by contributing qualities of dedication, concentration, breadth, and depth to democratic practice. Perhaps the liberally educated can once again be heard in the noisy marketplace. Only then might those souls who inherit contemporary liberal democratic regimes yearn for the prudent defeat of tyranny, seek the recovery of human excellence, and demonstrate a public-spirited concern for the common good instead of the joyless quest for joy.

Notes

1. For background on Strauss, see the author's three coedited books, listed in the bibliography.

2. Leo Strauss, "Political Philosophy and the Crisis of Our Time," in *The Post-Behavioral Era*, ed. George Graham and George Carey (New York: David McKay, 1972), 222–23.

3. Leo Strauss, "Relativism," in *Relativism and the Study of Man*, ed.

Helmut Schoeck and James W. Wiggins (Princeton, N.J.: Van Nostrand, 1961), 140.

4. Ibid., 4–5.

5. Leo Strauss, "Preface to Spinoza's Critique of Religion," in *Liberalism: Ancient and Modern* (New York: Basic Books, 1968), 255.

6. Leo Strauss, *Natural Right and History* (Chicago: University of Chicago Press, 1953), 6.

7. Strauss, *Liberalism: Ancient and Modern*, 24.

8. Herbert J. Storing, ed., *Essays in the Scientific Study of Politics* (New York: Holt, Rinehart and Winston, 1962), 221.

9. Strauss, *Liberalism: Ancient and Modern*, 34.

10. Ibid., 218–20.

11. Ibid., 218–19.

12. John H. Schaar and Sheldon S. Wolin, "Review Essay," *American Political Science Review* 57 (March 1963): 128.

13. Leo Strauss, "The Mutual Influence of Theology and Philosophy," *Iyyun: Hebrew Philosophical Quarterly* 5 (January 1954): 125.

14. Leo Strauss, *Spinoza's Critique of Religion* (New York: Schocken Books, 1965), 30.

15. Strauss, *Natural Right and History*, 13.

16. Ibid., 196.

17. Strauss, "The Mutual Influence of Theology and Philosophy," 125.

18. Strauss, *Natural Right and History*, 1–3.

19. Leo Strauss, *Thoughts on Machiavelli* (Glencoe, Ill.: Free Press, 1958), 13.

20. Letter to Karl Lowith, August 18, 1946, "Correspondence Concerning Modernity: Karl Lowith and Leo Strauss," *Independent Journal of Philosophy* 4 (1983): 107–8.

21. Leo Strauss, "The Crisis of Political Philosophy," in *The Predicament of Modern Politics*, ed. Howard Spaeth (Detroit: University of Detroit Press, 1964), 92–93.

22. Leo Strauss, "Liberal Education and Responsibility," in *Liberalism: Ancient and Modern*, 9.

23. Leo Strauss, "What Is Liberal Education?" in *Liberalism: Ancient and Modern*, 5.

24. Strauss, "Liberal Education and Responsibility," 18.

25. Strauss, "What Is Liberal Education?" 5.

26. Ibid., 8.

27. Ibid., 3.

28. Strauss, "Liberal Education and Responsibility," 19.

29. Leo Strauss, *Persecution and the Art of Writing* (Glencoe, Ill.: Free Press, 1952).

30. Strauss, "Liberal Education and Responsibility," 24.

Bibliography

"Correspondence Concerning Modernity: Karl Lowith and Leo Strauss." 1983. *Independent Journal of Philosophy* 4: 107–8.

Deutsch, Kenneth L., and John Murley, eds. 1999. *Leo Strauss, the Straussians, and the American Regime.* Lanham, Md.: Rowman and Littlefield.

Deutsch, Kenneth L., and Walter Nicgorski, eds. 1995. *Leo Strauss: Political Philosopher and Jewish Thinker.* Lanham, Md.: Rowman and Littlefield.

Deutsch, Kenneth L., and Walter Soffer, eds. 1987. *The Crisis of Liberal Democracy: A Straussian Perspective.* Albany, N.Y.: SUNY Press.

Schaar, John H., and Sheldon S. Wolin. 1963. "Review Essay." *American Political Science Review* 57 (March): 125–50.

Storing, Herbert J., ed. 1962. *Essays in the Scientific Study of Politics.* New York: Holt, Rinehart and Winston.

Strauss, Leo. 1952. *Persecution and the Art of Writing.* Glencoe, Ill.: Free Press.

———. 1953. *Natural Right and History.* Chicago: University of Chicago Press.

———. 1954. "The Mutual Influence of Theology and Philosophy." *Iyyun: Hebrew Philosophical Quarterly* 5 (January).

———. 1958. *Thoughts on Machiavelli.* Glencoe, Ill.: Free Press.

———. 1961. "Relativism." In *Relativism and the Study of Man,* edited by Helmut Schoeck and James W. Wiggins. Princeton, N.J.: Van Nostrand.

———. 1964. "The Crisis of Political Philosophy." In *The Predicament of Modern Politics,* edited by Howard Spaeth. Detroit: University of Detroit Press.

———. 1965. *Spinoza's Critique of Religion.* New York: Schocken Books.

———. 1968. *Liberalism: Ancient and Modern.* New York: Basic Books.

———. 1972. "Political Philosophy and the Crisis of Our Time." In *The Post-Behavioral Era,* edited by George Graham and George Carey. New York: David McKay.

The Relation of Intellect and Will in the Thought of Richard Weaver

ROBERT A. PRESTON

In May 1960 Richard Weaver (1910–1963) published an article in *The Individualist* in which he defined the intellectual conservative. To be clear, Weaver was speaking of the intellectual conservative, not the social, fiscal, or political conservative. Here is Weaver's definition:

> It is my contention that a conservative is a realist, who believes that there is a structure of reality independent of his own will and desire. He believes that there is a creation which was here before him, which exists now not by just his sufferance, and which will be here after he is gone. This structure consists not merely of the great physical world but also of many laws, principles, and regulations which control human behavior. Though this reality is independent of the individual, it is not hostile to him. It is in fact amenable by him in many ways, but it cannot be changed radically and arbitrarily. This is the cardinal point. The conservative holds that man in this world cannot make his will his law without any regard to limits and to the fixed nature of things.[1]

It is clear from this definition that Weaver stayed faithful to the position he set down in *Ideas Have Consequences*, published twelve years earlier. It is also clear that Weaver is stating definitively that there is a basis for truth in reality. There is, in Weaver's words, *"the fixed nature of things."* Ultimately, this gets to the heart of metaphysical realism, and because the metaphysics of realism has not been taught to the general under-graduate population for the past thirty years, these are strange concepts to many.

This decline in philosophical education has been nationwide, and as a result, most college students today would find the reading of Weaver an arduous task. The problem is compounded when the best and bright-est of our undergraduates go on to law school, medical school, business school, or graduate studies in the sciences or humanities without any grounding in a philosophy of realism. These are our leaders of tomor-row. In fact, many of those who were once our leaders of tomorrow have already arrived, and we are suffering the consequences of their being denied the education they needed to make decisions and choices based on *the fixed nature of things.*

In the introduction to *Ideas,* Weaver tells us that his basic assump-tion is "that the world is intelligible and that man is free."[2] This simple statement contains a world of wisdom. It implies that there is a Creator who has brought into being a planned universe in which each being has a purpose and function. This hearkens back to Aristotle's observation in the first book of *The Nicomachean Ethics* that if we are to understand the proper meaning of happiness, we must answer the question: *What is the function of Man?*[3] The implication here is that independent of what we might want, there is a purpose set down *in the nature of things* that we must fulfill if we are to become happy—that is, become the persons the Creator planned for us to be.

Weaver, in the same article quoted above, develops this theme as fol-lows: "There is in Elizabethan literature a famous poem entitled 'A Mir-ror for Magistrates.' . . . The story . . . I remember with special vividness concludes with this observation as a moral—'He made his will his law.' And that has stayed with me as a kind of description of the radical: he makes his will the law, instead of following the rules of justice and pru-dence."[4] This is the great temptation we all face today—the temptation to deny that there is an authority outside ourselves that can command our obedience and assert that we are "autonomous selves," that is, we make our own wills the law.

Weaver argues that this breakdown has its origin in the fourteenth century with the defeat of logical realism by nominalism. The result is that reality is judged to be the object of the senses, and the universals are relegated to logical constructs, with an ensuing denial of the realm of the transcendent. This ushers in the realm of materialism and the age of the physical sciences in the seventeenth century, when the question "what is the world for?" is no longer asked; rather, the major concern is "how does the world work?"

In the nineteenth century, Weaver argues, there occurred

> two developments of overwhelming influence. The first was a patent increase in man's dominion over nature which dazzled all but the most thoughtful; and the second was the growing mandate for popular education. The latter might have proved a good in itself, but was wrecked on the unsolvable problem of authority; no one was in a position to say what the hungering multitude was to be fed. Finally, in an abject surrender to the situation, in an abdication of the authority of knowledge, came the elective system. This was followed by a carnival of specialism, professionalism and vocationalism, often fostered and protected by strange bureaucratic devices, so that on the honored name of university there traded a weird congeries of interests, not a few of which were anti-intellectual even in their pretensions.[5]

Weaver, both in *Ideas Have Consequences* and again in *Visions of Order*, makes a strong attack on the notion of equalitarianism. He tells us in *Ideas* that "the most insidious idea employed to break down society is an undefined equalitarianism."[6]

It is this notion of "undefined equalitarianism" that I examine here to get at the basis of Weaver's objections. Let us begin with the proper use of the term *equal*, which is first and foremost a mathematical term. In mathematics, *equal* means "the same as." When we say that $2 + 2 = 4$ or that 2 pints = 1 quart, we mean that the terms on one side of the equation are equivalent to the terms on the other side of the equation. Note well the terms *equation* and *equivalent*. Because mathematics deals with formal, not material, concepts, in mathematics, two pints are the same as a quart. In the mathematical world, one does not ask "a quart of what?"

When we move the word *equal* from the world of mathematics to the realm of reality, it loses its univocal meaning and takes on an analogical meaning. It no longer means "the same as." To say that men and women are equal does not mean that men are the same as women, although some seem to think this might be the case. In its analogical sense, the term *equal* comes closer to the term *equivalent*, or "of equal value," but even that can be misleading.

If you bear with me, I now attempt to get behind the notion of *equal* as it is used in the Declaration of Independence. There it is written that "all men are created equal." It does not say that they are born equal, because it is obvious even to the careless observer that they are not. So what is the difference between being created equal and being born equal? We now enter the world of metaphysics, where we must confront the dual reality of the universal and the individual, a favorite Weaverian topic. The Creator creates human nature; the procreator gives birth to an individual human, that is, human nature incarnate, individualized by the material principle of the body. Each of us is equal in our humanity; each of us is unequal as an individual. It is when we confuse these two realms that problems arise.

Ideas Have Consequences is an unrelenting attack on nominalism, that doctrine that asserts the reality of the individual alone, consigning the universal to the realm of the logical construct. The proper world of the logical construct is the world of mathematics, where inches and feet, pints and quarts, triangles and trapezoids abound. In the real world, an inch of thread is not the same as an inch of string, nor is a pint of milk the same as a pint of bourbon.

The metaphysical doctrine of realism to which Weaver subscribes distinguishes between the universal and the individual, but it does not separate them. John is a human being and Mary is a human being, but John and Mary are quite different individuals. Thus, they are equal in the sense that both participate in human nature, but they are unequal in the sense that one is different from the other. This is what Weaver is referring to when he speaks of "undefined equalitarianism." Weaver observes that even though the notion of equalitarianism makes no sense, that is no deterrent to its spread.[7] The reason for this is quite easy to see. Nominalism, the current popular metaphysical position, holds that only the individual exists independently of the human mind. If that is so, then it is quite easy to gloss over differences and proceed by way of reductionism to some notion of equality and sameness.

In modern educational theory we find this creeping equalitarianism in the popular notion of students and teachers being co-learners. This is expressed in that wonderful injunction, "Get the sage off the stage." Good-bye, Mr. Chips. Teachers and students are all on a first-name basis, good buddies in the search for knowledge, and the grading system is a hanger-on from a less enlightened era.

It is instructive that the Latin term for student is *discipulus* and its correlative is *magister*. In this classical view, a *discipulus* needs a *magister*. The English word *discipline* refers to both content (what is your discipline?) and a regimen necessary to learning. Without discipline, no learning is possible. The serious student disciplines himself, but discipline is not enough. The student also needs the master, the one who knows.

In this regard, more insight is provided in the world of athletic competition. No matter how competent and professional the athlete, he or she still needs a coach. Tennis provides a good example here. Even the greatest tennis player has a coach, and usually a trainer as well. Once the player wearies of the discipline, the end is near. In sports it is not equality that is sought but superiority, and superiority requires constant discipline under the leadership of a competent coach. Here in the world of tennis we find the relationship of the *discipulus* and the *magister* writ large.

Weaver, in his attack on equalitarianism, argues that the problem stems from a confusion of roles. Weaver writes: "the comity of peoples in groups large or small rests not upon the chimerical notion of equality but upon fraternity."[8]

Before examining this notion of fraternity, it is useful to look closely at the notion of roles. Here I refer to the idea of the "created order." When a person is created, that person is created as a human being. When a person is born, that person is either a male or a female. Thus, we immediately have two roles: that of creature to the Creator, and that of son or daughter to parents. Other roles are also involved: if this is the firstborn, the wife has become a mother and the husband a father. Each of these roles has corresponding obligations and rights.

Notice the intricate web of roles involved here: creature to Creator, child to parents, husband to wife, wife to husband, mother to child, father to child. If the child is a son, the relationship to his parents is different from that of a daughter to her parents. (If you don't think so, ask any father if he worries more about his teenage son or teenage daughter being out late at night. Don't ask the mother; she worries about each one equally.) The point here is that we must view reality in terms of the "created order." We all exist in a web of relationships or roles, and it is our task to recognize our roles and the accompanying obligations and rights.

At first, we are sons or daughters with obligations and relations to our mothers and fathers. Then we are brothers and sisters related each to the other; we are students related to teachers, or vice versa; we are voters in the political order; we are employees related to employers, or vice versa; we are husbands or wives, fathers or mothers; we are parishioners or pastors; we are citizens or civic officeholders. The list of roles is endless.

Long before St. Paul told wives to be subject to their husbands and husbands to love their wives, Aristotle had written that the husband is superior to the wife. Aristotle has a clear notion of role in mind. He does not say that the male is superior to the female, but that the husband is superior to the wife. His meaning is clear from the context of the discussion. The husband has responsibility for the family, and the wife has responsibility for the household. Likewise, the role of the mother is superior to that of the father. This is not to say that the role of the father is not important, but the role of the mother is crucial.

Aristotle speaks of these relationships in terms of function. In Book VIII of *The Nicomachean Ethics* he says this: "From the outset the functions are divided, the husband's being different from the wife's; so they supply each other's deficiencies by pooling their personal resources. For this reason it is thought that both utility and pleasure have a place in conjugal love. But it may be based also on goodness, supposing the partners to be of good character; for they have each their own special excellence, and this may be a source of pleasure to both."[9] Those who are offended by Aristotle's or St. Paul's view that the husband has greater responsibility and obligation than the wife with regard to the family simply do not grasp the created order and our roles in that order. Aristotle says quite matter-of-factly that mothers love their children more than fathers do. This is the proper order of things. It often comes as a shock to the young husband that when children arrive on the scene, he takes a backseat to the children in terms of his wife's affection. However, as his wife takes on greater responsibility and importance as a mother, he takes on greater responsibility and importance not as a father but as a husband, because his duties to the family increase with each additional child.

Thus, we must view individuals not as monads floating unconnected in empty space but as individual beings with myriad relationships to one another in an ever-changing series of roles, each with its special responsibilities and duties.

Michael J. Sandel of Harvard writes in *Democracy's Discontent* of "the unencumbered self." This self has come to be in the world with no Creator; it has no obligations it does not choose to have. Referring to the view of John Rawls, Sandel writes: "considered as unencumbered selves, we must respect the dignity of all persons, but beyond this we only owe what we agree to owe."[10] What we see here are competing definitions of freedom: the liberal view that we are free to do what we want, and the conservative view, taken from Aristotle, that we are free to do what we know to be good.

I now turn to a topic that Weaver discusses in great depth but never mentions by its proper name: natural law. He does not mention it in *Ideas Have Consequences,* nor does he mention it in the hundreds of articles he wrote before his untimely death in 1963. I suspect Weaver knew that the concept of natural law was a red flag for those he was trying to convince of the error of their ways. He tells us in *Ideas* that he is reluctant to refer to religious notions unless absolutely necessary, and although natural law theory is a matter of reason rather than faith, Weaver knew it entailed an acceptance of the notion of a Creator.

A contemporary of Weaver's who was not reluctant to mention the theory of natural law was political pundit Walter Lippmann. In his book *Essays in the Public Philosophy,* published in 1955, Lippmann argues that natural law originated with the Greeks and was put into practice by Alexander the Great, who realized "that a large, plural society could not be governed without recognizing common law. This common law is 'natural' in the sense that it can be discovered by any rational mind, that it is not the willful and arbitrary positive command of the sovereign power. This is the necessary assumption, without which it is impossible for different peoples, with their competing interests to live together in peace and freedom within one community."[11]

For Lippmann, the basis of what he calls the public philosophy is natural law. Among the several schools of natural law there are certain common precepts: "that in Cicero's words 'law is the bond of civil society,' and that all men, governors and the governed, are always under, are never above, laws; that these laws can be developed and refined by rational discussion, and that the highest laws are those upon which rational men of good will, when fully informed, will tend to agree."[12] Lippmann argues that natural law theory began to disappear from public discourse in the nineteenth century, and by the twentieth century, it was no longer the dominant view in either politics or law. Yet without natural law, Lippmann sees no way for Western democracies to survive. But any attempt to restore the natural law basis to our political life is met with opposition. Lippmann writes: "The problem of communication is posed because in the modern world, as it is today, most men — not all men, to be sure, but most active and influential men—are in practice positivists who hold that the only world which has reality is the physical world."[13]

The physical world is, of course, the world of change and flux, of time and space, of individuals who live and then die. There is no basis for truth in that world. There are only facts to be analyzed and counted. As Weaver notes, the expression "It is a fact that . . ." is now the substitute for "It is true that. . . ."

Truth can only be based on the universal, which transcends our realm of change. It is the universal that is always and everywhere the same, that is outside the order of time—it is literally *ex tempore*, eternal. For Aristotle and Aquinas, the universal is in the individual. A person is at once an individual who possesses the universal human nature. Our knowledge of the individual qua individual is only factual knowledge: how old he is, how much he weighs, where is he at this moment. In contrast, our knowledge of human nature is universal: all human beings are rational animals, and what can be learned about the rational animal will be true of all human persons.

Natural law is based on the intelligible within reality. Only a philosophy of realism provides a basis for natural law theory, because only a philosophy of realism admits the reality of both the individual and the universal.

Lippmann makes clear the importance of this distinction when he speaks of the difference between the people and the voters. He writes: "Those who are strongly nominalist in their cast of mind, which modern men tend to be, look upon the abstract concept of a corporate people as mere words, like conjuring up spooks. Thus, according to that resolute nominalist Jeremy Bentham, 'the community is a fictitious body, composed of the individual persons who are considered as constituting as it were its members. The interest of the community then is—what?—The sum of the interests of the several members who compose it.'"[14]

But, as Lippmann goes on to say, Bentham's view does not bear critical analysis. The community is not the same from one hour to the next because individuals are born into it and pass out of it. It is constantly changing because it is composed only of individuals. The realist view of the community—that is, the people—is that it is composed of three groups: the dead, the living, and the unborn. Therefore, the well-being of the community cannot be entrusted to the voters, who can be counted on to express their own self-interest. To whom must the well-being of the people be entrusted?

This is, of course, an important question. Traditionally, in our form of government, this is the primary responsibility of the Senate. Members of the House of Representatives are sent to Washington to do as its name indicates, represent those who elected them to office. The senators, however, owe their allegiance to the people broadly considered. Their primary concern should not be the well-being of the voters or even the well-being of those alive at the moment; senators must include the well-being of those yet to come, and they must maintain an allegiance to those who have gone before. So it is that the old plant trees in whose shade they will not sit, and we build houses with an eye to the third generation. Those who are of a nominalist cast of mind cannot understand this.

I have been citing the works of two thinkers who wrote more than fifty years ago. Richard M. Weaver was a reclusive English professor at the University of Chicago. Walter Lippmann was a noted political journalist who was widely read and very influential. The similarities between their criticism of current events are striking.

Both men wrote in the period just after World War II, and in reaction to the destructiveness of that period. Each in his own way was trying to understand what had gone wrong in the Western European tradition that had resulted in two world wars within a twenty-five-year period. Both found the problem of their time rooted in man's inability to grasp the true nature of reality. It was, in short, a problem in metaphysics, the science that studies the nature of being and tries to answer Plato's question: what is really real?

Plato's question has echoed down the centuries. His metaphor of the cave tells us that we often confuse the shadows on the wall with reality, but only those who live in the sunlight can grasp what is really real. In short, those who claim that only the individual is real and assign the universal to the realm of the mental construct are the cave dwellers. These are the nominalists, the empiricists, the positivists, and the materialists.

In Weaver's view, the critical period in our history occurred in the fourteenth century with the defeat of critical realism by nominalism. It was the victory of William of Occam over Thomas Aquinas. It began a slow movement from the sunlight back into the cave, where modern man now finds himself.

Lippmann argues that the Western European tradition was able to hold on to the realist tradition at least until the founding of our nation at the end of the eighteenth century. Our basic political documents—the Declaration of Independence and the Constitution—are natural law documents, within the tradition of philosophical realism. But this tradition fell out of favor in the nineteenth century and was no longer taught in U.S. colleges, universities, and law schools in the twentieth century. Today, we still have the documents, but we no longer agree on what they mean.

On the face of it, it seems absurd to say that most people do not know what is really real—and I use that expression in its Platonic sense. But if Weaver and Lippmann are to be believed, that is exactly the case. And in fact, it is worse than that. Most people think they do know exactly what is really real—namely, what they see, taste, touch, hear, and smell. And that, of course, is the problem. Not only are most people out of touch with what is really real; they are unaware that such is the case. They are ignorant of their ignorance.

Weaver addresses this problem in these words:

> There is no term proper to describe the condition in which he (i.e., modern man) is now left unless it is "abysmality." He is in the deep and dark abysm, and he has nothing with which to raise himself. His life is practice without theory. As problems crowd upon him, he deepens confusion by meeting them with ad hoc policies. Secretly he hungers for the truth, but consoles himself with the thought that life should be experimental. He sees his institutions crumbling and rationalizes with talk of emancipation. Wars have to be fought, apparently with increased frequency; therefore he revives his old ideals—ideals which his present assumptions actually render meaningless—and by the machinery of state, forces them again to do service. He struggles with the paradox that total immersion in matter unfits him to deal with the problems of matter.[15]

Weaver notes the irony in the current predicament. As we have sought to establish human reason as the arbiter of the true and the false, the good and the evil, we have lost any basis for authority because we have individualized the concept of reason. My reason is as good as your reason, and my view of reality is as good as your view of reality. There is no authoritative view that must be consulted. If there is no Creator, then there is no divine eternal law, no natural law for us to examine to find a basis for objective truth. Human positive law, therefore, is no more or less than what five members of the Supreme Court say it is.

No wonder there are special-interest groups that spend millions of dollars and all their time in an attempt to influence our senators in deciding who shall sit on the Supreme Court. These groups fear that certain recently discovered "rights" in the Constitution might be taken away by a more considered judgment of what the Constitution actually means. On the other side are those who want to cite an authority above the Constitution, the one who is the foundation of the law that is above both the rulers and the ruled. Thus the battle is joined, and its outcome is uncertain. And it is a battle that is becoming more visceral in its intensity. Many have pointed to the incivility of our current political dialogue, if it can truly be called a dialogue at all. It has more of the characteristics of a dockside brawl. Emotion has replaced reason, with the result that there is no principled argument but only name-calling and propagandistic spinning.

There is a certain irony, I suppose, in citing two thinkers who see the problem of our time as being the citizenry's inability to grasp reality in its fundamental meaning. If that is the problem, is it solvable? There is a sort of exasperated tone to Weaver's observation in chapter 7 of *Ideas Have Consequence*, where he begins to address a solution to the problems he has cited: "I have endeavored to make plain in every way that I can that I regard all the evils in our now extensive catalogue as flowing from a falsified picture of the world which, for our immediate concern, results in an inability to interpret current happenings."[16]

Quite obviously, this problem has not been addressed, much less solved, in the fifty-plus years since Weaver and Lippmann wrote. The issues they addressed have been exacerbated by the continuing domination of nominalism over realism. One need only cite the current controversy over evolution versus intelligent design—where some claim that evolution is not simply the cause of the origin of species but the cause of life itself—to see the results of our inability to grasp reality. The proponents of neo-Darwinism and—it must be said—most of our fellow citizens can see no difference between the order of change and the order of being. Evolution can explain change, but only creation can explain the existence of things. Such distinctions are lost on the philosophically handicapped.

It is interesting that both Weaver and Lippmann proposed solutions that involve private property. Weaver calls private property our "last metaphysical right." He sees it as a way to get modern man to admit he has a "birthright of responsibility." Weaver writes: "We say that the right of private property is metaphysical because it does not depend on any test of social usefulness. Property depends upon the idea of the *hisness of his: proprietas, Eigentum,* the very words assert an identification of owner and owned. Now the great value of this is the fact that something being private property removes it from the area of contention. In the *hisness* of property we have dogma; there discussion ends."[17] Thus, Weaver treats private property from the point of view of the protection it provides the owner from the designs of a collectivist state. He calls it a "sanctuary" from the "relativists from the social sciences who wish to bring everyone under secular group control."[18]

Lippmann approaches the issue of private property from a natural law perspective. He tries to show that natural law is the best theoretical foundation for a legal system of private property. First of all, private property is not a natural right; it is a legal right granted by the state to achieve the ends of society. All property belongs to humankind, not to any individual. Lippmann writes: "Because the legal owner enjoys the use of a limited necessity belonging to all men he cannot be the sovereign lord of his possessions. He is not entitled to exercise his absolute and therefore arbitrary will. He owes duties that correspond with his rights. His ownership is a grant by the laws to achieve not his private purposes but the common social purpose."[19]

I think it is accurate to say that Lippmann understands the doctrine of private property much better than Weaver does. Weaver claims too much for the right of private property. He writes: "By some mystery of imprint and assimilation man becomes identified with his things, so that a forcible separation of the two seems like a breach in nature."[20] This rhetorical statement would lead one to believe that Weaver thinks of private property as a natural right, a position that contradicts his basic theory. But he was writing at a time when he saw the problem to be "the Omnipotent State" and private property to be the last bastion against its collectivist aims. Private property, let us say, was the largest arrow in the conservative's quiver, and Weaver made many claims for its use.

We have heard the arguments of two men writing at the same time who saw the political and social problems of our time to be rooted in a false metaphysical view of reality. If this is so, then the problem is one of education. However, the colleges and universities are firmly in the camp of the nominalists. This includes the church-related colleges and universities, with certain notable exceptions. What, then, is to be done? Let me conclude with this observation from Lippmann:

> The cultural heritage which contains the whole structure and fabric of the good life is acquired. It may be rejected. It may be acquired badly. It may not be acquired at all. . . .
>
> The acquired culture is not transmitted in our genes, and so the issue is always in doubt. The good life in the good society, though attainable, is never attained and possessed once and for all. So that what has been attained will again be lost if the wisdom of the good life in a good society is not transmitted.
>
> That is the central critical condition of the Western society: that the democracies are ceasing to receive the condition of civility in which the good society, the liberal democratic way of life at its best, originated and developed. They are cut off from the public philosophy and the political arts, which are needed to govern the liberal democratic society. They have not been initiated into its secrets, and they do not greatly care for as much of it as they are prepared to understand.[21]

Notes

1. Ted J. Smith III, ed., *In Defense of Tradition: Collected Shorter Writings of Richard M. Weaver 1929–1963* (Indianapolis: Liberty Fund, 2000), 477; emphasis in original.

2. Richard M. Weaver, *Ideas Have Consequences*, Midway Reprint (Chicago: University of Chicago Press, 1976), 1.

3. Aristotle, *The Nicomachean Ethics*, ed. J. A. K. Thomson (London: Penguin Classics, 1953), 15 (1097b-24).

4. Smith, *In Defense of Tradition*, 477.

5. Weaver, *Ideas Have Consequences*, 8.

6. Ibid., 41.

7. Ibid., 44.

8. Ibid., 41.

9. Aristotle, *Nicomachean Ethics*, 23–28 (1162a).

10. Michael J. Sandel, *Democracy's Discontent: America in Search of a Public Philosophy* (Cambridge, Mass.: Belknap Press of Harvard University Press, 1996), 14.

11. Walter Lippmann, *Essays in the Public Philosophy* (New York: New

American Library, 1955), 83.
    12. Ibid., 123.
    13. Ibid., 125.
    14. Ibid., 34.
    15. Weaver, *Ideas Have Consequences*, 6–7.
    16. Ibid., 129.
    17. Ibid., 132.
    18. Ibid.
    19. Lippmann, *Essays in the Public Philosophy*, 93.
    20. Weaver, *Ideas Have Consequences*, 134.
    21. Lippmann, *Essays in the Public Philosophy*, 75.

Bibliography

Aristotle. 1953. *The Nicomachean Ethics*. Edited by J. A. K. Thomson. London: Penguin Classics.

Lippmann, Walter. 1955. *Essays in the Public Philosophy*. New York: New American Library.

Sandel, Michael J. 1996. *Democracy's Discontent: America in Search of a Public Philosophy*. Cambridge, Mass.: Belknap Press of Harvard University Press.

Smith, Ted J. III, ed. 2000. *In Defense of Tradition: Collected Shorter Writings of Richard M. Weaver 1929–1963*. Indianapolis: Liberty Fund.

Weaver, Richard M. 1976. *Ideas Have Consequences*. Midway Reprint. Chicago: University of Chicago Press.

———. 1995. *Visions of Order: The Cultural Crisis of Our Time*. Wilmington, Del.: ISI Press.

Robert Nisbet and the Conservative Intellectual Tradition

BRAD LOWELL STONE

Robert Nisbet (1913–1996) was a prose stylist of the first rank, arguably the original American communitarian, and a major figure in the renaissance in conservative thought that occurred after 1950. He published his first and most influential book, *The Quest for Community*, in 1953 at the end of a three-year period that produced what he later called a "small harvest of conservative books"[1]: Russell Kirk's *The Conservative Mind*, Eric Voegelin's *The New Science of Politics*, Leo Strauss's *Natural Right and History*, William F. Buckley's *God and Man at Yale*, John Hallowell's *The Moral Foundation of Democracy*, and Daniel Boorstin's *The Genius of American Politics*. Upon its publication, *The Quest for Community* received warm attention from reviewers across the political spectrum.

According to Nisbet, however, he "had not particularly written [*The Quest for Community*] as a conservative book."[2] Until he read Russell Kirk's *The Conservative Mind* in 1953, Nisbet thought of conservatism as a European way of thinking associated with the reaction to the French Revolution. Nisbet had studied this thought in great detail. The subject of his dissertation was the "Reactionary Enlightenment," chiefly the thinking of Bonald, de Maistre, and Chateaubriand, but whatever sympathies he may have had toward conservatism before 1953, he agreed with Lionel Trilling, Louis Hartz, and others who argued in the 1950s that liberalism was the only authentic political and intellectual tradition in America. Certainly, Nisbet did not believe that a defense of business and opposition to the New Deal by themselves qualified one as a conservative. In fact, we would do well to remember that Herbert Hoover closed his 1928 campaign with a speech in which he praised liberalism and individualism, Dwight Eisenhower described himself as "militantly progressive," and not until the 1970s could the Republican Party claim to be the more conservative major party. After all, it was the pro-business Republican Party that introduced the equal rights amendment into every Congress between 1923 and the early 1970s; it was the Republican Party that favored contraceptive and abortion rights before 1973 (Estelle Griswold, of *Griswold v. Connecticut* fame, was a Republican activist and close friend of the Bush family); and it was the Republican Party that supported civil rights legislation opposed by states' rights Democrats.

According to Nisbet, his view of conservatism changed after he read *The Conservative Mind* because Kirk "gave scholarly and timely pedigree to conservatism in England and the United States, demonstrating the key role of Burke in both countries."[3] For example, in 1976 Nisbet published an essay, "The Social Impact of the American Revolution" (republished in *The Making of Modern Society*), in which he investigated the conservative nature of the American Revolution in contrast to the zealous passions and much greater social disorder of other revolutions.[4] He attributed the cautious and restrained nature of the American Revolution to the localization of power, the widespread influence of religion, the absence of anticlericalism, the vibrant presence of intermediate associations and traditional communities, and a class structure that prevented any group from identifying too thoroughly with the revolution and perpetual tumult. Indeed, Nisbet was so convinced by Kirk that he began to describe American soil as being particularly congenial to conservative ideas. In 1982 he claimed that there have been "two significant eruptions of conservative ideology in modern Western thought: first in 1790–1810 in Western Europe chiefly, but to some degree in the United States; and then in 1950–1970, largely in America."[5]

Having mentioned Nisbet's debt to and admiration for Kirk, I should also mention Kirk's admiration for Nisbet. In *The Politics of Prudence* Kirk says, "people may desire to commence their serious study of conservative thought by reading a succinct but sensible manual on the subject. If so, I recommend particularly an agreeably slim volume by Robert A. Nisbet, entitled simply *Conservatism: Dream and Reality*."[6] Needless to say, Kirk's endorsement held weight. He was for decades the dean of

American conservatism, and by all accounts, including Nisbet's, he was the person most responsible for inciting the post–World War II conservative intellectual movement in America.

I agree with Kirk's assessment of *Conservatism: Dream and Reality*. Nisbet's version of conservatism is simple, powerful, and very appealing. At the same time, I am compelled to state my belief that Nisbet's version of conservatism is somewhat peculiar, perhaps even singular. This in no way diminishes the worth of Nisbet's thought. On the contrary, I believe that any conservative can profit from an encounter with Nisbet's works and that the more conservatives who read Nisbet, the better. Reading Nisbet compels one to deliberate about the ends or purposes informing one's worldview and directing one's activities as a conservative. Nonetheless, I do not believe that Nisbet is best viewed as a typical or representative conservative thinker.

In an essay titled "Still Questing," published in 1993 to commemorate the fortieth anniversary of *The Quest for Community*, Nisbet said that any conservative group in the United States confronts a double task: "The first is to work tirelessly toward the diminution of the centralized, omnicompetent and unitary state with its ever-growing debt and deficit. The second and equally important task is that of protecting, reinforcing, nurturing where necessary the varied groups and associations which form the true building blocks of the social order."[7] Any conservative would recognize the importance of these tasks. What is peculiar in Nisbet's view is that these are the exclusive, exhaustive, and definitive conservative tasks. As he puts it in *Prejudices: A Philosophical Dictionary*, "the sole object of the conservative tradition . . . is the protection of the social order and its constitutive groups from the enveloping bureaucracy of the nation state."[8] Nisbet maintained throughout his career that conservatism includes just two complementary components: social pluralism and antistatism. Certainly, by this definition, Nisbet qualifies as a quintessential conservative. As I make clear in this chapter, however, by this definition, many who call themselves conservatives do not qualify because they fail to nurture the communities constituting the social order or they favor statist initiatives. Nisbet was in fact very quick to deny the label of conservative to many who claimed it.

Nisbet's own social pluralism and antistatism were maintained unwaveringly over the course of his long and productive career. In fact, in *The Quest for Community* he announced the theme that united virtually everything he wrote. He states there: "I have chosen to deal with the *political* causes of the manifold alienations that lie behind the contemporary quest for community."[9] The real significance of the unitary state, he believed, was that it dislocated the authority and functions of traditional communities—those of kinship, conscience, locale, and voluntary association—leaving individuals isolated and unattached. Like Tocqueville before him, Nisbet did not see the individual and state as opposed to each other; he saw them as mutually reinforcing poles, each opposed to the social groups and associations lying between them. Individual isolation and the fervent modern desire for communal fellowship, Nisbet believed, result from the debasement of intermediate communities wrought by the sovereign Western state. According to Nisbet, however, the sad irony of this circumstance is that the isolated modern individual who yearns for community typically embraces the "national community," thus enhancing the power of the state and further eroding traditional communities.

According to Nisbet's ideal-typical portrait, traditional communities possess several requisite features. First, communities have *functions* that they fulfill. They arise to address perennial human needs and to solve problems. As Nisbet says, quoting Ortega y Gasset, "human beings do not come together to *be* together; they come together to *do* something together."[10] Second, a community's function must be transformed into a deeply held belief or *dogma*. The function must "seem good"—the literal meaning of dogma.[11] Third, *authority*, not power, characterizes communities. Authority arises through and is legitimized by spontaneous custom, use, and wont, not, as with power, through external force. Fourth, communities are *hierarchical*. Within a community one's identity is bound up with one's status and roles, and it is impossible to array such roles in a line of equality. To "follow the specification of one's role" in a community is "to engage in and be part of a pattern of authority."[12] Fifth, communities are animated by a sense of *honor* that elevates the concerns of individuals beyond the merely utilitarian or pecuniary. And finally, communities sponsor feelings of *solidarity* and *superiority*.[13]

Their essential features expose communities to both widespread suspicion and state encroachment in the modern age. To modern critics, these features are unsavory: communities are exclusive, intolerant, arrogant, inegalitarian, and authoritarian. To these same critics, the state is seen as a more fair and efficient provider of social functions. Still, although the very nature of communities offends modern sensibilities, war has been the chief historical occasion and means for the state to consolidate its power at the expense of communities, according to Nisbet. War, he says, leads individuals to abandon their "smaller patriotism" for love of the state; it eats at "the cake of custom, the net of tradition," while promoting science and invention; and it fosters democracy.[14] Nisbet says, "Democracy, in all its variants, is the child of war," and he states elsewhere that "most of the great wars in the modern west have been attended by gains in the political and social rights of citizenship as well as by increased nationalism and the concentration of power."[15] Indeed, the war state, he argues, is the main cause of the welfare state. In *The Twilight of Authority*, he estimates that 75 percent of all national programs in Western societies designed to equalize income, property, and opportunity in the last 200 years "have been in the first instance adjuncts to the war state and of the war economy."[16]

In *The Present Age*, a book adapted from his 1988 Jefferson lecture, Nisbet addresses the United States specifically and speculates about the probable reactions of the framers to the product of their labor and aspirations 200 years after ratification of the Constitution. He asserts that three causally related things would most strike the framers about 1988 America: first, "the prominence of war in American life since 1914, amounting to a virtual seventy-five year war"; second, "the Leviathan-like presence of the national government in the affairs of states, towns, and cities, and in the lives, cradle to grave, of individuals"; and third, "the number of individuals who seem only loosely attached to groups and values such as kinship, community, and property, and whose lives are so plainly governed by the cash nexus."[17] The First World War is the most important war in U.S. history, according to Nisbet, because it "released the greatest number and diversity of changes in American life."[18] What changes would have occurred between 1914 and 1918 had there been no war, we cannot know. However, "What we do know is that the war and America's entrance into it, gave dynamic impact to the process of secularization, individuation, and other kinds of psychological change which so dramatically changed this country from the America of the turn of the century to the America of the 1920s."[19]

According to Nisbet, war always facilitates the centralization of power, but Woodrow Wilson's actions during the First World War greatly intensified this process. "Wilson's political, economic, social and intellectual reorganization of America in the short period of 1917–1919 is one of the most extraordinary feats in the long history of war and polity. . . . Within a few short months he had transformed traditional, decentralized, regional and localist America into a war state that at its height permeated every aspect of life."[20] Congress approved Wilson's request for war powers exceeding those dreamed of by any Caesar. The mines, telephones, telegraph, and railroads were nationalized; wages, prices, and profits were controlled by the national government; and civil liberties were suspended. Indeed, Nisbet asserts, "The blunt fact is that when under Wilson America was introduced to the War State in 1917, it was introduced also to what would later be known as the total, or totalitarian, state."[21]

Nisbet claims that Franklin Delano Roosevelt's moral model and practical political program were drawn directly from Wilson and argues, for example, that the New Deal was no more than an assemblage of government structures modeled on those that existed in 1917.[22] More consequential and long lasting than any particular New Deal program, however, was an idea contained within the New Deal. "In it the mesmerizing idea of *national community*—an idea that had been in the air since the Progressive era, featured in books by Herbert Croly, Walter Lippmann, John Dewey, and others, and had come into full but brief existence in 1917 under the stimulus of war—was now at long last to be initiated in peacetime, as a measure to combat the evils of capitalism and its 'economic royalists.'"[23]

According to Nisbet, as important as the New Deal was in promoting the idea of national community, World War II gave the idea its largest impetus. The real novelty and importance of World War II, in Nisbet's eyes, were that it created a "formal, official—and lasting!—union between the intellectual and the national government, at least when the latter could be thought of as in trustworthy hands, like Wilson's or FDR's."[24] The cold war followed, and the tie between the intellectual and the national government became even firmer. "Political omnicompetence, with the state the spearhead of all social and cultural life; industrialization, however farcical in context; nationalization of education; rampant secularization; and growing consumer-hedonism—all this bespeaks modernity to the Western clerisy and the welcome sign of the developed, the progressive."[25] Before World War I, socialist and liberal intellectuals viewed the state as a threat to liberties, but after seventy-five years of war and the moral equivalents of war, the left-leaning clerisy came to see the state as redemptive. "It is not enough to say that the national state is simply a *good* community; it must be presented as the *only* possible community in the late twentieth century, the single form of community that has emerged from the whole historical process and is thus, whether we recognize it or not, an inevitable stage in the evolution of human society."[26]

The combination of war and the concentration of power within the national, bureaucratic state, according to Nisbet, causes the fraying of social bonds. "Threads are loosened by the tightening of power at the center." Individuals are "loose" in the sense "of the loose cannon, the ship that slips its hawser, the dog its leash, the individual his accustomed moral restraint. . . . Without doubt," he says, "there are a great many loose individuals in American society at the present time: loose from marriage and family, from the school, the church, the nation, job, and moral responsibility."[27] Lacking genuine community ties, such persons are left with nothing but the "cash nexus" to regulate their relationships.

These things said, I must note that Nisbet was not a fatalist or a strict determinist. He says, "Everything vital in history reduces itself ultimately to ideas, which are the motive forces. Man *is* what he *thinks!*"[28] Consequently, in addition to containing a social history of the displacement of community by the state, his works contain a history of those ideas that have aided or combated this process. This history is conveyed largely through a description of two great traditions in Western thought—what Nisbet calls "political monism" and "social pluralism." This distinction bears little relationship to the more conventional distinctions between "liberal" and "conservative" or between "progressive" and "traditional" thought. Political monism begins with Plato and includes Hobbes, Rousseau, Michelet, Fichte, Treitschke, Bentham, and Lenin, among many others. According to Nisbet, each of these thinkers blended social nihilism with political affirmation, and "the affirmation in each instance is the state conceived as being, not force or repression, but justice, freedom, and tranquility for the individual."[29] Nisbet states in *Twilight of Authority* that within this tradition, "such groups as family, locality, neighborhood, church and other autonomous associations are almost uniformly reduced to their individual atoms, made into unities dependent upon concession of existence by the state, or in some other way significantly degraded."[30] Among the political monists, Nisbet considered Hobbes and Rousseau the "prime catalytic agents" in modern political thought, and in a 1953 letter to Kirk he called Rousseau "the real demon of the modern mind."[31]

The tradition of social pluralism, in contrast, begins with Aristotle and includes Aquinas, Althusius, Burke, Tocqueville, Acton, Proudhon, and Kropotkin. For these thinkers, freedom issues less from the form of government than from the relationship of government—whatever its form—to the communities constituting society. As Nisbet says, "a government monarchical or oligarchical in structure can be a free government if—as has been the case many times in history—it respects the other institutions of society and permits autonomies accordingly in the social and economic spheres."[32] For pluralists, liberty cannot exist if the powers of the state have reached out to encompass all spheres of social, moral, economic, and intellectual existence. The chief aim of social pluralists is to nurture and preserve the groups and associations constituting the social order.

Nisbet considered Aristotle, Burke, and Tocqueville the most important social pluralists, but he admired social pluralism in any form, be it called "conservative," "liberal," or "radical." Indeed, it is worth stressing that Proudhon and Kropotkin—both advocates of anarchist mutualism—were among the thinkers Nisbet most admired. He states, "I do not hesitate to say that there is a great deal more in common, so far as fundamental perspective is concerned, between Burke and Proudhon than there is between the former and some of those who today style themselves conservatives and between the latter and the vast majority of radicals, overwhelming[ly] dominated by Marx, in the late nineteenth and twentieth centuries."[33] Nisbet's rather ecumenical view of social pluralism is worth stressing because he was very discriminating when assessing "conservatives" in terms of their social pluralism and antistatism. In *Conservatism, Prejudices,* and various essays, he denies the "conservative" label to militarists, libertarians, populists, and many who are now called "social conservatives." Regarding militarists, he flatly states that the military spirit and conservatism have "nothing in common" because war undermines parochial affections while enhancing the power of the state.[34] As for libertarians, in an essay titled "Conservatives and Libertarians: Uneasy Cousins" first published in 1980, Nisbet describes libertarians as reliable and strident antistatists, but he denies that they are genuine conservatives because they are not social pluralists. "More and more," he says, "one has the impression that for libertarians today . . . individuals are alone real; institutions are but their shadows. I believe a state of mind is developing among libertarians in which the coercions of family, church, local community and school will seem almost as inimical to freedom as those of the political government."[35] He adds: "libertarians . . . appear to see social and moral authority and despotic political power as elements of a single spectrum, as an unbroken continuity. If, their argument goes, we are to be spared Leviathan we must challenge any and all forms of authority, including those which are inseparable from the social bond." In short, among certain libertarians, the authority of communities is mistaken for the power of the bureaucratic state, and such authority is deemed to be as great a threat to liberty as state power is.[36] Populists, for their part, dream the conservative nightmare, which Nisbet describes as "a society in which all constitutional limitations upon the direct power of the people, or any passing majority, are abrogated, leaving something akin to the mystique of Rousseau's General Will."[37] Nisbet also denies that certain "social conservatives" aligned with the Far Right are genuine conservatives. He states that the label "conservative," in the Burkean sense of the term, cannot be applied to most evangelicals because Burke distrusted enthusiasm in any form. "Conservatives," he says, "have for the most part believed in the Divine much as all educated people believe in gravity or the spherical shape of the earth—firmly but not ecstatically."[38] By contrast, among evangelicals, Nisbet identifies "an incessant desire to prove to others the exclusive truth of a single way of life or thought."[39] At any rate, he observes that many so-called conservative groups seek to replace "the social and economic provider-state" with "the moral provider-state."[40] He concludes that the "Far Right is less interested in Burkean immunities from government power than it is in putting a maximum of government power in the hand of those who can be trusted."[41]

Nisbet believed that no one could be trusted with such power, and he refused the label of "conservative" to any group that would use state power to impose its moral vision. To illustrate this in concrete terms, let me position Nisbet relative to a debate that occurred several years ago in the pages of *Responsive Community* between communitarian Amitai Etzioni and eminent social conservative Robert P. George. In response to Etzioni's suggestion that social conservatives are more willing than communitarians to use the power of the state to achieve their ends, George said that among the activities social conservatives disdain, abortion is the only one that "social conservatives would ban outright. . . . (in most cases)."[42] There is no doubt that Nisbet would have sided with Etzioni against George on this issue. Nisbet made it clear in *Prejudices* that he saw a national ban on abortion as a very dangerous use of government power. As a social pluralist, what concerned him most about *Roe v. Wade* was that "abortion was lifted from the twilight zone of pluralism, compromise, and conflicting dogma in which it had lain for millennia and was made the subject of centralized, national mandate."[43] If George's portrayal of social conservatives is correct, it is clear that they wish to replace one centralized, national mandate with another more to their liking.

Nisbet did lament the fact that defenders of abortion rights often use the issue as a means of venting their fury against the family. Still, as tragic and grotesque as pro-abortion views can sometimes be, Nisbet argued that the graver "danger to the social fabric and to individual liberty . . . is posed by the ranks of aggressive antiabortionists. In denying the right of the woman and her family to terminate pregnancy, these soldiers of righteousness strike at the very heart of both the family and individual rights."[44] Of these two rights, the loss of family rights concerned Nisbet more. "Nothing less than [an] abhorrent Rousseauian power lies potentially at least in the antiabortionist proposal that the origins of life be made a matter of political or constitutional law. The 'power which penetrates into one's innermost being' penetrates into the very womb, fragmenting in the process the moral authority that properly belongs to the family."[45] Nisbet maintained that moral virtue cannot thrive in the sort of sociological vacuum created by national mandates enforced by state power. The cultivation of moral virtue requires the "smaller patriotisms" and authority of communities. He concluded, therefore, that the issue of abortion should not be decided by coercive law but by Burkean expediency—"respectful recognition of the power and necessary role in human existence of privacy, use and wont, tradition and practicality."[46] Nisbet was far from being a pro-abortion libertarian; he was, as I heard Wilfred McClay put it, "anti-antiabortion" because of his commitment to the ancient and prescriptive rights of the family and other traditional communities so essential to the formation of moral character.

Nisbet believed that whatever their sources, monistic solutions to social ills almost always fail. Consequently, in the conclusions of both *The Quest for Community* and *The Twilight of Authority*, he suggests that the great need of our age is to redress the balance between the power of the unitary state and the authority of communities. What we need, he suggests, is a "new laissez-faire," a "form of laissez-faire that has as its object, not the abstract individual whether economic or political man, but rather the social group or association."[47] This new laissez-faire would supplement, not replace, the old laissez-faire, because the liberal values of freedom and autonomy are best achieved when community flourishes—when conditions foster "diversity of culture, plurality of association, and the division of authority."[48]

Of course, Nisbet recognized the legitimate role of the national state in issues of justice, national defense, and public works. Extensive administration and arbitrary power, both of which Nisbet feared, should not be confused with strong and energetic government within its proper sphere. The latter is as essential to spontaneous sociability as the former are dangerous. "But," Nisbet says, "from the centrality of government it does not follow that it must be omnicompetent, responsible for daily existence, and ever in our lives, and, worst of all, pretended moral teacher, guide to virtue and mother of spirit."[49]

From these few comments it should be clear that Nisbet's fear of the government as moral teacher and mother of spirit was indiscriminate; he feared such a government be it of the Left or the Right. What my brief comments cannot convey is just how rich a resource Nisbet's works are for any committed social pluralist and antistatist. From issues of perennial concern, such as the sources of corrosive individualism and the vital role of the family to the maintenance of social order and individual achievement, to the more timely issues of school vouchers, the use of faith-based organizations to administer government programs, and community approaches to crime, Nisbet's works are a potential source of great illumination.

I believe, in fact, that Nisbet contributed greatly to salutary changes over the last several decades in the way Americans conceive and speak about social issues and their solutions. In the early 1990s Nicholas Lemann asserted in *Washington Monthly* that "Nisbetism" had become "the stated creed of American politics at the highest level."[50] Although clearly overstated, this assertion contains a measure of truth. Among politicians in both major parties, public intellectuals, and many typical citizens, materialistic explanations of social problems and statist solutions have lost much of their appeal. The 1996 replacement of Aid to Families with Dependent Children by state and locally administered Temporary Assistance for Needy Families is just the most obvious retreat from federal bureaucracy to greater social pluralism. By various measures we have seen real signs of genuine social replenishment over the last fifteen years or so. For example, "community policing" has probably contributed at least in part to the dramatic declines in crime since the early 1990s, and associational memberships, volunteerism, and philanthropy have actually increased during this time.[51] Similarly, abortion,

teen birth, and teen suicide rates have all been declining since the early
to mid-1990s, and the annual divorce rate has been declining modestly
since the early 1980s. Clearly, Nisbet is not directly responsible for these
signs of social replenishment, but for decades he was the most eloquent
and persuasive advocate of the guidelines and directions that should be
followed.

As tempted as I am to conclude on this laudatory note, I will not do
so. I conclude on a critical note because I believe that Nisbet's views
on abortion and his criticisms of social conservatives relate to a fundamental failure that must be acknowledged. Simply put, for all his genius
and insight, Nisbet failed to fully recognize the role of human nature
in human affairs, or, to use Dennis Wrong's term to criticize the tendencies of sociological thought, Nisbet had an "oversocialized" view of
human beings.[52] More simply, Nisbet was a "social constructivist." In his
view, human nature is neither a leash nor a guide, and it is certainly not
a source of natural law; what human beings are and do is the result of
culture and social inventions. For example, in *Twilight of Authority* he
writes of our "natural impulses toward social initiative" and social invention, but this inventiveness is completely detached from nature, biol-
ogy, and instinct. He says, "We are prone to take something as complex
as, say, primitive kinship systems and, because these involve sexual and
procreative activities, assume kinship is some sort of evolutionary exfo-
liation of biological instincts. No mistake could be greater. The origins
of kinship in man's history are of course lost, but we do better to conjure
up a vision of some primitive Solon"—the Athenian lawgiver—"than of
mere instinct in the fashioning of structures as ingeniously designed as
clan, moiety, and tribe, with their complex requirements of endogamy
and exogamy, and their delicate balancing of authority and responsibility." He continues, "If mankind's earliest social inventiveness is to be
seen in kinship," then, after the invention of agriculture and the met-
allurgical arts, the local community was invented. "In every legitimate
sense of the word[,] local community, with its complex functions and
roles, was a social invention." He concludes: "The history of social organization comes down, basically, to the history of the rise and spread of
social inventions—relationships among individuals which, once found
useful and accepted, have in many cases gone on for thousands of years
in a variety of civilizations."[53]

The flip side of Nisbet's social constructivism is what might be
called his biophobia, an aversion to biological explanations of virtually

any social phenomenon. Biophobia and social constructivism are maintained today by a bewildering array of people, from most feminists and literary deconstructionists on the Left, to many anti-Darwinian Christians and paleoconservatives on the Right. One need not be a Darwinian biologist to believe, however, that although nature is always expressed via nurture—no biologist believes in "genetic determinism"—natural social inclinations and even natural institutions exist. As I have argued elsewhere, the evidence provided by evolutionary scientists is overwhelming that kinship, the requirements of endogamy and exogamy, reciprocal friendship, in-group tribal affections, out-group tribal animosities, and local community are not historical products of inventive geniuses; they are grounded in the most vigorous passions and inclinations of human nature.[54] They have existed as long as human beings have existed, although the precise form of these inclinations is influenced, of course, by culture and social innovation. Nisbet's social pluralist heroes, Aristotle, Burke, and Tocqueville, maintained this view. Each of these thinkers argued for the importance of intermediate institutions because such institutions express essential natural human sentiments, although, if one were splitting hairs, it is arguable that Aristotle grounded the social order in human nature even more thoroughly than did Burke and Tocqueville.

Nisbet's justifications for local and parochial institutions, by contrast, are made in terms of their utility, functionality, and efficiency. Such terms are often reliable, but without a bedrock standard in human nature—be it divine in origin or merely natural—one's argument can be overturned by references to utility, functionality, and efficiency. For example, I believe that the biological, psychological, and sociological evidence is overwhelming that nature recommends children be raised by their biological parents and other kin. Although Nisbet also defended traditional notions of kinship, if utility and efficiency are the standards justifying the traditional family, those who believe that raising children is a collective obligation will likely gain ground by invoking these same standards. After all, if one does not believe that nature recommends that biological parents raise their children to maturity, then our circumstance—in which a majority of American children will spend a portion of their childhoods in single-parent households by the time they are eighteen—allows only utilitarian grounds for lament. Indeed, the sheer fact of absent fathers compels one to search for some sort of "social invention" to replace them because an essential social function is not

being filled by any utilitarian standard, and nature bestows no obligations on biological fathers in Nisbet's view. In any event, I believe that
Nisbet's neglect of human nature weakened his case for communities
or intermediate institutions and that his belief in social invention led
him to several dubious conclusions. For example, he cited the youth
communes of the 1970s as indicative of the recovery of community, and
he was friendly toward Emile Durkheim's "corporatism," a scheme by
which professions and industries would be arranged on communal principles.[55] Without a full acknowledgment of human nature, there are no
means by which to recognize the limits of social invention.

In this regard, I note my own view that Burke's acquaintance David
Hume, in *An Inquiry Concerning the Principles of Morals*, and Burke's
good friend Adam Smith, in the *Theory of Moral Sentiments*, provide the
most convincing and complete pre-Darwinian accounts of the natural
social passions or instincts and their relationship to social institutions,
historical and otherwise. As Nisbet once observed, the moral philosophy
of the Scottish moralists was "richly sociobiological," just as Aristotle's
had been. The Scottish moralists, he said, "located the source of every
significant pattern of behavior in some passion, drive or instinct. Altruism, Smith thought, was the innate drive in man that made society possible, just as the 'instinct' to truck and barter, to buy and sell, was the true
source of the economic system."[56] Smith never used the term *altruism*—
it was coined by Auguste Comte in the mid-nineteenth century—but
he did argue that benevolence, or selfless regard for others, is grounded
in natural social passions that weaken with social distance. From stron-
gest to weakest, our ties to parents, children, siblings, extended family,
friends, colleagues, and neighbors are recommended to our care by
nature, according to Smith. Our goodwill is unlimited, he maintained,
but our good offices, our active duties, are inherently limited. Universal
benevolence, he argued, is utterly impotent. "The most sublime speculation of the contemplative philosopher can scarce compensate the
neglect of the smallest active duty."[57] It is also worth noting that in 1791,
a year after Smith criticized "universal benevolence" in the sixth edition
of the *Theory of Moral Sentiments*, Burke expressed essentially the same
view in a very harsh critique of Rousseau. Rousseau, who turned his five
illegitimate children over to a state-run foundling home and justified his
action with reference to Plato's ideal of citizenship, displayed, according
to Burke, "the stores of his powerful rhetoric in the expressions of universal benevolence, whilst his heart was incapable of harboring one spark

of parental affection. . . . He melts with tenderness for those only who touch him by the remotest relation, and then, without one natural pang, casts away, as a sort of offal and excrement, the spawn of his disgustful amours and sends his children to the hospital of foundlings."[58] Nature, for both Smith and Burke, recommends certain persons to our care, especially those to whom we are tied by kinship. Now, to be sure, Nisbet also feared telescopic philanthropy or universal benevolence, but if kinship and local community are social inventions ungrounded in nature, and if social inventions are to be assessed in terms of their utility, why should we not hope that institutions with the broadest imaginable scope will replace local communities? At the very least, Nisbet provides no reason not to experiment with such social inventions because he provides no natural grounding for kinship and local community.

Regarding Smith, let me note one more important point: although Smith argued for the existence of innate drives and natural social and moral sentiments, he hardly denied the significance of social institutions. For example, the propensity to truck, barter, and exchange may be innate, but Smith's attacks on the "mercantile system" in *Wealth of Nations* make it perfectly clear that he believed free and unregulated markets, which simultaneously release our innate drives and harness them for the public good, are anything but inevitable, even within commercial societies.[59] Acknowledging nature limits what can be deemed salutary social inventions, but it does not entail denying the importance of social institutions. Smith argued that custom and social institutions can easily "warp" the natural moral sentiments, even if these sentiments can never be "entirely perverted." As Jerry Muller notes, Smith's approach was one of "psychological institutionalism."[60] In both his major works, Smith sought to identify the institutional means by which the better angels of our nature could be educed and by which even our baser instincts might be made to serve the greater good.

Returning now to Nisbet, his neglect of human nature may be something of an occupational hazard, because sociologists are given to social constructivism. Specifically, Nisbet was greatly influenced by Emile Durkheim, who asserted, "Collective representations, emotions, and tendencies are caused not by certain states of the consciousness of individuals but by the conditions in which the social group in its totality is placed. Such actions can, of course, materialize only if the individual natures are not resistant to them; but these individual natures are merely the indeterminate material that the social factor molds and transforms."[61] The individual, for Durkheim, is merely a receptive blank canvas on which society paints. Thus, the psychological yields completely to the power of the sociological in Durkheim's view, and in a very similar manner, Nisbet grossly overappraised the importance of the social factor in molding individual nature and misassessed the plasticity of human nature. As a consequence, Nisbet's worldview does not permit any invocation of natural law, for without a systematic theory of human nature, there can be no natural law. Ultimately, I believe that Nisbet lacked the grounds to fully engage antiabortion social conservatives. Although one can believe in the existence of human nature without believing in natural law, most antiabortion social conservatives believe in human nature and oppose abortion because it violates natural law.

In conclusion, I must confess that I teach a course on the family, and in that course I try to avoid the issue of abortion. I recognize its importance, but given the intensity of opinions on the issue, I have found that discussions of abortion can destroy the decorum and civility of a class. In light of that experience, I know that bringing up the abortion issue here carries large risks. It is possible that because I have described Nisbet's views on abortion, some conservatives will be less inclined to engage seriously with Nisbet's writings. If so, my choice of strategy has been a mistake. As I stated earlier, anyone would profit from an encounter with Nisbet's works, and conservatism as a whole would be made better by such encounters. When reading Nisbet, one is compelled to deliberate about the purposes guiding one's worldview and one's activities as a conservative. There are very few people about whom this can be said. And, despite my belief that he failed to fully comprehend obdurate human nature and to ground communities in natural social and moral sentiments, Nisbet is an extraordinary thinker to whom we owe a great debt.

Notes

1. Robert Nisbet, *The Quest for Community: A Study in the Ethics of Order and Freedom* (New York: Oxford University Press, 1953). The "small harvest" comment is from Robert Nisbet, *Conservatism: Dream and Reality* (1986; reprint, New Brunswick, N.J.: Transaction Publishers, 2002), 106.

2. Nisbet, *Conservatism*, 106.

3. Ibid.

4. Robert Nisbet, *The Making of Modern Society* (New York: NYU Press, 1986), 178–92.

5. Robert Nisbet, *Prejudices: A Philosophical Dictionary* (Cambridge, Mass.: Harvard University Press, 1982), 55.

6. Russell Kirk, *The Politics of Prudence* (Wilmington, Del.: ISI Press, 1993), 49.

7. Robert Nisbet, "Still Questing," *Intercollegiate Review* 29 (fall 1993): 45.

8. Nisbet, *Prejudices*, 59.

9. Nisbet, *Quest for Community*, vii.

10. Robert Nisbet, *The Degradation of Academic Dogma: The University in America, 1945–1970* (New York: Basic Books, 1971), 43.

11. Nisbet, *Prejudices*, 92.

12. Robert Nisbet, *The Social Bond: An Introduction to the Study of Society* (New York: Knopf, 1970), 141.

13. Nisbet, *Degradation of Academic Dogma*, 44–45.

14. Robert Nisbet, *The Present Age: Progress and Anarchy in Modern America* (New York: Harper and Row, 1988), 6; Nisbet, *Prejudices*, 309–11.

15. Nisbet, *Prejudices*, 9; Nisbet, *Making of Modern Society*, 144.

16. Robert Nisbet, *The Twilight of Authority* (New York: Oxford University Press, 1975), 220.

17. Nisbet, *Present Age*, xi–xii.

18. Ibid., 5.

19. Ibid., 7.

20. Ibid., 42–43.

21. Ibid., 45.

22. Nisbet, *Twilight of Authority*, 184–85.

23. Nisbet, *Present Age*, 50–51.

24. Nisbet, *Twilight of Authority*, 185.

25. Nisbet, *Present Age*, 73.

26. Ibid., 69.

27. Ibid., 84.

28. Nisbet, *Twilight of Authority*, 233.

29. Robert Nisbet, *The Social Philosophers: Community and Conflict in Western Thought* (New York: Crowell, 1973), 10.

30. Nisbet, *Twilight of Authority*, 245.

31. Nisbet, *Social Philosophers*, 10; George Nash, *The Conservative Intellectual Movement in America: Since 1945* (Wilmington, Del.: ISI Press, 1996), 231.

32. Nisbet, *Twilight of Authority*, 246.

33. Ibid., 248.

34. Nisbet, *Prejudices*, 60.

35. Robert Nisbet, "Uneasy Cousins" [1980], in *Freedom and Virtue: The Conservative/Libertarian Debate*, ed. George W. Carey (Wilmington, Del.: ISI Press, 1998), 47.

36. Ibid., 51.

37. Nisbet, *Conservatism*, 112–13.

38. Ibid., 84.

39. Nisbet, *Prejudices*, 59.

40. Ibid., 60.

41. Nisbet, *Conservatism*, 113.

42. Amitai Etzioni and Robert P. George, "Virtue and the State: A Dialogue between a Communitarian and a Social Conservative," *Responsive Community* 9 (spring 1999): 56.

43. Nisbet, *Prejudices*, 4.

44. Ibid., 5.

45. Ibid., 7.

46. Ibid., 9.

47. Nisbet, *Twilight of Authority*, 276.

48. Nisbet, *Quest for Community*, 276.

49. Nisbet, *Conservatism*, 56.

50. Nicholas Lemann, "Paradigm Lost," *Washington Monthly* 23 (April 1991): 46.

51. See Everett Carll Ladd, *The Ladd Report* (New York: Free Press, 1999); Arthur Brooks, *Who Really Cares: The Surprising Truth about Compassionate Conservatism* (New York: Basic Books, 2006).

52. Dennis Wrong, "The Oversocialized Conception of Man in Modern Sociology," *American Sociological Review* 26 (April 1961): 183–93.

53. Nisbet, *Twilight of Authority*, 276, 280.

54. Brad Lowell Stone, "The Most Unique of All Unique Species," *Society* 45 (March/April 2008): 146–51; Brad Lowell Stone, "The Evolution of Culture and Sociology," *American Sociologist* 39 (spring 2008): 68–85.

55. Robert Nisbet, *The Sociology of Emile Durkheim* (New York: Oxford University Press, 1974), 28, 136–45.

56. Nisbet, *Prejudices*, 288–89.

57. Adam Smith, *The Theory of Moral Sentiments* (1790; reprint, Indianapolis: Liberty Press, 1982), 223, 235, 237.

58. Edmund Burke, *Further Reflections on the Revolution in France* (1791; reprint, Indianapolis: Liberty Press, 1992), 49.

59. Adam Smith, *An Inquiry into the Nature and Causes of the Wealth of Nations* (1776; reprint, Indianapolis: Liberty Press, 1981), 429–688.

60. Jerry Muller, *Adam Smith in His Time and Ours* (New York: Free Press, 1993), 49.

61. Emile Durkheim, *The Rules of Sociological Method* (1896; reprint, New York: Free Press, 1962), 105.

Bibliography

Brooks, Arthur. 2006. *Who Really Cares: The Surprising Truth about Compassionate Conservatism.* New York: Basic Books.

Burke, Edmund. 1992 [1791]. *Further Reflections on the Revolution in France.* Indianapolis: Liberty Press.

Durkheim, Emile. 1962 [1896]. *The Rules of Sociological Method.* New York: Free Press.

Etzioni, Amitai, and Robert P. George. 1999. "Virtue and the State: A Dialogue between a Communitarian and a Social Conservative." *Responsive Community* 9 (spring): 54–66.

Kirk, Russell. 1953. *The Conservative Mind.* New York: Regnery.

———. 1993. *The Politics of Prudence.* Wilmington, Del.: ISI Press.

Ladd, Everett Carll. 1999. *The Ladd Report.* New York: Free Press.

Lemann, Nicholas. 1991. "Paradigm Lost." *Washington Monthly* 23 (April).

Muller, Jerry. 1993. *Adam Smith in His Time and Ours.* New York: Free Press.

Nash, George. 1996. *The Conservative Intellectual Movement in America: Since 1945.* Wilmington, Del.: ISI Press.

Nisbet, Robert. 1953. *The Quest for Community: A Study in the Ethics of Order and Freedom.* New York: Oxford University Press.

———. 1970. *The Social Bond: An Introduction to the Study of Society.* New York: Knopf.

———. 1971. *The Degradation of Academic Dogma: The University in America, 1945–1970.* New York: Basic Books.

———. 1973. *The Social Philosophers: Community and Conflict in Western Thought.* New York: Crowell.

———. 1974. *The Sociology of Emile Durkheim.* New York: Oxford University Press.

———. 1975. *The Twilight of Authority.* New York: Oxford University Press.

———. 1982. *Prejudices: A Philosophical Dictionary.* Cambridge, Mass.: Harvard University Press.

———. 1986. *The Making of Modern Society.* New York: NYU Press.

———. 1988. *The Present Age: Progress and Anarchy in Modern America.* New York: Harper and Row.

———. 1993. "Still Questing." *Intercollegiate Review* 29 (fall): 41–45.

———. 1998 [1980]. "Uneasy Cousins." In *Freedom and Virtue: The Conservative/Libertarian Debate*, edited by George W. Carey, 38–54. Wilmington, Del.: ISI Press.

———. 2002 [1986]. *Conservatism: Dream and Reality.* New Brunswick, N.J.: Transaction Publishers.

Smith, Adam. 1981 [1776]. *An Inquiry into the Nature and Causes of the Wealth of Nations.* Indianapolis: Liberty Press.

_____. 1982 [1790]. *The Theory of Moral Sentiments*. Indianapolis: Liberty Press.

Stone, Brad Lowell. 2008. "The Evolution of Culture and Sociology." *American Sociologist* 39 (spring): 68–85.

_____. 2008. "The Most Unique of All Unique Species." *Society* 45 (March/April): 146–51.

Wrong, Dennis. 1961. "The Oversocialized Conception of Man in Modern Sociology." *American Sociological Review* 26 (April): 183–93.

John Courtney Murray as Catholic, American Conservative

Peter Augustine Lawler

John Courtney Murray (1904–1967) was a member of the Society of Jesus. He taught at the Jesuit theologiate at Woodstock, Maryland, and was editor of the Jesuit journal *Theological Studies* from 1941 until his death. He became a leading American public figure—the subject of a 1960 *Time* cover story. He was known mainly for his work on the relationship between the Catholic Church and American political life, his interpretation of the American view of religious liberty, and his resolutely Catholic view of the true ground of that liberty.[1] His affirmation of the basic continuity between the Catholic and the American views of human nature and human liberty led to tensions with and even his silencing by the Vatican Curia, but something resembling his view of religious liberty was affirmed by the Second Vatican Council.[2] His most celebrated book, *We Hold These Truths: Catholic Reflections on the American Proposition* (1960), reflects, even in its title, his order of priorities.[3] For an American Catholic, the U.S. Constitution can be affirmed as intrinsically good only if it recognizes each person's freedom to participate in the moral community or "order of culture" (35) that corresponds to his or her deepest natural longing. *We Hold These Truths*—a book of astutely political, popular, and thus rather polemical essays—cannot be understood without some attention to Murray's deeper and somewhat neglected classic *The Problem of God* (1964). The failure of the modern world has been its efforts to solve that problem and to somehow produce a world where the human person can exist in freedom without God.

My purpose here is to illuminate Murray's enduring contribution to conservative American political thought—especially our proper relationship to our political Fathers and our proper relationship to God. Murray is surely America's best proponent of "natural law" criticism of the intentions of modern thought, and it was his conservative intention to show that, by placing the American people "under God," the Constitution cannot be understood as modern, in the most important respect. Murray acknowledges that the leading American founders were, in fact, influenced by the modern theory of John Locke more than anything else, but that theory, in truth, is not embodied in the political order they constructed. The American problem is that our political Fathers built better than they knew (or thought they knew), so we have to know more or better than they did to properly appreciate and sustain what they accomplished. The greatest gift an American Catholic citizen can give to his country, Murray claimed, is a theory adequate to its wonderful practice (10–11).

The Problem of Political Veneration in America

Murray seems to begin We Hold These Truths with classic conservative questions: How do we show proper veneration for what our Founding Fathers have given us? How do we make their gift to us our own? According to Murray, we begin by taking seriously their "American proposition," which was based on a "realist epistemology": human beings are ordered by nature to be capable of discovering the truth and sharing it in common. The truth, as the Declaration of Independence claims, is "self-evident"—it can be discovered by human selves or souls. And those truths we hold in common can be the foundation of political institutions that protect liberty and promote justice. Our political Fathers' proposition, Murray claims, was asserted as a "coherent structure of thought" that aimed at "historical success" through the "working out" of all its practical implications over time. Our nation would increasingly become a place worthy of beings for whom the truth is self-evident (7–8).

A proposition in geometry is a theorem to be proved true, and a political proposition is to be proved true through historical action. But a political proposition—unlike a geometrical one—is never proved true once and for all. Its demonstration over time will always be limited by the constraints of beings who act in time. The proof—like everything human in this world—will never be "a finished thing." History, as they say, will never come to an end. So it will always be true, Murray asserts, that our doctrine—what Murray sometimes calls our "public philosophy"—and our practical project will require "development on penalty of decadence." Two reasons that "historical success is never to be taken for granted" is that history is constantly revealing the limitations of doctrine, and doctrine is constantly being distorted by history (7–8).

So it cannot be regarded as ingratitude or an offense against civic piety to see that our Fathers were not completely wise men. Our founding principles and institutions, as *Federalist* 49 predicts, have come to benefit from "the veneration time bestows on everything," whether deserved or not. Veneration, the *Federalist* adds, is not merely a "superfluous advantage." But veneration by itself is not enough, our Fathers knew, to sustain their Constitution. Although Murray—following the "classic" example set by Abraham Lincoln—appeals to that veneration by calling our political founders our Fathers (8), he knows that they really taught us to attend to their words and honor their deeds only if our filial piety corresponds to what we can affirm with our minds. They certainly did not want to hide what they really thought and did under some veil of tradition or prescription. Even if they had, Murray observes, tradition or prescription could hardly govern us effectively in a time like ours. Our Fathers' affirmation and intention must become our "personal acquisition" (85–86).

Lincoln on the Imperiled American Proposition

The idea that our Founding Fathers dedicated our "new nation" to a proposition, Murray acknowledges, was formulated not by our Fathers but by Lincoln (8). Lincoln, Murray suggests, criticized our Fathers by calling them Fathers, by blurring the distinction between them and the biblical patriarchs and even God the Father more than they themselves would have wanted. They did not do enough to inspire filial devotion to their project—a devotion that has a religious as well as a rational dimension. Lincoln also criticized our Fathers by calling on their authority to develop or transform their doctrine and make it more an object of dedication and more secure. He tried to combine the spirit of civil theology with devotion to a universal proposition.

Murray claims that Lincoln "asserted the imperiled part of the theorem and gave impetus to the impeded part of the project." He turned one of the self-evident truths into our proposition that "all men are created equal." Lincoln's reduction of the whole of our project to one of its parts was an understandable response to the crisis of his time (7–8). Americans had come to doubt the fact of human equality and therefore the fact that slavery is self-evidently unjust. The reconfiguration of our Fathers' doctrine into a proposition was intended to remove that doubt. Doubt might always be the result when reason operates alone, and the leading southerners twisted that doubt in the direction of their pride and their self-interest. Lincoln's antidote to doubt was largely dedication; proving the proposition true became our pious and noble national imperative. Devotion to equality means working to demonstrate historically that which we believe is true.

The cause of the Civil War, in Murray's eyes, was disagreement over what the truth is and what moral demands it makes on us. The issue was not whether it is actually possible for human beings to reason their way to a truth they can share in common. It was not whether the truth is, in some sense, self-evident. Despite their friendship, Alexander Stephens and Abraham Lincoln disagreed over whether the black person, by nature, is equal to the white. But they shared the conviction that politically fundamental truths about human nature can be discovered by beings like themselves. Stephens's considered view was that the allegedly self-evident truth about human equality asserted by the Declaration of Independence is actually self-evidently untrue. He thought he had evidence that proved that Thomas Jefferson and the other Fathers had erred in their thinking. And Lincoln thought that Stephens's powerful doubt was evidence that the Fathers had erred in not marshaling all the moral means necessary to defend their rational devotion to their proposition.[4]

Lincoln's great victories on the levels of doctrine and history seem to have eradicated doubts, though not all at once, about human equality, at least "on this continent." But arguably, Murray suggests, intensified devotion to equality as a historical project came at the expense of real reflection on the truth about human nature. In our time, for example, Richard Rorty has urged us to accept our egalitarian project with a kind of calculated—but still pious—American patriotism. We should reject as useless any reflection on whether our common faith has any real foundation. Our impossible quest for intellectual certainty about what we are doing, Rorty claims, only produces paralyzing doubt about our sentimental devotion to historical transformation.[5] Lincoln's appeal to piety eventually had the historical cost of making us believe we could dispense with the truth of self-evidence.

Murray is implicitly somewhat critical of Lincoln by explaining, in effect, why his ambiguous success created the crisis Murray himself faces—the crisis of self-evidence. But Murray, of course, also expresses a great debt to Lincoln. He reaffirms, in his own way, Lincoln's concern with dedication to the way established by our political Fathers. It is foolhardy, in fact, to recommend a wholly new beginning to beings with limited powers of knowing and loving. A rational tradition is more solid than no tradition at all, so he affirms the conservative view that all political reform is best understood as a renewal of a nation's original, constituting self-conception. Murray follows Lincoln by appealing to our Fathers' "ancient heritage" while also emphasizing that their faith was a rational one—a faith in epistemological realism or self-evidence. Our public philosophy or public consensus is in the ambiguous position of having to be partly—but only partly—"patrimony" or "prejudice" (7–8 11, 47). The best way to deepen our veneration for our political Fathers, Murray claims, is to show that they were more dependent than they knew on "the Fathers of the Church" (30, 43). Our Fathers' ancient, particular political accomplishments are best interpreted in light of the much more ancient and universal church (11).

Murray does what he can to situate his project in America's rational tradition and to situate our country's rational tradition in the older rational tradition of Thomistic Catholicism. Murray even criticized the church—in its largely just criticism of the genuinely illiberal character of modern European liberal absolutism—for not appreciating American exceptionalism: our founding—"the most striking and successful political realization of modern times"—was, in fact, "of linear descent from the central political tradition of the West, which the Church had helped fashion out of Greek, Roman, and Germanic elements." America is genuinely distinguished by being *the* nation in modern times that began as a descendant of the West's traditional political rationalism.[6] Murray affirms the classic view of American conservatives that what our Fathers accomplished "was less a revolution than a conservation" (31), while deepening and enlarging conservatives' view of what about tradition is most worth conserving.

Murray on the Crisis of Self-Evidence

Murray really thought that the challenge he—and the America of his time—faced was more radical and comprehensive than the one Lincoln faced. In his (cold war) time, "civil war had become the basic fact of global society." The foundation of that worldwide civil war was what the philosopher Martin Heidegger called the clash of worldviews or radically incompatible and warring faiths or ideologies (19, 24). Every part of the American doctrine—not just equality—was, Murray observed, "menaced by active negation" everywhere. Negation had become almost exclusively active because of the loss of confidence that differences could be resolved by argument (8). The self-evidence of truths "we hold" in common seems to have become a self-evident impossibility. From one view, the only way to avoid civil war is to submit to the "dictatorship of relativism,"[7] to reduce opinions about God, nature, politics, and morality to mere preferences or, as Rorty says, private fantasies. From another view, the victory of relativism seems to make the world more impersonally rational than ever: technological efforts to achieve rational control are increasingly unguided by person or moral considerations, by real or self-evident thought about who we are.

We seem, more than ever, to be under the sway of the modern, pragmatic opinion that the only way to know what is true is through historical and technological conquest. We *make* the truth; there is no rational appeal beyond the fact of success in manipulating nature—including human nature. In our world, Murray contends, "there are, so to speak, no truths, there are only results." We used to believe, he claims, that the truth would win out "if it were subject to the unbridled competition of the marketplace of ideas," that truth's victory is the "cardinal merit of a pluralistic society" (126). But those whom Murray calls our proponents of "modern evolutionary scientific naturalism"—what purports to be the "new rationalism"—have shown us the naïveté of that view (322). There is no evidence that we are hardwired to know the truth, but only to survive and flourish like members of the other species. Our strange residual concern with moral, political, and religious truth—the truth about our dignity, our origin, and our destiny—is at best a salutary illusion that we need to put in its place. The evolutionary pragmatist says that we should call true whatever makes us feel comfortable and secure, so we should call true whatever public consensus happens to emerge. The nominalist claim that we can name the truth into being certainly should not be sullied by being compared to any reality outside itself.

Murray's conservative objection is that our newly pragmatic devotion to equality seems consciously and willfully oblivious to the standard by which our Fathers expected us to judge their doctrine and their project. Their project is "eviscerated . . . in one stroke"—or no longer makes any sense at all—if we deny its dependence on their confident assertion of a realist epistemology (7–9). Our project has no future, in fact, if it is merely our prejudice. All prejudice is equally weightless in our radically unprescriptive or untraditional time. We are stuck with our Fathers' prejudice against prejudice, and it is impossible—not to mention undignified—to take our bearings from the distinction between useful and useless prejudices. We are still stuck asking the question: useful for what or for whom? We know we are not really free to define ourselves however we please.

Our proposition about the truth being self-evident—the only genuine foundation of our equality in liberty—is eviscerated, Murray contends, if we cannot address together "the basic question of modernity": "What is man?" From that question flow many others that concern "the rank of man within the order of being"; the continuity or discontinuity of man with the rest of nature; the ability of human knowledge and love to transcend the constraints of space and time; the existence of God as a person, power, or principle who cares for or is indifferent to each person's particular existence; and the truth about the significance of the personal experiences of love, death, and anxiety. We even must consider—in the absence of any stable, traditional answer—the question of whether the dignity of the particular person depends on the possibility of that person being directed by nature to discover his or her personal, loving duties to a personal God (126–28).

For Murray, our proposition is less about this or that answer to these particular questions than about the confidence that we are all equally dignified beings who are compelled to raise such questions and even find some real answers. Our crisis is about "the loss of confidence in the power of reason to fix the purposes of political life" (130). He claims that "the basis and inspiration" of the American project are nothing more or less than this confidence. "We hold these truths," we say; "therefore we can argue about them" (10). The self-evidence of some of the particular truths our Fathers affirmed "may legitimately be questioned," and in fact, it has to be. We have to be realistic and admit that "the serene, and often naïve, certainties of the eighteenth century have crumbled" (8). Some of what seemed self-evident to our Fathers does not seem so to us. We are loyal to their confidence in holding the truth in common by questioning their particular understanding of "the law of nature" with the intention of improving on it. For us, it is "imperative" to find "other, more reasoned grounds" for our Fathers' confidence about self-evidence (15).

Locke as Our Fathers' Theorist

The theory that seemed most self-evident to our Fathers was John Locke's. But, Murray claims, we cannot take Locke "with any philosophical seriousness" today. The "eighteenth-century gospel" he inspired unleashed a "dynamism of destruction based on 'philosophical nonsense.'" Murray presents two ways of considering our Fathers' view of that dynamic nonsense. The first is that they were theoretically superficial men who sometimes actually thought Locke explained it all. The second is that they quite self-consciously knew they were using Locke's theory as a means to level unjust orders, and their liberating efforts presupposed a different and truer view of nature than Locke's. In their eyes, Locke's "philosophic weakness vanished before its performance of the political task" they needed performed. Nobody can deny the Lockean achievement of "destroy[ing] an order of privilege and inaugurat[ing] an era of political equality" (311–19). Locke's emphasis on political consent, based on his denial that "the people are the great beast of aristocratic theory" (181), was, in fact, in accord with the Christian, Thomistic natural law tradition.

Locke said something to the effect that words are weapons, nothing more. In some measure, our Fathers took him at his word, using his words as weapons and nothing more. For them, Locke's "theoretic dogmas" may well have been "false" but still "powerful." Murray's most nuanced judgment is that Locke's theory could not "quite veil" the natural law "imperatives of a human reason that has a greater and more universal power than was dreamt of in Locke's philosophy." Our Fathers, finally, were ambivalent Lockeans. Their own deeds were inspired by a more realistic view of the purpose of words than Locke's, but they pursued historical success with the weapon of Locke's theory in mind (311–20).

When and if our Fathers really believed that Locke taught the whole truth and nothing but, from Murray's view, they must have accepted two unempirical premises: (1) that we consent to government and every other human institution as radically free individuals, and (2) that all human connections or relationships are to be understood as based on one's own self-interested calculation. As Murray explains, this means that "all forms of sociality are purely contractual" or "have no basis in nature" (306). We are not naturally social beings; we are not hardwired, so to speak, to share a life in common. The idea that all "mutual relations" can be understood in terms of contracts that utterly free individuals enter into and dissolve according to their sovereign willfulness is, we can see, clearly "a false theory of personality."[8] But it is a theory that has the advantage of privileging one's own freedom over all established privileges. Locke's radically individualistic insight must lead to theoretical nominalism: our natural capacity for language or naming is not for the joy of shared discovery, which, of course, would point in the direction of shared duties. Words are for maximizing one's own individual power, and they correspond to no "metaphysical reality" (309). The "naked essence" of Locke's thought, Murray reveals, is that all human capabilities are for the generation of power. The "law of nature," from this view, is nothing but a name given to the self-interested decisions I make as a free individual to perpetuate my own being and enhance my comfort. The law of nature is nothing but a corollary of the liberty each individual has to act in his or her own self-interest rightly understood. Locke, Murray claims, said more "politely" what Hobbes said more "forthrightly": man's natural condition is war, and every capability he has is a weapon of war (304).

Locke's most basic theoretical incoherence seems to be his effort to sustain both nominalist premises and at least the semblance of the realist epistemology suggested by the idea of the "law of nature"—the suggestion of continuity with the realist, Thomistic tradition of "natural law." Locke says that all free individuals can know that all free individuals are basically in the same situation. This seems to mean that there are some truths about nature and liberty we can share in common. But it is also true that the truths each individual holds to be self-evident radically separates that person's thoughts and concerns from those of others, and the words he or she uses to communicate with others are not presented with the truth in mind. What nature has given each of us, Locke explains, is pretty worthless, and that includes our natural inability to understand much of anything at all without freely imposing our will on it. What we can know is what we have imposed on nature; even truth is the individual's powerful creation.

Murray suggests the paradox that Locke's realism is not very realistic, and even Locke knew it. His attempt to feign continuity with the

philosophical tradition has to be understood, for the most part, as one
means among many that Locke used to maximize his power (309). His
"state of nature" does not seem to be a real place. It is just a name he
gave to a myth—a "fictitious abstraction"—that he invented to maximize our power and freedom. It certainly does not correspond to what
we know about our nature (305). Locke's views of nature and liberty
are less descriptions than transformational weapons meant to become
more true over time. They, like all other words, are tools for individual
liberation. Locke's denial of realism in the name of freedom has worked
to some extent, but from one view, the fantasy of the modern world
is that it could work completely. Contrary to Locke's intention, it has
worked most powerfully to undermine whatever real freedom we have.
Our Fathers and even Locke himself were genuine liberals—or advocates of limited, constitutional government—only because they "did not
draw out all the implications from his theory" (308).

The Jacobin French revolutionaries, Murray explains, actually
understood all the implications of Locke's theory better than Locke himself. If all human questions are to be resolved through power, then the
individual, in truth, has no perspective, either theoretical or practical,
by which he can resist the power of the state. The naturally content-
less individual is defenseless against superior power. The French project was the "monism," or politically imposed unity, of their revolution
and the "omnipotent," and so omnicompetent, "totalitarian democracy"
that was the prelude to the much harder totalitarianism of the twentieth century. The French, inspired by Jean-Jacques Rousseau, attempted
to reduce particular human beings to citizens and nothing more, and
to reduce religion to "civil religion"—yet another instrument of political power—and nothing more (308–9). Locke's nominalism led them
to conclude that there are no real limits to the state's power to shape
human beings according to its political requirements.

Locke's intention was to free the individual from political, natural,
and divine determination. But because the freedom he promoted was
merely negative or destructive, it did not really empower the individual
to constitute himself against the powerful forces surrounding him. "The
logical outcome of Locke's individualistic law of nature," Murray contends, "was the juridical monism of the . . . French Republics." Every
communal or social or purposeful reality—"the pluralism of social institutions"—between the "individual" and the "state" was abolished (308).

Lockean theory, in the eyes of the French revolutionaries, asserted "the absolute autonomy of individual human reason." This means that "each man is a law unto himself," and everything "is a matter of individual choice." No obligations are imposed on particular human beings by God or nature, and there is no foundation for any political authority but the will of the individual. Reason makes us all equal, but reason gives no content to our freedom. Therefore, "by nature," what really exists is "an absolutely egalitarian mass of absolutely autonomous individuals." Society can be constituted only by "the people," and this public power is as unlimited as that of the individual human being, who lacks what it takes to resist or even differentiate himself from the homogeneous whole. Because "the state, like individual reason, knows no God," it knows no authority above its own popular will.[9] Government becomes "the political projection of the autonomy of reason," and so it becomes "the Supreme Judge" of even "religious truth."[10]

Locke's wholly indeterminate freedom has no middle place between anarchism and slavery and no place for genuinely limited government based on particularly human purposes.[11] Locke's effort to absolutely free human beings from natural and divine determination subordinates them completely to the will of man as expressed in a wholly conventional or simply willful Rousseauian social contract. For Murray, the view that there is nothing higher than the will of man eradicates every barrier to the particular individual's totalitarian determination by the will of other men.

Lockean destructiveness, it is easy to see, went beyond the establishment of a kind of limited, consensual equality and toward a comprehensive egalitarianism that took aim at the root of human liberty itself. We now know that the modern experiment, as Murray observes, will never "erect an order of social justice or inaugurate an order of freedom" (319). It is now particularly necessary to defend our real, natural freedom and openness to order and justice against promiscuous, willful leveling, to show that America is dedicated to more than groundless equality.

Darwin, Freud, and Marx as Devastating Critics of Locke

Locke's theory, Murray says, need not be refuted by us. It was demolished by his theoretical successors. "The Lockean idea of man," he observes, has been "destroyed completely" by "the genuine and true insights" of "Darwin, Marx, and Freud" (309). That does not mean, obviously, that Charles Darwin, Karl Marx, and Sigmund Freud teach anything like the whole truth. Each, in his "monistic" way, denies what we really know about human liberty. Their denials of liberty flow naturally, so to speak, from Locke's abstract, nominalist separation of liberty from nature. Marx's radical view that we are nothing more than what we have produced in the economic history of the division of labor—that we are wholly historical and wholly economic beings—depends on Locke's antinatural view that free individuals reveal themselves to themselves through their work to transform nature. Darwin's view that we are, by nature, qualitatively no different from the other species depends on Locke's seemingly unscientific or unempirical detachment of human freedom and purpose from all natural guidance. The Darwinian says that everything that exists is natural, and the Lockean claims that our freedom is not natural. So the Darwinian, in a way, reasonably concludes that what Locke calls freedom could not really exist.

Marx's criticism of the anxious and miserable individuals invented by Locke is not so different from that of a Darwinian sociobiologist. These individuals are distorted by experiences characteristic of beings who are unnaturally alienated from their true home. Marx was not wrong to notice that Locke's capitalist ideology had, to some extent, worked to detach individuals from their natural, social ties, and Marx exposed the real "loss of freedom" that came with the success of that "empty nominalism" (311). Marx, of course, exaggerates the effects of that detachment: the lives of individuals have not been reduced to merely whimsical playthings of the market; women have not become simple wage slaves, like men; and of course the great mass of people have not become only cogs in a machine. But all these exaggerations contain some truth, and contemporary life is full of the anxiety that comes with the experience of being emptied out of properly human content. These exaggerations correspond to what the modern individual would become if Locke's theory could become wholly true.

But Marx, as everyone now knows, offered no real remedy for the human misery he described. "Communism," Murray writes, "is political modernity carried to its logical conclusion" (211). From the most obvious view, totalitarianism is the logical, wholly political antidote to the emptiness of the Lockean individual. But when Marx himself describes life under communism, of course, it is the very opposite of totalitarianism. It is even, in a way, the very opposite of communism; the particular human being is free from alienating social or communal duties. The state, the family, and the church will have all withered away. People will, quite unobsessively, be able to do whatever they want, whenever they want. Everything we do would become undistorted by any real experiences of God, truth, love, or death. Without such alienation, man would no longer be "a stranger to his own will."[12]

From Murray's view, Marx's theoretical communism would merely radicalize—or make more modern—the loneliness and boredom—the alienation of one human being from another—that existed under capitalism. And under communism, of course, people would be deprived of the "opiate" of religious or revolutionary hope. For Murray, theoretical communism cannot become real because it can eradicate who we are by nature. That is the deeper reason why the pursuit of theoretical communism produced its opposite—political or totalitarian communism. The logical conclusion of modernity is a political war against who we really are, against what we cannot help but know. Murray unreservedly endorsed America's political struggle against modernity's logical culmination, but with the suggestion that the real or spiritual foundation of our struggle cannot be wholly modern or Lockean.

For Murray, what is most true in Marx is expressed more deeply or psychologically by Freud. The modern conquest of nature depends on expanding the realm of the "techniques of conscious reason" and "renounc[ing] the forces of instinct." The result is that our natural sources of happiness and satisfaction are increasingly repressed, so our most basic needs are denied gratification. The success of the Lockean project brings not "self-fulfillment and happiness, but psychic misery and loss of personal identity." Freud rightly replaces the economic misery of the Marxian proletariat with his own "Freudian proletariat, chained in neurotic misery amidst material abundance" and without, of course, the solace of religious or revolutionary hope.[13] Freud has an unrealistically monistic or reductionistic or merely sexual view of human eros and happiness. But he is right that we are miserably anxious or disoriented when we deny or repress the truth about who we are by nature, and he is right to dismiss the merely economic or historical accounts of Marx that make the revolutionary overcoming of our alienation from nature seem inevitable or even possible. Freud "shattered forever the 'angel-mindedness' of Cartesian man"—the idea that we are essentially other than natural or embodied beings—and thus "the brittle rationalistic optimism" based on the idea that our bodies are machines to be manipulated at will by free beings (310–11).

The Marxian and Freudian view that the Lockean war against nature or instinct is an error that makes us more unhappy is shared by Darwin, and Murray's realistic affirmation of what is true in Darwin is particularly striking. Darwin's "principle of continuity in nature" shows that we are like the other animals in many ways and share some purposes with them. Evolutionary theory expresses a partial but very real truth about our being: "man is solidary, by all that is material in him, with all of life." "Purified of its monistic connotations," Murray writes, the Darwinian principle of natural continuity "is compatible with a central thesis of Christian anthropology," which is "the law of solidarity of both flesh and spirit." Our social natures connect us as both material and spiritual beings, so it is not realistic to disparage our bodies on behalf of our spiritual freedom. "Evolutionary theory," Murray adds, "is not compatible with Lockean individualism," which views all expressions of solidarity with and dependence on others or nature as worthless illusions that can and should be overcome. And evolutionary theory, in truth, dealt a "mortal blow" to that atomistic individualism (310). Darwin is right in two respects: we are social animals, and what we are given by nature is both good and, in the most important details, inescapable, despite our best efforts.

Darwin's supposed naturalism or empiricism achieves its allegedly comprehensive explanations by abstracting from everything that essentially distinguishes particular human beings from the rest of nature. The Darwinian abstraction is, in a way, a mirror image of the Lockean abstraction: Darwin exaggerates—while Locke denies—the continuity between members of our species and members of all the others. Our self-consciousness—as well as our singular, erotic openness to the truth about ourselves and all that exists—transforms even the natural ends we share with the other animals.

Darwin shares Locke's unrealistic nominalism: words do not give us access to self-evident truths; they are tools we have been given by nature to aid in the survival and flourishing of a species. The truth is not genuinely self-evident to us because we are not hardwired to have selves or souls—or personal freedom—at all. Locke is surely wrong to think that words alone can sustain us against the impersonal forces of nature.

The Modern Will to Atheism

Darwin, Freud, and Marx are astute critics of the empty unreality of the Lockean individual, but Locke remains right about the reality of human liberty. Locke cannot defend individual or personal freedom from monistic destruction because he has detached that person from his real natural ends, from the truth about who he is. Murray's criticism of Locke, finally, is a criticism of the modern decision for atheism, and all the monistic tendencies of modern thought are efforts to eradicate the personal, social longing for God as a natural explanation of who we are. All modern thought attempts to understand us as less than we really are by nature, and so all modern thought is self-consciously scientistic or willfully reductionistic.

For Murray, the "original act of freedom" that produced modern thought was "the will to atheism." The modern theory from which God is absent depends on the prior "intention that he be absent." Murray's "own proposition, derivative from the Bible is that atheism is never the conclusion of any theory, philosophical or scientific." It is, instead, "a decision, a free act of choice that antedates all theories."[14] This means, in Murray's eyes, that "ignorance of God is not a want of knowledge or even a denial, it is a free choice of a mode of living."[15] God has given human beings the freedom to choose to live without him, but that does not mean that humans can realistically say they do not know of God.

The original modern intention was to "explain God away," to show that "God can have nothing to do with the order of intelligence." He is "to be relegated to the order of fantasy," to become an imaginary projection for which there is no evidence. That is why the key modern dogma is that religion is merely a "private matter" that exists nowhere but in "the individual conscience" and has no juridical or "public status." Public life or the reality human beings share in common is godless. The church or any religious community has no official or legal presence.[16]

The modern will to atheism *is* the will to complete autonomy—or freedom from God and nature. Murray explains that "man fell in love with himself," that is, "with his own creative powers." He fell in love, in fact, "with the dazzling brilliance of his own creations." The will to atheistic freedom is based on the thought that nothing creatures have been given is either good or lovable, so only an "anthropocentric" or self-created universe can do justice to who we really are. The modern, technological will has, in fact, "altered the face of the earth," and nature has been "made to feel in her very being that man is the master." That will, at its beginning, was "rational and purposeful," able to create a world worthy of genuinely autonomous beings—beings who have no need of God.[17]

The original modern will Murray calls "aristocratic atheism," and it allowed the philosophical elite to understand all there is—including who we are—without God. Its lack of definitive success caused it to be succeeded by "bourgeois atheism," or the effort to show that people can prosper—be happy and comfortable—without God. Because bourgeois life turned out to be, in some ways, more restless and miserable than ever (as Marx and particularly Freud explained), it was succeeded by an increasingly insistent "political atheism"—various attempts, inspired by Rousseau, to reduce human beings to secular citizens and nothing more. The movement of modern atheism from aristocratic to political is a movement from theory to practice, from understanding to imposition, from scientistic abstraction to relentlessly forcible destruction.[18] Despite the logic of that movement, aristocratic, bourgeois, and politicized atheism all operate simultaneously in the modern world. The collapse of political atheism that accompanied the fall of communism, Murray would not be surprised to see, led to an intensification of bourgeois atheism—evident in the efforts of libertarians and "bourgeois bohemians"—and to an intensification of aristocratic atheism—evident in the popularized, basically Darwinian science of the so-called new atheists.[19]

For Murray, the whole modern experience is evidence that the Christian discovery of the truth about our freedom cannot be expunged from any genuinely empirical account of "natural law"—or who we are according to nature. The misery that Marx, Darwin, and Freud described is our misery in the willed absence of God. We now know that this misery has no historical, political, economic, or technological cure. We also know there is no returning to, for example, the Aristotelian or classical account of nature and human nature. For Aristotle, "man in the end was only citizen, whose final destiny was to be achieved within the city" (155). In truth, Aristotle did not know about each human being's freedom from political life; this was discovered by the Christians and displayed in an unrealistically extreme and reductionistically distorted way by Locke. It is unclear, to tell the truth, whether Murray regards Aristotle as primarily ignorant of God or choosing against him, but in any case, his choice was clearly less willful than the characteristically modern one.

Murray explains that "Christianity freed man from nature by teaching him he has an immortal soul," which apparently he would not have known by natural means alone. That teaching revealed to man that he longs to be more than a biological, species-oriented being, that he has singular purposes not given to the other animals. So Christianity "taught him his own uniqueness, his own individual worth, the dignity of his own person, the equality of all men, and the unity of the human race" (192). Christianity freed human beings from what Aristotle perceived to be the limits of their natures. That revelation about the truth of who we are has survived every modern effort to distort or suppress it. We continue to know, despite the best efforts of secular civil theologians and other ideologists, that "every fatherland" is, to some extent, "a foreign land" (15). *The* political truth the Christians discovered is that "the whole of political life is not absorbed in the polis" (333), and human dignity is not primarily "civil dignity" (52).

That is why the integrity of the political order cannot be restored in post-Christian times except by "totalitarian" means. The modern secularist must make inauthentic denials that the pagan secularist—such as Aristotle—did not have to make. It is inevitable, Murray observes, that any post-Christian "unification of social life" both is more "forcible" and takes place on "a lower level" than Aristotle's (133). The attempt to restore the monistic polis in the modern world is never really a political restoration, because the Christian criticism of civil theology, which is true even if the personal God does not exist, cannot be eradicated from the world. The revolutionary totalitarian democrats might have thought they were guided by a republican "myth of antiquity," but they were really concerned with the reactionary negation of the true discoveries of "Christian civilization," the true sources of egalitarian political and spiritual freedom.[20]

Every willful attempt to exaggerate the autonomy of reason ends up denying the reality of the genuine transcendence—or orientation in the direction of God and transpolitical moral responsibility—of human freedom. In thinking about the "imperatives" of his own nature, Murray realizes that "my situation is that of a creature before God" (32). And he calls the modern denial of the human situation "a basic betrayal of the existential structure of reality itself" (215). What Murray himself knows, he claims, the "common man" also knows, "instinctively and by natural inclination" (204).

Sartre's True, Biblical View of the Absurdity of Atheism

Murray observes that existentialist Jean-Paul Sartre's understanding of the will to atheism—the will to be a man striving to be a God—as basically "absurd" is, "in a strange way . . . hauntingly biblical." Sartre was right "not even to attempt to cast up a rational justification" of such a "decision" and its "ensuing project." The existentialist truthfully sees that the modern decision culminates in absurdity. Sartre affirms absurdity as the price worth paying for willfully being free from God and nature. In Sartre's willful eyes, there is no intelligibility, no meaning, no God, no nature at all.[21] He has decided to see nothing that limits his own determination of his own "essence." At the end of the modern world, our freedom remains displayed by a useless longing that points to no particular existence at all, a longing we are stuck with despite the various scientistic and totalitarian efforts to eradicate it. The authentic existentialist affirms the resulting "climate of anguish and anxiety" as undeniable evidence that *he* is really there. But, in Murray's view, he cannot quite free himself from both fear and guilt. He remains afraid that "God may not be missing," despite his best efforts, and his guilt flows from "the feeling that God is missing only because he has been dismissed."[22]

Here is what Murray himself sees at the end of the modern world: nature has been remade, but man, the creator, "seems to have exhausted himself." He feels enslaved to what he has created, because he has deprived himself of all purposes higher than technological productivity. His release of himself—his "primal energy"—into nature, he can now see, leaves him haunted by "the spectre of self-annihilation." Not only might he be in the process of destroying the natural environment on which he cannot help but depend, but he no longer knows who he is apart from his environment. The master of nature seems to have freed himself from natural and divine domination for nothing in particular, so in his "own interior there is a wasteland." "His most intimate experience is of insecurity" because there is nothing to secure his being beyond his own power, So he is too anxious even to take pride in what he has done; he is less at home than ever in the world he has created for himself. As the Bible says, when man falls in love exclusively with himself, he ends up finding even particular human beings—beginning with himself—unworthy of love.[23]

Murray echoes the existentialist's truthful conclusion that all the modern efforts to make human beings at home without God through scientific or historical transformation were mirages. The real, culminating modern experience is a "spiritual vacuum . . . at the heart of human existence" (215–16). Sartre is right enough that our necessarily anxious reflection calls for a decision. But for Murray, the existentialist's attempt to perfect the will to atheism—natural or bourgeois or political—does nothing for us but highlight even more the absurdity of being defined by a vacuum. For Murray, the culmination of the modern world in absurdity—and so in "impotent nihilism" (12)—forces us to consider anew, in a completely untraditional way, "the nature and structure of reality itself" as a prelude to making "a metaphysical decision" about "the nature of man," a decision necessarily "much more profound" than the one made by our political Fathers (321).

Our anxious reflection is about how our "hollow emptinesses [should] be filled." Our search can no longer be about liberation from this or that constraint. We need a "definition of freedom" for our liberty to have some "positive content" or to be "ordered." A metaphysical decision cannot merely be an assertion. It depends on discovery of "a metaphysic of nature, especially the idea that nature is a teleological concept" (327). We need to discover or rediscover what our natural freedom is for. That discovery, Murray finally concludes, depends on our rejection of the modern will to atheism or a "prior affirmation" of God. Once that affirmation is made, Murray contends, then "man is free to affirm, to love, and to seek all that is human and natural." Without that affirmation, everything the modern experience has shown us, "the human and the natural become . . . bonds of imprisonment and slavery, agents of disorder and human destruction."[24] That is why Murray says, against Nietzsche (and Sartre and others), that there is no "purely secularistic" solution to the ineradicable problem of human liberty (216). The problem of human liberty is inseparable from the problem of God. The decision for natural teleology depends on the affirmation that the highest purpose of human beings is to seek, know, and love God. And on the basis of that decision, our self-understanding becomes more in accord with who, by nature, we are. The choice for God is at the foundation of "natural law" and can be validated on genuinely empirical grounds. The choice for God is a choice for a being who is not, essentially, "a solitary, separated individual" but a social, loving being embedded in a community while retaining his own personal identity.[25]

The postmodern choice is not for revelation against reason but against wholly "autonomous reason" and for reasoning about who we are as whole natural beings. There is no such thing, Murray observes, as "abstract reason, but only reason as it exists in men," and it is willful fantasy of abstracted or utterly autonomous reason that unrealistically abolishes the distinctions between true and false and right and wrong.[26] For Murray, the truth is that will is prior to reason and to theory. But we now have more evidence than ever that the will to atheism can neither extinguish the truth about our personal or transcendent orientation nor even begin to explain it. It even opens us to appreciate the genuine practical and intellectual accomplishments of the modern world for what they are. Murray once wrote in exasperation against someone who had accused him of being an antiscientific authoritarian: "I am for intellectual curiosity, full exploration of nature, the satisfaction of biological needs, the progressive elimination of disease, honesty, the Bill of Rights, more dignity for man, politics as the science of the possible, leaving morality to moralists, and a [long] life expectancy."[27]

Our Nation under God

Our political Fathers' will, Murray claims, was not fundamentally atheistic. He follows Lincoln, most of all, by showing that our Fathers, despite their Lockean theory, built "a nation under God." He does so, first of all, in opposition to the strict separationist jurisprudence that emerged in the 1940s. According to this view of constitutional interpretation, derived from the theory of Thomas Jefferson and James Madison, government and religion are to have nothing to do with each other, the church is to have no "juridical" status, and religion is to be a purely private affair. The public schools are to be an instrument of national civic unification based on some fuzzy, "mystical" civil theology, and parents may well lose the right to educate their children according to their view of the whole truth about the human being. Civic unity trumps religious diversity, and the dominant interpretation of the U.S. Constitution inches closer to Rousseauian totalitarian democracy.[28]

Democracy in America, Murray observes, though "once a political and social idea, now pretends to be a religion, the one true religion, transcendent to all warring 'sects.'"[29] And a secularism grows in America that is fundamentally antagonistic to any organized force that threatens to disturb the "community of democratic thought" (21). The danger is that the strict separationism that denies any real status to genuinely transcendent religion might be understood to represent our nation's progress toward a more consistent Lockeanization over time, to a more perfect fulfillment of our Fathers' intention. It is, the Supreme Court saw, perfectly consistent with the antiecclesiastical bias of Madison's *Memorial and Remonstrance*, which, following Locke, tends to view the individual's conscientious duty to his Creator as purely "interior" or solitary and private.[30] That isolated conscience, all modern experience has shown, cannot bear the weight placed on it in defense of human liberty and dignity. Its wholly subjective concerns cannot, in fact, be distinguished from a private fantasy. Murray counters by saying that the religion clauses of the First Amendment were partly the product of Madison the statesman (as opposed to the theorist) and partly the product of legislative compromise. They do not reflect any modern theory. Instead, they were merely understood to prevent the establishment of a national religion and to facilitate the free exercise of religion.[31] They were meant, in a way, to constitutionalize that "landmark in political theory," the Declaration of Independence. The theory of the Declaration is that there is "a truth that lies beyond politics: it imputes to politics a fundamental human meaning. I mean the sovereignty of God over nations as well as over individual men" (28). The Declaration too was a legislative compromise, and its seemingly self-evident, personal view of the providential and judgmental God of nature was due to additions made to Jefferson's Lockean draft by more Christian members of Congress. Jefferson's theoretical will was moderated by the necessity of operating as a statesman in a somewhat Christian environment. The result was the Declaration's virtually Thomistic or natural law theory, a result that cannot be found in or reduced to the will of any particular Father or founder. The compromise between Locke and John Calvin, we are tempted to say, produced something like the synthesis of Thomas Aquinas. America, as Murray says, was "very superficially Christian" (317) in the eighteenth century, but it was Christian enough not to embrace the politicized will to atheism.

From the beginning of "the authentic American tradition," Murray claims, parties and statesmen who "erect atheism into a political principle" are rejected. Privately, Jefferson and Madison might have been atheists, but their atheism had no public status. Americans privatize atheism and have political institutions that point beyond themselves in the direction of God. In America, atheism is the private fantasy that cannot be openly affirmed by those engaged in political life. Murray quotes the Supreme Court as stating, "We are a religious people whose institutions presuppose a free being." Because of that presupposition, there is no need for the Constitution to mention God. From the beginning, Americans—and especially their political leaders—acknowledged their dependence on God without resorting to official civil theology (29–30).

Murray quotes a key statement of the Third Plenary Council of Baltimore (1884): "We consider the establishment of our country's independence, the shaping of its liberties and laws, as a work of special providence, its framers 'building better than they knew,' the Almighty's hand guiding them." The bishops rejected the theory but affirmed the results of our Fathers' work. God's hand guided them, whatever they might have thought. But Murray explains that what was providential was hardly miraculous: "The providential aspect of the matter, and the reason for the better building, can be found in the fact that the American political community was organized in an era when the tradition of natural law and natural rights was still vigorous" (30). Our Fathers—partly because of the need to compromise with vigorous proponents of this tradition, and partly because they and even Locke himself did not think through all the implications of his theory—were more influenced than they knew by thought they thought they rejected.

Our Constitution, Murray explains, "was a great providential blessing" for Catholic American citizens. Because it points in the direction of the community called the church, Catholics as Catholics can be good American citizens. The liberty it protects is religious liberty in the sense of freedom for religion, the freedom to orient one's will with others toward the truth about one's situation as a creature. The U.S. Constitution, because it is about the free exercise of religion, does not require civic theological affirmations from its citizens—affirmations no Christian can make with "conscience and conviction" (43). Murray was and is criticized by conservative Catholics for his "Americanism"—for identifying American political solutions with ultimate or religious truth.[32] But Murray's inclination was, in fact, in exactly the opposite direction.

The key providential fact about our Constitution, for Murray, is that "the distinction between church and state, once the central assertions of the [Christian, natural] law tradition," found its way into the Constitution. Our Fathers understood this separation as "the distinction between state and society," and, following the tradition, they thought of society as composed "of a whole area of human concerns which were remote from the competence of government." For our Fathers, it was emphatically not true that there was "nothing above the state" (58).

As others, such as Alexis de Tocqueville, have noted, the American Revolution was limited; it did not aim to reconstruct religion or the family or even local government. So our Fathers held that government cannot "presume to define the Church or in any way supervise her authority in pursuit of her own distinct ends." Religious freedom is accorded not

only to the individual but also to "the Church as an organized society with its own law and jurisdiction." The social area from which our
Fathers excluded government "coincides with the divine mission of the
Church" as the church itself understands it (69–70), so "there's an evident coincidence of the principles which inspired the American republic
and those which are structural to the Western Christian political tradition" (30). The providential compatibility of America's political mission
and the church's divine mission was actually a coincidence based on a
compromise. None of those involved in the compromise were thinking
in terms of the Catholic Church's self-understanding, but that does not
mean the church cannot affirm the result as providential, as what our
political Fathers gave us.

Put another way, the American way of separating church and state is
not philosophical but political. The Jacobin decision to politicize everything "was basically philosophical"—or a theoretical claim about all
reality and the whole human being. The American decision is "simply
political," or a prudential compromise that did not mean to privilege particular theory. Because the compromise included Christian concerns, it
can be seen as "recognizably part of the Christian tradition." In that
respect, Murray affirms the conservative view that "Christian history"
prevailed in the Constitution over "rationalist theory." And so the man
whose rights are protected by the Constitution "is, whether he knows it
or not, [a] Christian man." That is, he "has certain original responsibilities precisely as man, antecedent to his status as citizen"; he is a man
whose understanding of his "personal dignity" has an irreducibly Christian foundation (30, 36–37, 39).

Today, that conservative victory of Christian history over Lockean
theory has to be defended not only as providential but also as corresponding to true or rational theory, to what is genuinely self-evident.
The true foundation of religious freedom, Murray explains, is natural
status or "dignity of the human person." That moral dignity is "rooted in
the given reality of man as man." Each of us is given "the basic imperative to act in accordance with his nature." And that objective imperative given to the true "moral subject" is the source of the freedom from
political determination that each dignified person has when it comes
"to the search for the truth, artistic creation, scientific discovery, and
the development of a man's political views, moral convictions, and religious beliefs." We are free by our natural gifts for all these aspects of "the
human spirit."[33]

The key truth we hold in common—what Murray calls "the essential idea upon which a democratic culture must be erected"—turns out to be "the dignity of human nature," which includes "man's spiritual nature."[34] It is because of that nature—probably cultivated or habituated—that we can conceive of the possibility of real freedom, which is the freedom of a virtuous people "inwardly governed by the recognized imperatives of a universal moral law" (36).

The Catholic Contribution to America

American Catholic citizens as citizens, Murray claims, are especially well equipped to give their country what it most needs—a theory that adequately accounts for the success of its experiment in liberty. Our lack of such a theory has produced a crisis of self-evidence. That crisis has moved from Locke through Darwin in one way and the Jacobin, totalitarian version of Rousseau in another way to the pragmatic, relativistic conclusion that there is no reality we can know that corresponds to our experiences of self or soul or freedom. If that is the case, then our Fathers' dedication to the protection of our equality in human liberty makes no sense.

Locke, Darwin, and the totalitarian secular civil theologians all share the nominalist view that words are nothing more than weapons. For Locke, words exist to secure the individual's power or survival; for Darwin, they exist to secure the species' survival; for the totalitarian civil theologians, they exist to impose civic unity on naturally anarchistic individuals. They all deny that we are naturally equipped to hold the self-evident truth in common. We need a science or theory of natural law that does not exaggerate either our freedom from nature or our continuity with the rest of nature. We need a theory that does not make us so homeless that our freedom is displayed in nothing but absurd, anxious misery, yet one that does not attempt to make us so at home that our real experiences of freedom and dignity are unrealistically denied. We need a theory that grounds our personal dignity in our natural openness to God. The God who is *logos* and *eros* made us in his image, so there must be a ground for human freedom rooted in our natural capabilities for knowing and loving. The best present expression of that view of who we are is found in the thought of our philosopher-pope.[35] And that view makes the best sense of our Fathers' choice of our natural openness over a consistently Lockean individualism that would reduce religion—and finally all our experiences of freedom and dignity—to private fantasies with no common or public weight.

That theory, as Murray summarizes, has to "be asserted within a religious framework" (or a choice for God); it has to be "realist (not nominalist)," or based on the truth that words are not merely weapons but give us access to the way things and persons really are; it has to be "societal (not individualist)," because we are given the ability to hold personal truth in common; and it has to be "integrally human (not rationalist)," because the truth is that the whole human being or person—the being open to truth, God, and the good—cannot be reduced to either mind or body (320). What our country most needs from its Catholic citizens, in Murray's view, is genuinely conservative in two senses. It conserves the whole truth about who we are against unrealistic abstractions and empty nominalism. It also reinvigorates the American rational tradition by conserving a tradition both old and more rational—or at least more realistic—than our own.

Notes

1. The two best introductions to Murray's life and thought are Robert W. McElroy, *The Search for an American Public Philosophy* (New York: Paulist Press, 1989), and Thomas P. Ferguson, *Catholic and American: The Political Theology of John Courtney Murray* (Lanham, Md.: Rowman and Littlefield, 1993).

2. Murray's disappointment with the weak foundation for religious liberty found in the council document *Dignitatis Humanae* is described by Francis Canavan, S.J., "Religious Freedom: John Courtney Murray and Vatican II," in *John Courtney Murray and the American Civil Conversation*, ed. Robert P. Hunt and Kenneth L. Grasso (Grand Rapids, Mich.: Eerdmans, 1992). One way that Murray tried to spin what the document actually says in the direction of his own view is described by Russell Hittinger, "The Declaration of Religious Freedom, *Dignitatis Humanae*," in *Vatican II: Renewal within Tradition*, ed. Matthew L. Lamb and Matthew Levering (New York: Oxford University Press, 2008).

3. John Courtney Murray, *We Hold These Truths: Catholic Reflections on the American Proposition* (Kansas City, Mo.: Sheed and Ward, 1960); subsequent references to this book are given parenthetically in the text. Throughout this chapter I borrow from two earlier chapters I wrote on *We Hold These Truths*: Peter Augustine Lawler, *Aliens in America: The Strange Truth about Our Souls* (Wilmington, Del.: ISI Books, 2002), and *Homeless and at Home in America* (South Bend, Ind.: St. Augustine's Press, 2007). In *Homeless*, I show that many

of Murray's views are anticipated in the work of the great nineteenth-century American Catholic writer Orestes Brownson. For an application of Murray's and Brownson's thought to some contemporary issues, see Peter Augustine Lawler, "Locke, Our Great Founders, and American Political Life," in *Defending the Republic: Constitutional Morality in a Time of Crisis*, ed. B. Frohnen and K. Grasso (Wilmington, Del.: ISI Books, 2008). For my lengthy introduction to Brownson's *The American Republic*, see the ISI edition (Wilmington, Del.: ISI Books, 2003).

4. See Harry V. Jaffa, *A New Birth of Freedom* (Lanham, Md.: Rowman and Littlefield, 2000), 214–25, for the relationship between Stephens and Lincoln, which is perfectly consistent with Murray's general analysis.

5. Richard Rorty, *Achieving Our Country: Leftist Thought in Twentieth Century America* (Cambridge, Mass.: Harvard University Press, 1998); Lawler, *Aliens in America*, 75–94.

6. John Courtney Murray, S.J., "School and Christian Freedom," *National Catholic Educational Proceedings* 48 (August 1951): 551.

7. Josef Cardinal Ratzinger, "The Dictatorship of Relativism," 2005 (this is Ratzinger's last homily before becoming pope); Peter Augustine Lawler, *Postmodernism Rightly Understood: The Return to Realism in American Thought* (Lanham, Md.: Rowman and Littlefield, 1999), chap. 2.

8. John Courtney Murray, S.J., *Bridging the Sacred and the Secular*, ed. J. Leon Hooper (Washington, D.C.: Georgetown University Press, 1994), 111.

9. Murray, "School and Christian Freedom," 553–54.

10. John Courtney Murray, S.J., *Religious Liberty: Catholic Struggles with Pluralism*, ed. J. Leon Hooper (Louisville, Ky.: Westminster/John Knox Press, 1993), 70.

11. John Courtney Murray, S.J., "Law or Prepossessions," *Law and Contemporary Problems* 14 (winter 1949): 560.

12. John Courtney Murray, S.J., *The Problem of God: Yesterday and Today* (New Haven, Conn.: Yale University Press, 1964), 110.

13. Murray, *Bridging the Sacred and the Secular*, 158.

14. Murray, *The Problem of God*, 85, 95.

15. Ibid., 77.

16. Ibid., 90–99.

17. John Courtney Murray, S.J., "St. Ignatius and the End of Modernity," in *The Ignatian Year at Georgetown* (Washington, D.C.: Georgetown University Press, 1956).

18. Murray, *The Problem of God*, 86–87.

19. David Brooks, *Bobos in Paradise: The New Upper Class and How They Got There* (New York: Simon and Schuster, 2000); Edward Fesler, *The Last Superstition: A Refutation of the New Atheists* (South Bend, Ind.: St. Augustine's Press, 2008).

20. John Courtney Murray, S.J., "The Church and Totalitarian Democracy," *Theological Studies* 14 (December 1952): 545.

21. Murray, *The Problem of God*, 85.

22. Ibid., 111–16.

23. Murray, "St. Ignatius and the End of Modernity."

24. Ibid.

25. Murray, *Bridging the Sacred and the Secular*, 113.

26. John Courtney Murray, S.J., "How Liberal Is Liberalism?" *America* 75, no. 6 (April 1945).

27. John Courtney Murray, S.J., "On the Necessity for Not Believing: A Roman Catholic Interpretation," *Yale Scientific Magazine* 23, no. 5 (February 1949).

28. Murray, "Law or Prepossessions."

29. Murray, "School and Christian Freedom."

30. Murray, "Law or Prepossessions."

31. Ibid.

32. This sort of anti-Americanist criticism is found throughout Donald J. D'Elia and Stephen Krason, eds., *We Hold These Truths and More* (Steubenville, Ohio: Franciscan University Press, 1994).

33. John Courtney Murray, S.J., "The Declaration on Religious Freedom: A Movement in Legislative History," in *Religious Liberty: An End and a Beginning*, ed. J. C. Murray (New York: Macmillan, 1966), 40–41.

34. Murray, *Bridging the Sacred and the Secular*, 108.

35. For the thought of Pope Benedict XVI, see the essays collected in Bairnard Cowan, ed., *Gained Horizons: Regensburg and the Enlargement of Reason* (South Bend, Ind.: St. Augustine's Press, 2000).

Bibliography

Brooks, David. 2000. *Bobos in Paradise: The New Upper Class and How They Got There*. New York: Simon and Schuster.

Canavan, Francis, S.J. 1992. "Religious Freedom: John Courtney Murray and Vatican II." In *John Courtney Murray and the American Civil Conversation*, edited by Robert P. Hunt and Kenneth L. Grasso. Grand Rapids, Mich.: Eerdmans.

Cowan, Bairnard, ed. 2009. *Gained Horizons: Regensburg and the Enlargement of Reason*. South Bend, Ind.: St. Augustine's Press.

D'Elia, Donald J., and Stephen Krason, eds. 1994. *We Hold These Truths and More*. Steubenville, Ohio: Franciscan University Press.

Ferguson, Thomas P. 1993. *Catholic and American: The Political Theology of John Courtney Murray*. Lanham, Md.: Rowman and Littlefield.

Fesler, Edward. 2008. *The Last Superstition: A Refutation of the New Atheists*. South Bend, Ind.: St. Augustine's Press.

Hittinger, Russell. 2008. "The Declaration of Religious Freedom, *Dignitatis*

Humanae." In *Vatican II: Renewal within Tradition*, edited by Matthew L. Lamb and Matthew Levering. New York: Oxford University Press.

Jaffa, Harry V. 2000. *A New Birth of Freedom*. Lanham, Md.: Rowman and Littlefield.

Lawler, Peter Augustine. 1999. *Postmodernism Rightly Understood: The Return to Realism in American Thought*. Lanham, Md.: Rowman and Littlefield.

————. 2002. *Aliens in America: The Strange Truth about Our Souls*. Wilmington, Del.: ISI Books.

————. 2003. "Introduction" to *The American Republic* by Orestes Brownson. Wilmington, Del.: ISI Books.

————. 2007. *Homeless and at Home in America*. South Bend, Ind.: St. Augustine's Press.

————. 2008. "Locke, Our Great Founders, and American Political Life." In *Defending the Republic: Constitutional Morality in a Time of Crisis*, edited by B. Frohnen and K. Grasso. Wilmington, Del.: ISI Books.

McElroy, Robert W. 1989. *The Search for an American Public Philosophy*. New York: Paulist Press.

Murray, John Courtney, S.J. 1945. "How Liberal Is Liberalism?" *America* 75, no. 6 (April): 6–7.

————. 1949. "Law or Prepossessions." *Law and Contemporary Problems* 14 (winter): 23–43.

————. 1949. "On the Necessity for Not Believing: A Roman Catholic Interpretation." *Yale Scientific Magazine* 23, no. 5 (February): 11, 12, 22, 30, 32, 34.

————. 1951. "School and Christian Freedom." *National Catholic Educational Proceedings* 48 (August): 63–68.

————. 1952. "The Church and Totalitarian Democracy." *Theological Studies* 14 (December): 525–63.

————. 1956. "St. Ignatius and the End of Modernity." In *The Ignatian Year at Georgetown*. Washington, D.C.: Georgetown University Press.

————. 1960. *We Hold These Truths: Catholic Reflections on the American Proposition*. Kansas City, Mo.: Sheed and Ward.

————. 1964. *The Problem of God: Yesterday and Today*. New Haven, Conn.: Yale University Press.

————. 1966. "The Declaration on Religious Freedom: A Moment in Legislative History." In *Religious Liberty: An End and a Beginning*, edited by J. C. Murray. New York: Macmillan.

————. 1993. *Religious Liberty: Catholic Struggles with Pluralism*. Edited by J. Leon Hooper. Louisville, Ky.: Westminster/John Knox Press.

————. 1994. *Bridging the Sacred and the Secular*. Edited by J. Leon Hooper. Washington, D.C.: Georgetown University Press.

Rorty, Richard. 1998. *Achieving Our Country: Leftist Thought in Twentieth Century America*. Cambridge, Mass.: Harvard University Press.

Russell Kirk

Traditionalist Conservatism in a Postmodern Age

GERALD J. RUSSELLO

Russell Kirk (1918–1994) is widely credited as one of the architects of postwar American conservatism. The author of more than thirty works of intellectual history, literary criticism, and biography, Kirk was a long-time newspaper columnist, an early contributor to *National Review,* and the founder of two quarterly journals, *Modern Age* and *The University Bookman.* His 1953 book *The Conservative Mind: From Burke to Santayana* (in later editions expanded to include T. S. Eliot) created for a nascent conservative movement an intellectual genealogy to counter the dominant story of America as a liberal nation.

Kirk is often pigeonholed as a hidebound traditionalist, but he himself had a different view, which also casts light on his work as a whole. Kirk describes himself in an essay collection entitled *Confessions of a Bohemian Tory* as "a connoisseur of slums and strange corners, I have dwelt in more garrets and cellars, forest cabins and island hovels, than I can recall." Writing in the early 1960s, Kirk staked a claim for a conservative countercultural position: "A Tory, according to Samuel Johnson, is a man attached to orthodoxy in church and state. A bohemian is a wandering and often impecunious man of letters or arts, indifferent to the demands of bourgeois fad and fable. Such a one has your servant been. Tory and bohemian go not ill together: it is quite possible to abide by the norms of civilized existence, what Mr. T. S. Eliot has called 'the permanent things': and yet to set at defiance the sot securities and sham conventionalities of twentieth-century sociability."[1]

Though a Tory, Kirk was not yet attached to a particular orthodoxy in church; his conversion to Roman Catholicism still lay some years in the future. Nor do his condemnations of the "bourgeois fad and fable," "sot securities," and "sham conventionalities" trace the usual conservative pieties; were not these the very things conservatives ought to be conserving? Kirk was charting a different course: of orthodoxy, yes, but not of the expected kind. As he recalls in his memoir, "some readers began to fancy that there were two scribbling Russell Kirks."[2] And indeed, in a sense, there were two. The one composed long works of biography or intellectual history. The other produced stories of the occult for collections such as *Love of Horror* and was given the "high distinction" of being made a Knight Commander of the Order of Count Dracula by the Count Dracula Society, for his books *The Surly Sullen Bell* and *The Old House of Fear.*

The intervening decades, however, have partially obscured the significance of Kirk's interpretation of conservative principles. Some conservative writers, such as scholar Walter Berns and polemicists such as Frank Meyer, offered sharp critiques. More recently, Alan Wolfe published a vituperative review of a collection titled *The Essential Russell Kirk*, claiming, among other things, that Kirk had no lasting intellectual depth and that his brand of conservatism was really a dangerous reactionary posture. Nevertheless, some have proclaimed Kirk "redivivus" in American intellectual life.[3] Though remaining well respected, Kirk's vision of a person centered in a community guided by what he calls the "permanent things" of human existence remains an embattled position on the Right. For some, Kirk represents a futile nostalgia for a time that never was; for others, his thought, whatever its attractions, has no place in an ideological "movement" seeking political victories. Nevertheless, Kirk's intellectual legacy remains in a number of places, and its echoes are found throughout the intellectual landscape. Concretely, the journals he founded continue to appear, and his books remain in print. In a series of books, Bill Kauffman has outlined a defense of regionalism that is very much Kirk's in spirit. Kauffman wants to reclaim the particularities of the American experience from the domination of big government and the monotone culture emanating from Hollywood, Washington, and New York. His lyrical prose elevates half-forgotten episodes and figures in American history and weaves them into a compelling countercultural story that includes Dorothy Day, Norman Mailer, Henry Clune, Calvin Coolidge, and others. Rob Dreher, in his provocative book *Crunchy Cons*, explicitly draws support from Kirk for his view of a localist, organic lifestyle. Modeled on Kirk's suspicions of the cult of technology and his faith in science, the appeal of "crunchy" transcends traditional political labels of Left and Right. In a more particular, academic way, scholars such as Barry Alan Shain, in their writings on early America, remind us that the colonies were not Lockean utopias but small, close-knit, highly religious Protestant villages. The world the founders lived in was not, in other words, an earlier version of a secular society but something wholly different. These strands of modern conservative thought each echo themes in Kirk's writings.

Major Themes

The Canons and Other Features of Kirk's Conservatism

In a well-known passage of *The Conservative Mind*, Kirk sets forth what he considers six basic "canons" that have defined conservative thought since the French Revolution. They are largely the opposites of those features that, for Kirk, define the modern world. Kirk describes them as follows: (1) a belief in a transcendent order, which may be based in tradition, divine revelation, or natural law; (2) an affection for the "variety and mystery" of human existence; (3) a conviction that society requires orders and classes that emphasize "natural distinctions"; (4) a belief that property and freedom are closely linked; (5) a faith in custom, convention, and prescription; and (6) recognition that change is not reform, which entails a respect for the political value of prudence.[4]

In retrospect, these canons are perhaps the weakest part of the book. Such a catalog played right into the hands of Kirk's critics, who thought these canons exemplified a conservative abstraction at odds with the historical texture of the remainder of his argument, which, Kirk claimed, formed the basis of conservative belief. One reviewer, Gordon Lewis, concentrated on this precise point: "any attempt to build philosophic foundations for [the conservative] attitude is invariably evidence that the attitude no longer claims the instinctive allegiance" of the culture; "far too much of genuine conservatism . . . is a matter of feeling and instinct and emotion to be satisfactorily reducible to the forms of logical assertion and proof."[5] Kirk continued to tinker with the number and formulation of the canons throughout his career, perhaps as a sign of discomfort with such abstractions. In his last enumeration of these principles, for example, the requirement of orders and classes in society is muted.

Perhaps in recognition that, with the end of the cold war, the allure of large-scale government schemes appeared to be waning, Kirk added an explicit canon favoring "voluntary communities" to replace the one opposing social planning.[6] Indeed, in one of his last books, Kirk himself acknowledged that conservative principles are fluid. "The diversity of ways in which conservative views may find expression is itself proof that conservatism is no fixed ideology. What particular principles conservatives emphasize during any given time will vary with the circumstances and necessities of that era."[7]

The Moral Imagination

Despite the changes, there is no reason to doubt that the canons set out in *The Conservative Mind* provided the scaffolding for much of Kirk's thinking, but they should be distinguished from other important themes. For example, the imagination is barely implied in this list, although it does appear elsewhere in *The Conservative Mind* and assumed a large place in Kirk's thinking beginning in the 1950s. The imagination was at the center of Kirk's critique of modern life and therefore crucial to a proper understanding of his work. Kirk borrowed the term *moral imagination* from Edmund Burke and the American critic Irving Babbitt. In a famous passage in *Reflections on the Revolution in France*, Burke contrasts the "superadded ideas, furnished from the wardrobe of a moral imagination, which the heart owns, and the understanding ratifies, as necessary to cover the defects of our naked, shivering nature, and to raise it to dignity in our own estimation" with the "barbarous philosophy, which is the offspring of cold hearts and muddy understandings, and which is as void of solid wisdom as it is destitute of all taste and elegance, [that] laws are to be supported only by their own terrors, and by the concern which each individual may find in them from his own speculations, or can spare them from his own private interests."[8]

Burke's description, in tightly wrapped form, gives us several elements that inform Kirk's understanding of the imagination. The imagination is not primarily rational but embraces the feelings and affections of those subject to it; it is something outside the individual but something the individual "owns" and "ratifies" through individual effort and action; it is not based on calculation, understood as some sort of utilitarian calculus; and, finally, it provides something beyond the physical realities of our "shivering nature." Kirk himself explains Burke's meaning as "that power of ethical perception which strides beyond the barriers of private experience and momentary events. . . . The moral imagination aspires to the apprehending of right order in the soul and right order in the commonwealth."[9] Further, the moral imagination "informs us concerning the dignity of human nature; which instructs us that we are more than naked apes. As Burke suggested in 1790, letters and learning are hollow, if deprived of the moral imagination. And as Burke said, the spirit of religion long sustained this moral imagination, along with a whole system of manners. Such imagination lacking, to quote another passage from Burke, we are cast forth 'from this world of reason, and order, and peace, and virtue, and fruitful penitence, into the antagonist worlds of madness, discord, vice, confusion and unavailing sorrow.'"[10] The imagination, moreover, "as high dream or low dream," is always present, especially in literature. The only question for Kirk is whether the imagination will be respected and employed, or enslaved and ignored. For Kirk, the moral imagination "draws man back to the 'ethical center,' or what Kirk would later call the 'permanent things.'"[11]

On either side of the moral imagination, Kirk places the idyllic and diabolical imaginations. The idyllic imagination is a model for modernity. It assumes human perfection, both individually and socially, and wishes away the faults and sins of people caused by the artificial bindings of society and religion. The idyllic is "the sort of imagination that, ignoring the hard necessities of human existence, would have us surrender to the appetites in primitive simplicity."[12] The idyllic imagination leaves us in lotusland, oblivious alike to the joys and the pains of a full human existence; it "rejects old dogmas and old manners and rejoices in the notion of emancipation from duty and convention."[13] The idyllic imagination casts our glance backward, to the supposed origins of humanity. Once freed from actual history or society, Jean-Jacques Rousseau, one of the progenitors of the idyllic imagination, creates a "golden age" of untrammeled desire, and the absence of prescription or tradition, from his own private stock of reason. This imaginative reconstruction has had political effects: the "idyllic fantasy of a free, happy, lawless, propertyless state of nature" results, almost inevitably, in tyranny: Rousseau's general will brook no dissent from the individual or minorities.[14] The idyll, however, cannot last. Once there has been complete emancipation from every restraint, something must fill the vacuum. Kirk calls that something the diabolic imagination.

The diabolic imagination (a term drawn from T. S. Eliot's early work *After Strange Gods*) is concerned solely with the darker appetites of human nature. Kirk describes it as a "narcosis."[15] It is purely materialistic and rejects the transcendent. Kirk is not squeamish, nor does he prudishly seek to hide these passions. He writes that "fulsome praise of goodness can alienate" and may even cause a rejection of principles. Yet those passions exist for a purpose—the same purpose Kirk discovered in the writings of Flannery O'Connor: to lay bare human nature and, despite the ugliness and evil, to find the "grotesque face of God."[16] Imagination is a means of reenchanting the world against the sterility of modernity, which has stripped away all the nonrational and nonscientific aids to human existence. Between the idyllic imagination, which creates a false utopia by ignoring the material realities of existence, and the diabolic imagination, which treats the material as the only existence and revels in the lower passions, Kirk sets the moral imagination.

An early postmodern theorist, Ihab Hassan, has written in remarkably similar terms. In *The Dismemberment of Orpheus*, Hassan writes that "imagination cannot abandon its teleological sense: change is also dream come true. . . . I can only hope that after self-parody, self-subversion, and self-transcendence, after the pride and revulsion of anti-art will have gone their way, art may move toward a *redeemed imagination*."[17] A redeemed imagination is startlingly close to Kirk's theologically infused vision of the moral imagination. The moral imagination redeems humanity from its weaknesses and from the provinciality of being trapped in a particular time and its opinions.

The Importance of Religion

Religion is another feature that is absent from the canons, except for the indirect implication of belief in an undefined transcendent. Some prominent conservatives have maintained that religious belief is not essential to a conservative position. Kirk may have had some sympathy with that opinion early in his career—hence his respect for nontheist conservatives such as libertarian Albert Jay Nock and Babbitt. Later, however, he came to hold a contrary opinion. Even before his conversion, he believed that "orthodoxy in church and state" is part of the very definition of a "Tory," whether bohemian or not. And subsequent study convinced him that organized forms of religious worship are the mainsprings of culture.

As Christopher Dawson, one of Kirk's favorite historians, contends, viewed historically, religion has always been bound up with the development of culture, yet religion is never solely a conservative force. Christianity tore apart the fabric of the pagan Roman Empire, and the emergence of Protestant Christianity had a similar effect on the political and theological unity of medieval Europe. The idea of a "Christian culture" is not, as some of Kirk's opponents imply, a monolithic theocracy espousing a reactionary politics. Indeed, at least with respect to the United States, Kirk sets himself apart from such an idea. In a essay on Eliot, Kirk writes that religion forms the basis of every society, that "liberalism and democracy cannot stand unsupported," and that support must come from either the religious beliefs of the people or "else the inverted religion of ideology." Nevertheless, Kirk does not endorse for America a national or established church; indeed, in that same essay, he condemns the "millenarianists," whom he describes as wishing to impose a theocracy out of a hatred of difference.[18]

Kirk rejects the contention that religion has a merely utilitarian purpose and decries efforts to invent religious faith, such as the cult of reason during the French Revolution. He likewise disdains finding a substitute for lost faith, as argued by the proponents of "civic virtue" in the 1980s. According to Kirk, these efforts are doomed to failure and, in any event, are subject to use as manipulative tools. He wrote in 1992:

> Some well-meaning folk talk of a "civil religion," a kind of cult of patriotism, founded upon a myth of national virtue and upon veneration of certain historical documents, together with a utilitarian morality. But such experiments of a secular character never have functioned satisfactorily. . . . Worship of the state, or of the national commonwealth, is no substitute for communion with transcendent love and wisdom.
>
> Nor can attempts at persuading people that religion is "useful" meet with much genuine success. . . . People will conform their actions to the precepts of religion only when they earnestly believe the doctrines of that religion to be true.[19]

However, the features of religion that provide structure and a story of existence to people who have faith is valuable, even in a practical way. Kirk also contends that faith will inevitably supply an organizing feature to such people's culture. As an empirical matter, religious faith is at the root of any culture. The problem with modern culture is that it has lost its connections with its religious roots and had instead substituted ideology.[20] In other words, people will always have belief. The question is whether that belief will be the traditional religion of the culture or another belief system imposed on them or invented for the moment.

Kirk considers what he calls "scientism," a reduction of human existence to material criteria, to be the enemy of religion and a particular characteristic of the modern age. Scientism uses science to serve particular ideological ends, and in general, it simply parrots the materialistic assumptions of a previous generation. Significantly, Kirk does not think that "scientism" has any real connection to contemporary science. Contemporary science, according to Kirk, has now entered upon "the realm of mystery" and imposes no difficulty for religious belief.[21] The two, split at the time of the Enlightenment, may yet see a reconciliation through the intermediaries of particle physics or "string theory." Indeed, a rejection of scientism would lead to an openness toward theism: "Physicists instruct us that we of this seemingly too-solid flesh actually are collections of electrical particles, held in an ephemeral suspension and arrangements by some 'laws' that we do not understand in the least. We are energy—and energy, which we can neither create nor destroy, is incessantly being transmuted into new forms. . . . For the science of quantum mechanics has undone nineteenth-century concepts of matter, and it becomes conceivable that whatever power has assembled the negative and positive charges composing us may reassemble those electrical particles, if it chooses." Kirk considers imagination to be as applicable to science as it is to literature or history, and he was fond of recalling the passage in Andre Maurois's *Illusions* in which Albert Einstein and poet St. John Perse discover from each other that the physicist and the poet work through similar methods.[22] The scientific imagination and method held no fears for Kirk.

Place and Sentiment

Two further ideas deserve mention: place and sentiment. Kirk criticizes the rootlessness of much of modern life, and the associated loss of place, as a defining characteristic of existence. The emotional and imaginative resources people invest in places are important components of individual and social self-identity and, therefore, a source of loyalty and affection. Political boundaries, family homes, old castles, familiar neighborhoods, and ruins can each contribute to the creation and formation of personal identity in the larger culture. To Burke, "the link between place and identity is a psychological one in which feelings (such as love) and cognitive associations and not merely preferences, such as those that get mobilized in the expression of consent, are galvanized. . . . Burke takes territoriality to be constitutive of individual and collective identity and associates its denial with the cavalier horror of imperial and Jacobin excesses."[23] Some of Kirk's best early work focuses on the importance of places, such as St. Andrews and the great houses of Scotland, Mountjoy Square in Dublin, and even the Detroit of his youth; he uses their physicality, and the affections they generate, as illustrations for the binding power of place. Because of their power, a society should be mindful of the construction of its places; not surprisingly, architecture is an abiding concern for Kirk. In an essay entitled "The Architecture of Servility and Boredom," he sets out the importance of the way buildings look. The art of architecture and city planning "must be concerned primarily with the person, and how he thrives under a large plan; with the republic (or public interest) and what sort of society arises from grand designs." Kirk asserts, "Assuming, however, that urban planning has no limits, the breed of urban planners have given us the architecture of servility and boredom. Over the past quarter of a century and more, anarchy and desolation have been the consequences of grandiose pseudo-planning." The critique of modern architecture contains a capsule of Kirk's broader complaints about modernity. A small class (urban planners) controls the manipulation of architecture and other of society's symbols. The ideas of this class are false: though seemingly focused on the public good, they are more often devoted to ego or profit. Rather than public architecture, "it has been an architecture of sham: the outward symbol of a society which, despite all its protestations of being 'free' and 'democratic' rapidly sinks into servility."[24] Most important, the planners ignore the sense of scale, preferring large and bureaucratic structures, which reduce the importance of the individual, to a human-scaled community. This is not to say that Kirk proposed a standpattism; individuals have a responsibility to create their communities and to constantly engage the past in that act of reconstruction. However, for Kirk, the settled certainties of place are where one must begin; indeed, Kirk considers conservatism to be loyalty to place as much as to principle.

Sentiment became more important as Kirk developed his critique of modernity based on a disjunction between "discussion" and "sentiment." Kirk defines sentiment as "a moving conviction; . . . a conviction derived from some other source than pure reason."[25] It is sentiment, not reason, that moves us first. Architecture, politics, literature, and history all inspire feelings in us before they make us think. Though Kirk proclaims himself more a man of thought than one of sentiment, his conception of rationality is bound up with the sentiments. One does not, in Kirk's view, think about something one has no feelings about, for good or ill. Indeed, he recognizes that sentiment may have more power than reason. Without educated feelings, rational discourse would be impossible: the passions would rule.[26]

Sentiment assumes a larger importance in Kirk's work because of his assertion that the coming (post)modern age will be an Age of Sentiments, superseding the old, modern, liberal Age of Discussion, as discussed more fully later. The coming age will be more concerned with the power of image on the heart than the power of logical discourse on the mind. Kirk considers rhetoric—the creation of image through language—a critical art for conservatives to perfect. And for Kirk, rhetoric is effective at creating those images only if it pays careful heed to the sentiments.

Kirk's construction of the role of the sentiments, therefore, is tied together with his qualified respect for reason. The first comes before the second, and he deplores those he considers reductive rationalists—John Dewey, for example—who abstract all thought from feeling and denigrate both. Likewise, he is suspicious of those who, like Rousseau, have reduced sentiment to mere feeling and emancipated it from thought. Thus, when writing of education, Kirk stresses the importance of arousing students' feeling for or against certain things through the use of story, only later providing a rational explanation for those feelings.

The Age of Discussion and the Age of Sentiments

Kirk, as a progenitor of modern conservatism, is often considered a steady adversary of liberalism. Although it is true that Kirk has little patience for the varieties of liberalism evinced in figures such as Rousseau, Dewey, or Locke, Kirk has a slightly different project in mind: reconstructing tradition in a postliberal society. In an early essay, "The Dissolution of Liberalism," Kirk concludes that liberalism was moribund from the beginning "for lack of a higher imagination." Because it lacks any real narrative power, it cannot maintain a hold on the popular imagination for long; liberalism soon "cease[s] to signify anything, even among its most sincere partisans, [other] than a vague good will."[27] Although written in the 1950s, Kirk's essay anticipates the subsequent scholarly arguments over the content and future of liberalism. Kirk examines the dissolution of the modern age in two prescient essays, one each on the Age of Discussion and the Age of Sentiments.[28] The Age of Discussion was dominated by the word, by rational argument that ultimately tired of itself and would, Kirk thought, give way to the Age of Sentiments, which would be dominated by the image.

The Age of Discussion began in the mid-nineteenth century. Kirk borrowed the phrase from English journalist Walter Bagehot, writing that he "understood well that during the nineteenth century the old order of things was being effaced—swept away by the nineteenth-century triumph of what Bagehot called Discussion." Discussion created democracy, as it did liberalism. Both revolve around the premise that through discourse based on rational principles, social and moral problems can be resolved. Both are based on the same understanding of reason. Discussion emerged with the age of the great eighteenth-century journals of opinion. The Age of Sentiments began with television.

> Into the Age of Sentiments there will survive some serious peri-
> odicals, and some decent books, and here and there obscure
> corners where a few people earnestly discuss some matters that
> cannot well be swept into oblivion. Yet this remnant of genuine
> thinkers and talkers may be very small. The immense majority
> of human beings will *feel* with the projected images they behold
> upon the television screen; and in those viewers that screen will
> rouse *sentiments* rather than reflections. Waves of emotion will
> sweep back and forth, so long as the Age of Sentiments endures.
> And whether those emotions are low or high must depend
> upon the folk who determine the tone and temper of television
> programming.

Kirk admired the old British periodicals, but he was no lover of the Age of Discussion and did not despair over its demise: "for the most part, the Age of Discussion was an age of shams and posturings."[29] Like its fruit, liberalism, discussion lacked "vitality"; mired in abstractions, it failed to move hearts. Even Eliot's *Criterion*, closest to Kirk's own cultural attitudes, was a failed defense of discussion.

Kirk saw in the proliferation of new media the increased chance that images would be packaged and presented to a gullible public without that critical process of discrimination and judgment being encouraged or engaged. Daniel Boorstin states that the process of image creation in a modern society is essentially a passive and synthetic one, that is, the image (of a company, a product, or a person) is constructed deliberately, with a purpose, and to encompass only a limited range of qualities—perhaps only one quality. Further, the image is passive, in that the "consumer of the image . . . is also somehow supposed to fit into it."[30] This problem of images and image creation has occupied much of postmodern criticism. Because postmodernism is, in one sense, concerned with the production and endless reproduction of cultural symbols—not only in art but also in more commonplace forms such as shopping malls and amusement parks—postmodern critics often examine images that have no content in themselves but are only "the shadows we make of other shadows." Kirk similarly observes that "the image often betrays."[31] In other words, the constant array of images provides only superficial form and no substance; it is bereft of real imagination. For Kirk, however, this was not the only path the Age of Sentiments might take. Conservative rhetoric, which is, at its best, imaginative, could also be suitable for this new age.

In the recovered tradition of Burke and others, another manner of imagery and image making can be found, which (like its counterpart) evokes sentiment and emotion, but for a different purpose and to different effect. Thus the Age of Sentiments need not be one of unbridled emotionalism, without tradition or authority, or adapted to suit the consumer society of contemporary capitalism. Sentiments of honor and duty are just as possible as the sentiments espoused by narcissism or materialism. As Kirk notes, the Age of Discussion was reserved only for a few; most were content to follow "the doctrines of one faction or another." Indeed, "an age moved by high sentiments can be more admirable than an age mired in desiccated discussions."[32] In elevated political rhetoric, such as that of Edmund Burke, such joining of the imagination with proper sentiments can be found.

Kirk contends that modernity—or, more specifically, the modern outlook—"is not confined to any especial party, faction, or class; rather it is a cast of mind and character." As a cast of mind, the relevant intellectual characteristics of modernity could arise anywhere, at any time, although they assumed particular cultural and political importance beginning with the end of the eighteenth century. The characteristics

Kirk identifies as constituent parts of the modern outlook include "neot-erism on principle; preference for change over permanence; exaltation of the present era over all previous epochs; hearty approval of material aggrandizement and relative indifference toward a moral order; positive hostility, often, toward, theism."[33] In these features, the modern age is an heir to the thought of both the positivists and the utilitarians.

Kirk never fully embraced this distinction between premodern and modern adopted by other thinkers (including some of his fellow con-servatives), if only because such periodization too often implied a per-petual moving forward to a terrestrial paradise, something Kirk thought impossible. In the 1950s, against the social planners, he wrote, "to think that society can really be reformed by any grandiose program of posi-tive legislation or expenditure of money is itself the grossest of utopian delusions. There is no Grand Design to remedy the ills of the twentieth century—a disappointing statement, perhaps, but ineluctable."[34] Kirk's conclusion is fully compatible with the postmodern reluctance to con-done "metanarratives," precisely because he does not see the two as inex-tricably linked.

Kirk, Federalism, and State Power

One reason for Kirk's relative lack of direct political influence is his almost perverse refusal to speak specifically or decisively with respect to public policy issues. As discussed earlier, his conservatism was mostly directed toward regenerating a lost tradition of thought. His imaginative conservative was meant as an antidote to ideology and was advocated on the plane of ideas.

Nevertheless, Kirk did not entirely neglect questions of pressing public interest. Characteristically, however, he examined them through a historical lens. Although federalism was not explicitly a major strand of his writing, Kirk elaborated an understanding of the structure and purpose of the American federalist system that attempted to preserve individual and communal freedom by separating powers of the national government and those of the states and by acting as a bulwark to political or economic centralization. Federalism also served to create local lead-ers, who strengthened localities and the states against a central govern-ment. Indeed, Kirk wrote in 1964 that most of the functions of society are more properly left at the local or state level.[35] This understanding of federalism is rooted in Kirk's belief that politics is based on sentiment—

what we love or hate—and that sentiment is best grounded in small communities whose decisions are accessible and debatable by the entire community.

Kirk thought that although most persons would prefer a truly federal system to a uniform central government, "incantations" about the supposed ability of the central government to solve every problem could carry the electorate toward results opposite to their intentions.[36] Political language, such as "democracy" or "the people," has powerful effects, and Kirk was especially sensitive to the importance of political language in shaping policy. Indeed, Kirk considered political rhetoric so powerful that it could overcome even the normal self-interest expected in the political arena.[37]

Ultimately, Kirk adopted a view of federalism that is neither nationalistic nor based on the usual arguments about states' rights. Kirk instead mixed conservative arguments about the need for separation of powers with what American thinker Orestes Brownson calls "territorial democracy." In doing so, he sought to articulate a version of federalism consistent with that of the founders, though based on different premises. Rather than the traditional understanding of federalism in the founding era—as a way to solve the problem of "large republics" that confronted classical political theory and is discussed, for example, in *Federalist* 10—Kirk analyzed the issue from the perspective of local communities. Using territorial democracy solidified Kirk's belief that "rights" as understood in the American context reflect the specific traditions of the United States rather than a complete theory of universal human rights. Further, territorial democracy could reconcile the tension between treating the states as mere "provinces" of the central government and seeing them as autonomous political units independent of Washington.

The value of place has an obvious resonance for federalism, which is an institutional expression of the "spirit of particularism." People generally prefer their own neighborhood, town, or state and choose to remain and build their lives in places for which they feel affection. Moreover, they are reluctant to concede power to distant bureaucrats. The people most directly affected should have the greatest participation in decision making, a principle not unlike the concept of subsidiarity in Catholic social teaching. Kirk opposed large governments for two primary reasons. First, they are inefficient in allocating resources and making decisions. Second, they tend to impose "moral absolutism."[38] In a lecture given at the Heritage Foundation in 1989, for example, Kirk advocated "family farms, farmers' cooperatives for marketing, encouragement of artisans and small traders, the technical and administrative possibilities of industrial decentralization, the diminution of the average size of factories," and other measures to reduce the reliance on centralization, which "terribly damages communal existence."[39]

Federalism—which, Kirk stressed, was the result of the practical circumstances and history of the colonies as much as political theory—allocates power appropriately. Issues of national concern are addressed by the central government, but everything else is left to the states or localities. The common-law system, which the colonies and later states adopted virtually wholesale from England, reinforces this allocation of power. Borrowing language from John Randolph, Kirk condemned the "legislative maggot" that serves private interest in the name of the public good. Legislation has two difficulties: it can be used to further selfish interests, or it can be employed in the service of an ideology without regard for human nature or historical circumstance. Even when well-intentioned, legislation often fails; it is often written in broad strokes or aspirational terms, leaving the more difficult tasks of interpretation and implementation to administrative agencies, which are not answerable to an electorate, or to undemocratic courts, which are given free rein to insert their own political beliefs into vaguely worded laws. Either way, self-government suffers.

This argument, in Kirk's view, means that "the general or federal institutions were republican, not democratic in character; that is, the Federal Constitution deliberately erected barriers against direct popular control of the national political apparatus. But in their townships and counties, and to some extent even in their state governments, the mass of the people enjoyed strong powers and rights."[40] Relying on the work of Felix Morley, whose book *Freedom and Federalism* appeared in 1959, Kirk argues that the "unwritten" constitutions of these localities, in turn, support self-government at the national level.

> Genuine federalism, then, is the protector both of private rights and of local interests and powers of free decision. "Our organic law seeks to harmonize all government action with the talent of a truly free people for self-government," Dr. Felix Morley writes in his book "Freedom and Federalism." "They remain free only as long as they maintain this spiritual aspiration. Without faith, the Constitution fails. Whether or not our Federal Republic will

be maintained is therefore at bottom a moral issue. It depends as much on the churches and the synagogues as on the legislators and the law courts. The growth of Big Government goes hand in hand with the loss of Big Conviction."[41]

If localities express local democratic sentiment, the states act as buffers between the national government and the localities, and they also represent, in a corporate fashion, state, regional, and territorial interests. "Brownson distinguishes between the old American territorial democracy founded upon local rights and common interests of the several states and smaller organs of society, and the pure democracy of Rousseau, which later writers call 'totalitarian democracy.'"[42] This pure democracy of Rousseau is characterized by centralized administration in the name of an abstract "people," with little authority or freedom at the national level or, ultimately, at the local level. For Kirk, this meant the dissolution of true democracy: "whatever is beneficent and prudent in modern democracy is made possible through cooperative volition. If, then, in the name of an abstract Democracy, the functions of community are transferred to distant political direction—why, real government by the consent of the governed gives way to a standardizing process hostile to freedom and dignity."[43] This assessment owes obvious debts to Alexis de Tocqueville and his celebration of the township, an insight into the local roots of self-governance that has engendered its own body of scholarship.[44]

The conversation Kirk envisions among the democratic localities, indirectly democratic states, and a representative national government is the genius of the American system. Federalism is a necessary instrument to protect that conversation. "If the federal character of American government decays badly, then American democracy also must decline terribly, until nothing remains of it but a name; and the new 'democrats' may be economic and social levellers, indeed, but they will give popular government short shrift."[45] As he argued in the 1963 essay "The Prospects for Territorial Democracy in America," even for the new western states, whose boundaries were set by fiat rather than by culture or history, territorial democracy can give "Montana and Arizona and Kansas, say, some distinct and peculiar character as political territories, by fixing loyalties and forming an enduring structure of political administration."[46] But *territorial democracy*, as Kirk uses the term, presents a more radical interpretation of local rights than their being a simple mechanism for federalist governance. Politically, a strong notion of place assists in reducing the power of a centralized government. At bottom, love of country—the large nation—is dependent on a love for one's own place and community. Quoting Randolph, Kirk writes that "in clinging to [the states] . . . I cling to my country; because I love my country as I do my immediate connexions; for the love of country is nothing more than the love of every man for his wife, child, or friend."[47]

Because Kirk so carefully tied the American political order to the traditions of territorial democracy and federalism, his understanding of federalism impacted his understanding of rights. Kirk's view of rights was almost diametrically opposite that of the current elite. Kirk did not readily separate individual rights from community norms and considered rights to have opposing duties. He adopted from Brownson a conviction that rights are tied to a geographic territory. Although there may be universal human rights, these cannot substitute for the actual political rights of a particular community. Drawing from George Mason—perhaps the founder he most respected—Kirk wrote that "individuals' liberties can exist only within a civil social order—that is, in community."[48] Thus, the rights of individuals can be understood and maintained only in community, particularly a community whose members share similar beliefs as to what constitutes a right. Indeed, Kirk essentially rejected the idea of "human rights" as improperly descended from the dangerous abstractions of the French Revolution. True rights grow from "old custom, usage, and political tradition, and from judges' common-law decisions."[49] Kirk distinguished "human rights" from both natural law and "civil rights," those practical immunities and privileges developed in every concrete legal system.[50] Natural law, Kirk argued, was meant primarily as a guide for individual action and should rarely enter into political or legal issues. He considered "human rights" only an ideological cover for the lust for power that characterized the Jacobins and their heirs.[51]

It is not easy to translate Kirk's prescriptions for territorial democracy directly into policy, but several principles clearly stand out. His conservative federalism rejects the "rights" revolution at the Supreme Court during the last four decades as detaching real rights from local political traditions and therefore creating an inevitable conflict between citizens and the communities they live in. Echoing conservative arguments made most strongly in the 1970s and early 1980s, Kirk also heatedly rejects the assumption of duties such as education by the national government. As much as possible, therefore, Kirk would dismantle the structures of centralization and return these functions to their localities. He was not, it should be stressed, against government as such, but he believed that its distance from the people governed and its vulnerability to special interests make the national state an unsteady protector of liberty or tradition.

Kirk's advocacy for territorial democracy also has implications for foreign policy, which is a subject Kirk addressed in the 1990s. If the focus of government is on local communities, and if a federal principle rejects centralization, the risks of foreign entanglements will not be as great. Kirk opposed the first Gulf War and strongly advocated a reduced international profile for America abroad. Kirk strongly condemned the equation of "democratic capitalism" with American culture and could, in that sense, be seen as a forerunner to the strong noninterventionist sentiment among conservatives, both before and after September 11, 2001.

Kirk's Contribution to American Conservative Thought

The foregoing discussion is meant to illuminate the major strands of Kirk's thought and explain how they might apply to conservatism in a post-9/11 world. The debate over the dissolution and possible futures of the Right only intensified during George W. Bush's two terms as president and after the election of Barack Obama. Even before 9/11, the Bush administration drew criticism from other conservatives on its immigration policy and its advocacy of "compassionate conservatism." After the invasion of Iraq, opposition exploded from conservatives who invoked a tradition of American nonintervention and rejected the "national greatness conservatism" and "unitary executive" theories promoted by Republican Party operatives. Loosely clustered around a set of magazines and Web sites, these conservatives organized a revolt against mainstream conservatism. This dissatisfaction was expressed politically in the short-lived presidential campaign of Texas congressman Ron Paul, but their best-known standard-bearer is perhaps former Richard Nixon aide Patrick J. Buchanan, whose recent books have advocated extreme nonintervention in foreign policy, a position that resonates with this new conservative mood. The election of Barack Obama caused a new round of self-critique among conservatives that will continue to explore fissures among various conservative factions on issues such as foreign policy, culture, and the role of the state.

Kirk's contribution to conservative thought has been primarily two-fold. First, he not only "record[ed] the past" for conservatives; in the words of David Frum, "he created it."[52] In a very real sense, conservatives know what conservatism is because Kirk excavated this partially hidden, partially created series of positions and attitudes. He brought to light a number of writers, statesmen, and thinkers who articulated an ongoing critique of and conversation with the modern age. For that reason alone, Kirk deserves a prime place in conservative genealogy.

Second, Kirk provides another source for conservative reflection because he supplies a framework for thinking about tradition, continuity, and culture as the age of liberal modernity fades away. Although the meaning of *postmodern* remains contentious, it can be defined for our purposes as an age that is less reliant on Enlightenment reason, one in which prerational commitments, such as tradition or religious belief, come once more to the forefront. Kirk clearly would have rejected the conclusion of most postmodern thinkers that the end of Enlightenment signaled the need for "radical" political commitments. However, that obvious difference does not by itself mean that conservatism and postmodernism, a priori, are incompatible. As early as 1982, in an essay he wrote for *National Review*, Kirk suggested that "the Post-Modern imagination stands ready to be captured. And the seemingly novel ideas and sentiments and modes may turn out, after all, to be received truths and institutions, well known to surviving conservatives." With liberalism moribund, it "may be the conservative imagination which is to guide the Post-Modern Age." In the caricatured placidity of the 1950s, Kirk saw disruptions: "We live, then, in an insecure society, doubtful of its future, an island of comparative but perilous sanctuary in a sea of revolution; and neither the old isolation nor the old received opinions of the mass of men seem likely to hold against the physical force of revolutionary powers and the moral innovations of moral ideologies. This is just such a time as commonly has required and produced, in the course of history, a re-examination of first principles and a considered political philosophy."[53]

Kirk concluded that modern thought was unable to address humanity's deepest longings and could not present those longings in a way that was palatable or even comprehensible to most people. Liberalism, as a political or social system, failed because it could not sustain the affections, and it could not sustain the affections because it lacked the capacity to connect individuals to the permanent things. For Kirk, the imagination in its various forms remedied this lack of appeal to the sentiments. Even politics, though at a greater remove, has the task of retaining a view of the "eternal contract" of society through daily compromises and electioneering. Indeed, all the ways in which the moral imagination can be employed serve to represent the truth to a bent world.

For example, Kirk's championing of Burke's "little platoons," wherever they are found, serves as a warning to both liberal and conservative proponents of government moralizing. His admiring essay on Donald Davidson's work on "regionalism" supports localism against both big-business capitalism and a liberal leviathan. Kauffman, in his book-length polemic *Look Homeward America*, identifies a "reactionary radical" tradition encompassing Dorothy Day, William Jennings Bryan, Millard Fillmore, and 1960s radical Paul Goodman that rejects both liberal social planning and conservative moralism, both big business and big government.[54] This rejection of the universal and favoring of the personal and particular, as we have seen, also fits well with the postmodern critique. The rise of postmodernism has supplied the possibility of returning conservatism to its more natural mode of discourse. Dialectic—the logical analysis of the human condition according to abstract notions of the individual or society that is characteristic of most forms of liberal modernism—presents, according to its critics, only a "thin" theory of life. In contrast, Kirk's writing is almost defiantly imaginative, frustrating even his admirers for not being sufficiently "analytic." He concentrated on the formation of images and the cultivation of imagination, for "whether to throw away yesterday's nonsense to embrace tomorrow's nonsense, or whether we find our way out of superficiality into real meaning, must depend in part upon the images which we discover or shape."[55] This problem is peculiarly appropriate to the postmodern age, where excessive self-awareness is reflected in everything from TV commercials to art exhibits.

Kirk mistrusted overarching narratives of any form: Rousseauian general will, Hobbesian or Lockean states of nature, Benthamite calculus, Marxist class struggle, or the global marketplace. These representatives of the modern age each thought that the core of modernity lay in rejection: of sin, of history, or of the limits of human progress. As a Christian, Kirk believed in sin; even before his conversion, the reality of evil was clear enough to him. Kirk advocated a reminder of limits and called for a reinvigoration of "the energy and talents of individuals" and a recognition of the "always inscrutable" work of Providence. Kirk placed the individual, and the physical and psychological limits of life, against the idealistic dreams of radicals of every stripe—even conservative ones. The statesman, the imaginative entrepreneur, the person at the cross-roads of a historical moment: this is where the truisms of modernity fail to capture the interstices of life that Kirk relished. In crafting this conservative counternarrative, Kirk created "spaces of resistance" against liberalism, pockets of nonmodernity out of which he hoped the imagination could create an alternative future.

Kirk often quoted a phrase adapted from *Hamlet*: "Nothing is but thinking makes it so." This can serve as a coda to Kirk's own imaginative restructuring of modernity. Ideas, words, and imagination have consequences; they can change the way individuals and cultures experience reality. Kirk tried to construct one such reality from the disintegrating fragments of what he conceived of as a coherent tradition. Against "liquid modernity," in Zygmunt Bauman's striking term, Kirk thought order could still be created and preserved. Kirk's religious views on sin and redemption and the existence of evil compelled him to consider a more layered view of issues such as progress or the emergence of truth. "Human thought and human actions, unpredictable ordinarily, determine the course of civilizations. Decadence is no more inevitable then progress. Great civilizations commonly experience periods of decay, alternating with periods of renewal."[56] This cautiously optimistic view avoids the disappointment of liberalism when its proposals meet with what Kirk would see as their natural and expected limitations. It also avoids the postmodern despair of meaning, which cannot distinguish between decadence and progress and which hesitates to make judgments of any kind. Whether the narrow path Kirk navigates can be resonant in a world that has, in many respects, chosen a direction different from that which he advocates remains to be seen.

Notes

Parts of this chapter appeared in slightly different form in the following publications: Gerald J. Russello, "Russell Kirk and Territorial Democracy," *Publius: The Journal of Federalism* 34, no. 4 (fall 2004):109–24; and in Gerald J. Russello, *The Postmodern Imagination of Russell Kirk* (Columbia: University of Missouri Press, 2007).

1. Russell Kirk, *Confessions of a Bohemian Tory* (New York: Fleet, 1963), 3–4.

2. Russell Kirk, *The Sword of Imagination: Memoirs of a Half-Century of Literary Conflict* (Grand Rapids, Mich.: Eerdman's, 1995), 251.

3. Michael P. Federici, "Russell Kirk Redivivus," *Modern Age* 49, no. 3 (summer 2008): 251–57.

4. Russell Kirk, *The Conservative Mind: From Burke to Eliot*, 7th rev. ed. (Washington, D.C.: Regnery Gateway, 1986), 8–9.

5. Gordon K. Lewis, "The Metaphysics of Conservatism," *Western Political Quarterly* (1953): 728, 729.

6. Russell Kirk, *The Politics of Prudence* (Wilmington, Del.: ISI Books, 1994), 17–24.

7. Kirk, *Conservative Mind*, 10; Kirk, *Politics of Prudence*, 17.

8. Edmund Burke, *Reflections on the Revolution in France*, vol. 2 of *Select Works of Edmund Burke*, comp. Francis Canavan, S.J. (Indianapolis: Liberty Fund, 1999), 171.

9. Russell Kirk, "The Moral Imagination," *Literature and Belief* 1 (1981): 37, 38.

10. Russell Kirk, *Redeeming the Time* (Wilmington, Del.: ISI Books, 1996), 71.

11. Claes Ryn, *Will, Imagination and Reason: Babbitt and Croce and the Problem of Reality* (Washington, D.C.: Catholic University of America Press, 1986), 147; W. Wesley McDonald, *Russell Kirk and the Age of Ideology* (Columbia: University of Missouri Press, 2004), 65.

12. Ryn, *Will*, 128.

13. Kirk, "The Moral Imagination," 38.

14. Kirk, *Conservative Mind*, 422, 424–25.

15. Kirk, *Redeeming the Time*, 71–73.

16. Russell Kirk, "Flannery O'Connor and the Grotesque Face of God," *The World & I* (January 1987): 429–33.

17. Ihab Hassan, *The Dismemberment of Orpheus: Toward a Postmodern Literature* (Oxford: Oxford University Press, 1971), 257–58 (emphasis added).

18. Russell Kirk, "Eliot and a Christian Culture," *This World* (winter 1989): 5, 10, 15.

19. Russell Kirk, "Civilization without Religion?" (lecture, Heritage Foundation, Washington, D.C., July 24, 1992), 4.

20. Russell Kirk, "Religion in the Civil Social Order," *Modern Age* 27, no. 4 (fall 1984): 306.

21. Kirk, "Civilization without Religion?" 5.

22. Kirk, *Sword of Imagination*, 13–14.

23. Uday Singh Mehta, *Liberalism and Empire: A Study in Nineteenth-Century British Liberal Thought* (Chicago: University of Chicago Press, 1999), 116, 127, 133.

24. Kirk, *Redeeming the Time*, 88–90.

25. Ibid., 131.

26. Russell Kirk, "Reinvigorating Culture," *Humanitas* 7, no. 1 (winter 1994): 27.

27. Russell Kirk, *Enemies of the Permanent Things* (Peru, Ill.: Sherwood Sugden, 1988), 33, 40.

28. Russell Kirk, *Beyond the Dreams of Avarice: Essays of a Social Critic* (Peru, Ill.: Sherwood Sugden, 1991), 43.

29. Kirk, *Redeeming the Time*, 128–29, 134, 136.

30. Daniel Boorstin, *The Image: A Guide to Pseudo-Events in America* (New York: Atheneum, 1962), 188.

31. Ibid., 183; Russell Kirk, "The Rediscovery of Mystery," *Imprimis* 6, no. 1 (January 1977): 2.

32. Kirk, *Redeeming the Time*, 137, 140.

33. Kirk, *Sword of Imagination*, 192.

34. Kirk, *Beyond the Dreams of Avarice*, 185.

35. Russell Kirk, "Is Washington Too Powerful?" *New York Times Magazine* (March 1, 1964), 22.

36. Russell Kirk, "The Prospects for Territorial Democracy in America," in *A Nation of States: Essays on the American Federal System*, ed. Robert A. Goldwin (Chicago: Rand McNally, 1963), 49.

37. Ibid., 49–50.

38. Russell Kirk, *Edmund Burke: A Genius Reconsidered*, rev. ed. (Wilmington, Del.: ISI Books, 1997), 173–75.

39. Russell Kirk, "A Conservative Program for a Kinder, Gentler America" (lecture, Heritage Foundation, Washington, D.C., April 27, 1989), 4.

40. Kirk, *Enemies of the Permanent Things*, 238.

41. Ibid., 239–40.

42. Russell Kirk, ed., *Orestes Brownson: Selected Political Writings* (New Brunswick, N.J.: Transaction Publishers, 1990), 8.

43. Kirk, *Politics of Prudence*, 23.

44. See Filippo Sabetti, "Local Roots of Constitutionalism," *Perspectives on Political Science* 33, no. 2 (spring 2004): 70–78.

45. Kirk, *Enemies of the Permanent Things*, 239–40.

46. Kirk, "Prospects for Territorial Democracy," 43.

47. Kirk, *Conservative Mind*, 164.

48. Russell Kirk, *Rights and Duties* (Dallas: Spence Publishing, 1997), 73.

49. Russell Kirk, *America's British Culture* (New Brunswick, N.J.: Transaction Publishers, 1994), 44.

50. Kirk, *Rights and Duties*, 231–32.

51. Gerald J. Russello, "The Jurisprudence of Russell Kirk," *Modern Age* 38, no. 4 (fall 1996): 354–63.

52. David Frum, "The Legacy of Russell Kirk," *New Criterion* 13, no. 10 (December 1994): 15.

53. Russell Kirk, "Conservatism: A Succinct Description," *National Review*, September 3, 1982, 1080–84, 1163–64.

54. Bill Kauffman, *Look Homeward America: In Search of Reactionary Radicals and Front-Porch Anarchists* (Wilmington, Del.: ISI Books, 2006).

55. Kirk, "The Rediscovery of Mystery," 1, 3.

56. Kirk, *Redeeming the Time*, 305.

Bibliography

Boorstin, Daniel. 1962. *The Image: A Guide to Pseudo-Events in America*. New York: Atheneum.

Burke, Edmund. 1999. *Reflections on the Revolution in France*. Vol. 2 of *Select Works of Edmund Burke*, compiled by Francis Canavan, S.J. Indianapolis: Liberty Fund.

Federici, Michael P. 2008. "Russell Kirk Redivivus." *Modern Age* 49, no. 3 (summer): 251–57.

Frum, David. 1994. "The Legacy of Russell Kirk." *New Criterion* 13, no. 10 (December): 10–16.

Hassan, Ihab. 1971. *The Dismemberment of Orpheus: Toward a Postmodern Literature*. Oxford: Oxford University Press.

Kauffman, Bill. 2006. *Look Homeward America: In Search of Reactionary Radicals and Front-Porch Anarchists*. Wilmington, Del.: ISI Books.

Kirk, Russell. 1963. *Confessions of a Bohemian Tory*. New York: Fleet.

———. 1963. "The Prospects for Territorial Democracy in America." In *A Nation of States: Essays on the American Federal System*, edited by Robert A. Goldwin. Chicago: Rand McNally.

———. 1964. "Is Washington Too Powerful?" *New York Times Magazine* (March 1), 22, 82.

———. 1977. "The Rediscovery of Mystery." *Imprimis* 6, no. 1 (January): 1–6.

———. 1981. "The Moral Imagination." *Literature and Belief* 1: 37–49.

———. 1982. "Conservatism: A Succinct Description." *National Review*, September 3.

———. 1984. "Religion in the Civil Social Order." *Modern Age* 27, no. 4 (fall): 306–9.

———. 1986. *The Conservative Mind: From Burke to Eliot*. 7th rev. ed. Washington, D.C.: Regnery Gateway.

———. 1987. "Flannery O'Connor and the Grotesque Face of God." *The World & I* (January): 429–33.

———. 1988. *Enemies of the Permanent Things*. Peru, Ill.: Sherwood Sugden.

———. 1989. "A Conservative Program for a Kinder, Gentler America." Lecture, Heritage Foundation, Washington, D.C., April 27.

———. 1989. "Eliot and a Christian Culture." *This World* (winter): 5–19.

———. 1991. *Beyond the Dreams of Avarice: Essays of a Social Critic*. Peru, Ill.: Sherwood Sugden.

———. 1992. "Civilization without Religion?" Lecture, Heritage Foundation, Washington, D.C., July 24.

———. 1994. *America's British Culture*. New Brunswick, N.J.: Transaction Publishers.

———. 1994. *The Politics of Prudence*. Wilmington, Del.: ISI Books.

———. 1994. "Reinvigorating Culture." *Humanitas* 7, no. 1 (winter): 27–42.

———. 1995. *The Sword of Imagination: Memoirs of a Half-Century of Literary Conflict*. Grand Rapids, Mich.: Eerdman's.

———. 1996. *Redeeming the Time*. Wilmington, Del.: ISI Books.

———. 1997. *Edmund Burke: A Genius Reconsidered*. Rev. ed. Wilmington, Del.: ISI Books.

———. 1997. *Rights and Duties*. Dallas: Spence Publishing.

———, ed. 1990. *Orestes Brownson: Selected Political Writings*. New Brunswick, N.J.: Transaction Publishers.

Lewis, Gordon K. 1953. "The Metaphysics of Conservatism." *Western Political Quarterly*, 728–41.

McDonald, W. Wesley. 2004. *Russell Kirk and the Age of Ideology*. Columbia: University of Missouri Press.

Mehta, Uday Singh. 1999. *Liberalism and Empire: A Study in Nineteenth-Century British Liberal Thought*. Chicago: University of Chicago Press.

Morley, Felix. 1959. *Freedom and Federalism*. Chicago: Henry Regnery.

Russello, Gerald J. 1996. "The Jurisprudence of Russell Kirk." *Modern Age* 38, no. 4 (fall): 354–63.

Ryn, Claes. 1986. *Will, Imagination and Reason: Babbitt and Croce and the Problem of Reality*. Washington, D.C.: Catholic University of America Press.

Sabetti, Filippo. 2004. "Local Roots of Constitutionalism." *Perspectives on Political Science* 33, no. 2 (spring): 70–78.

Wolfe, Alan. 2007. "Contempt." *New Republic*, July 7.

F. A. Hayek

A Man of Measure

Linda C. Raeder

The Austrian-born Nobel Laureate, economist, and social theorist F. A. Hayek (1899–1992) was neither an American nor a self-avowed conservative, yet any exploration of American conservative philosophy must place Hayek front and center. He is widely regarded as one of the fathers of the postwar conservative revival in the United States and, despite his objections, is conventionally, and with some justification, aligned with American conservative thought.[1] Hayek's ambition, he said, was to "restate" the traditional philosophy of individual liberty under law for a contemporary audience increasingly unfamiliar with its ideals and institutions, which he believed were powerfully instantiated in the U.S. Constitution as originally framed. Thus, in the American context, Hayek, a self-styled Old Whig or classical liberal, appears profoundly conservative. Within that context, his aim—the preservation of the free society as historically achieved in the West—is an essentially conservative endeavor, involving the attempt to preserve the American moral and political heritage of limited government, the rule of law, and free enterprise in the face of numerous modern threats to that vision.

Hayek provided powerful philosophical support for various objectives prominent among modern American conservatives. Hayek, like the conservatives, aimed to resist the growing trend toward collectivism manifest in the West throughout the twentieth century, as well as the concomitant schemes for various forms of social reconstruction. He also provided theoretical support for the conservative respect for the moral and religious traditions of the West. Indeed, one might say that Hayek's significance was to provide historical, philosophical, and even scientific support for a conservative politics to justify reverence toward historically grown cultural traditions; to explain more precisely why and in what sense, as his forebear Edmund Burke put it, "the individual is foolish . . . but the species is wise."[2]

Hayek's more exclusively political philosophy cannot be understood apart from his more comprehensive social theory, which involves what he calls the "twin ideas of evolution and spontaneous order," as well as a critique of the role of reason in human affairs.[3] I begin with a discussion of Hayek's theory of cultural evolution, which yields profoundly conservative implications. For Hayek, liberty under law was a fragile achievement, the hard-won product of history and cultural development. The institutions of freedom emerged from an undesigned and spontaneous evolutionary process dependent on the distilled knowledge embedded within inherited traditions and institutions. He was captivated by the wondrous order within complexity generated by this suprarational social process and wished to defend it against that rationalistic mentality which refuses to comprehend the significance of tradition and custom. For Hayek, in short, freedom and the creative growth it encourages depend on a preservation of our inheritance: "All progress," he counsels, "must be based on tradition."[4] Thus follows Hayek's "conservatism," his profound regard for the intricate evolved pattern that is the institutional structure of the free society. And thus follows the warm embrace extended to the classical liberal Hayek by his conservative American counterparts and fellow travelers.

I also examine Hayek's critique of reason. He attributed the rise of the illiberal and collectivist doctrines of the modern age to an unfounded valorization of the power of human reason, and a study of "the abuse of reason" in modernity would become a central theme of his work.[5] Yet Hayek was no irrationalist, and he always insisted that the conditions of human flourishing must be cultivated through rational insight into the forces that generate and sustain social order. Hayek's political prescriptions are thus inseparable from his general theory of the nature and operation of complex social formations—the theory of spontaneous order—which must be briefly examined. This leads, in turn, to a consideration of the relation of law to social order. I discuss what Hayek describes as "the role of law in an ordering mechanism"—that is, the "market," the means by which human action is coordinated in a complex and free society. For Hayek, the free society is an integral whole that demands coherence among its various institutional supports—political, legal, moral, and economic—and depends crucially on the recognition of various conservative insights and the upholding of various conservative values. Finally, I conclude by considering certain implications of Hayekian theory for policy making, and especially Hayek's conclusions on the nature of the common good in modern liberal society.

Reason and Cultural Evolution

Throughout a lifetime of scholarly investigation, Hayek explored certain epistemological issues that bear on social science methodology in general and economic and political theory in particular. Among the more important of these issues is the extent to which human reason is capable of consciously coordinating the actions of the numerous members of any complex social order and of determining either the rules or values that should govern a society or the ends its members ought to pursue. Such epistemological concerns were central to Hayek's investigations because he believed that the rise of the modern collectivist ideologies he was concerned to refute could be attributed, in large part, to mistaken notions concerning the nature and function of human reason. The Western liberal tradition, Hayek argued, was shaped by two distinct schools of thought—the French rationalist and the British evolutionary traditions—which embrace very different conceptions of liberty, social order, and the role of reason in human affairs. In *The Counter-Revolution of Science* he draws a distinction between the two "kinds of rationalism" that he believes are related to the two schools.[6] Adherents to the French tradition, he claims, typically exhibit a profound (if mistaken) regard for the constructive powers of reason and tend, moreover, to attribute social order to rational design and conscious intention (views that Hayek associates with "constructivist or naive rationalism").[7] The evolutionary school, which Hayek represents, is characterized, on the contrary, by an acute awareness of the limits of the constructive powers of human reason and an understanding of social order as the unintended outcome of rule-governed human behavior (views Hayek associates with an "evolutionary or critical rationalism").[8]

The liberal tradition that Hayek contrasts with the constructivist tradition is rooted in the Scottish Enlightenment. This liberalism, he says, derives from the discovery of a "self-generating" or spontaneous order in social affairs, first elaborated by thinkers such as David Hume, Adam Ferguson, and Adam Smith and significantly developed by Carl

Menger and his followers in the Austrian School.[9] Such theory endeavors to explain how social order emerges, in Ferguson's famous phrase, as "a result of human action, but not . . . of . . . human design"—how a stable abstract pattern of social relations may emerge as the unintended by-product of human interaction.[10] In so doing, it explores the significance of the fact that human beings are as much rule-governed as purposive agents and that systematized, explicit, articulated knowledge is but the "crowning part" of the body of human knowledge.[11]

This tradition is characterized, moreover, by an evolutionary perspective that conceives social institutions and practices—law, morals, money, the market mechanism, habits, language—not as products of conscious construction or enlightened invention but as products of a suprarational trial-and-error process of cultural evolution. From such a perspective, traditions, customs, and the entire panoply of human convention do not appear as mere arbitrary and irrational prejudices to be cavalierly abandoned in the quest for rational control over social forces. Inherited practices embody a "superindividual wisdom" acquired through the practical experience of former generations, and equally important, the observance of many of these nonrational conventions is indispensable to the formation and maintenance of the social order.[12] Hayek argues, in *The Constitution of Liberty* and elsewhere, that traditional liberal rules and institutions, as well as reason, abstract thought, and the structure of the mind itself, should be understood as evolutionary adaptations to certain irremediable circumstances of human existence (dispersed knowledge, limited foresight, scarcity, and the infinite complexity of social and physical reality), selected, at bottom and over the long run, in accordance with their human survival value. However difficult to discern, those traditional values and rules whose observance generated modern liberal society serve a function in regard to the maintenance of that kind of order, and, Hayek contends, we abandon them at the price of civilized order and perhaps survival itself.

The conception of reason that Hayek repudiates is that which conceives reason as an autonomous faculty standing outside the cosmos of nature and capable of judging society and human action in general from a superior perspective. Such a conception leads not only to the "synoptic delusion"—"the fiction that all relevant facts can be known to one mind and that it is possible to construct from this knowledge of the particulars a desirable social order"—but also to certain beliefs regarding the appropriateness of action, beliefs that boil down to the idea that "action, if it is to be rational, must be deliberate and foresighted."[13] The constructivist, in other words, is convinced that it is unreasonable to take any action unless one "knows what one is doing"—unless one can consciously identify the purpose of an action and both foresee and desire the consequences that will ensue. For Hayek and his intellectual forebears, on the contrary, man is more "lazy, . . . improvident, . . . and short-sighted" than he is rational, deliberative, and foresighted.[14] In their view, man has been successful not because he is rational but because he is guided in his actions by evolved rules and practices that compensate for the lack of extensive individual rationality and foresight. Evolutionary theorists, as noted, conceive inherited rules and social institutions as bearers of tacit knowledge that transcends the knowledge available to the conscious reasoning mind (because the knowledge embedded in such social phenomena has been gained by many more trials and errors than any individual could gain), not as instruments that persons deliberately employ to achieve certain desired goals. In Hayek's view, man does not possess the distance from rules implied by such an instrumental conception, for, as he explains in *The Sensory Order*, the human mind is itself *constituted* by systems of rules, only some of which enter into explicit reasoning processes.[15]

Hayek's conservatism is further exemplified by his view of human nature, that is, his attempt to conserve the traditional view of man as a being irremediably ignorant and imperfect, constitutionally limited in knowledge, power, and foresight. Hayek was a moral realist who rejected any notion of human perfectibility or other forms of utopianism. Hayek and other conservatives, then, shared a common enemy—Enlightenment rationalism—as well as a common understanding. For Hayek, again, Enlightenment thought is characterized by its valorization of the constructive power of human reason and its dismissal of tradition as mere superstition and prejudice. Through Enlightened eyes, inherited values, institutions, and customs appear as the very embodiment of ignorance, "reason" as the tool that can liberate man from the ancient fetters of oppression. From an erroneous view of the power of human reason, Hayek concludes, it is but a short step to the equally erroneous belief that human society can be rationally designed or constructed in a way superior to the kind of society grown by gradual cultural evolution and ordered by rules and institutions that are the outcome of a suprapersonal process of trial and error.

It is fair to say that Hayek, like many of his conservative predecessors, regarded the French Enlightenment and especially the "constructivist" mentality associated with that movement—one that recognizes no limits to the authority or competence of human reason and believes reason to be a viable tool for designing a social order—as a grave threat to liberty and the preservation of civilized order. The preservation of free government and civilized society, he contends, depends on man's willingness to be governed by certain inherited rules of individual and collective conduct whose origin, function, and rationale he may not fully comprehend. The rationalist contempt for tradition, by contrast, is typically accompanied by the demand for the radical reconstruction of traditional moral and legal rules, a major preoccupation of modern social theorists from Rousseau through Rawls. Perhaps no other thought is as uncongenial to the modern rationalist temper as the idea that man is not free to rationally determine or choose his ethical or legal framework. Modern thought bears little trace of that "strong impression of the ignorance and fallibility of mankind" that long served to suppress rationalistic hubris.[16] Hayek warned, however, that the endeavor to destroy inherited customs, morals, and prejudices in the name of reason or on any other grounds must also destroy the humanistic liberal society engendered and sustained by such phenomena, however little we can rationally comprehend their significance. Reason, Hayek warned in *The Constitution of Liberty*, "is like a dangerous explosive which, handled cautiously, may be most beneficial, but if handled incautiously may blow up a civilization."[17] The most important task of reason, he urged, is to recognize the limits of its own reach.

Liberal Society as a Spontaneous Order

Hayek was no mere critic of modern developments. He also offered a positive social theory that aims to clarify the nature and structure of the free society and to elucidate the conditions of its maintenance and flourishing, one that, like his theory of cultural evolution, yields various conservative implications. Among his many contributions to the preservation of the Western heritage of liberty under law, his theory of spontaneous order is perhaps the most original and profound.

A spontaneous order is a kind of order that is produced without conscious human intention or design. It is a self-generating and self-maintaining order, an abstract, purpose-independent pattern (system, structure) of stable and predictable relations that emerges as an unintended consequence of the regular or rule-governed behavior of the individual elements forming it. An example of a spontaneous ordering process in the physical realm may assist in understanding how such forces function in the social realm: To induce the formation of a crystal, one must create the conditions under which the individual elements will arrange themselves so that the overall structure of a crystal will emerge or grow. One cannot deliberately arrange the several elements to produce the desired formation. In the appropriate conditions, however, each rule-governed element, adapting itself to its initial position and particular circumstances, will arrange itself in a way consistent with the formation of the relatively more complex structure of a crystal. Hayek views liberal society as such a spontaneous order. It, like a crystal, *grows* under the right conditions, as individuals adapt themselves to the circumstances they encounter, guided in their activity by certain inherited rules of conduct. It is not constructed or made in accordance with deliberate human design.

The character of the spontaneous order of liberal society may be seen more clearly in contrast with a second type of social order found in modern society—organization, or "made order." An organization is an end-dependent order created by the deliberate arrangement of its several elements according to the conscious intention of a designing mind. An example from the physical world is a watch or a computer microchip, in which each component is deliberately positioned in accordance with the maker's knowledge and purpose. Because someone constructs an organization by putting its elements in a specific place or directing their movements to fulfill a particular purpose, organization is an ordering technique indispensable for achieving known aims. Thus the purpose-independent spontaneous order of liberal society consists of both individuals and organizations—business corporations, governmental institutions, and voluntary associations of all kinds—deliberately created to pursue particular ends. The coordination of the activities of the individuals and organizations within society, however, comes about through the spontaneous ordering processes generated and governed by the observance of certain types of abstract rules, similar to the formation of a crystal. All we can achieve in the social realm is to cultivate the conditions that permit the complex formation of society to emerge or grow. This entails securing a framework of appropriate rules, whose attributes are discussed later, because not all rule-following behavior will result in the formation and maintenance of a complex spontaneous order.[18]

As mentioned, Hayek emphasized the necessary coherence of the various social and political institutions of a flourishing liberal society, a coherence obtained by the consistent application of uniform principle. This is a profoundly conservative position that imposes constraints on those who would preserve the free society: they are not free to design a social order by combining at will various forms of political, legal, economic, and moral political institutions. In particular, Hayek is concerned to show that modern liberal society depends on particular *kinds* of legal and economic frameworks, for only certain kinds of legal rules will sustain the spontaneous ordering processes (the "market") that serve to coordinate human activity in the modern "extended order of cooperation." It is also dependent on the observance of particular *kinds* of moral rules and a particular *kind* of government, limited government that enforces and is itself constrained by the rule of law.

The Role of Law in an Ordering Mechanism

The device developed to protect individual freedom throughout the evolution of liberal society, Hayek explains, is the rule of law, and the preservation of liberty depends on its continued vitality. Hayek links the modern understanding of the rule of law to the Old Whigs, who were united by a passionate hostility to arbitrary power. The prevention of arbitrary action by government remained the guiding aim of their political thought and practice. The basic issue around which Whig opinion formed had been identified as early as 1610: "There is no[thing] which [we] account . . . more dear and precious than this, to be guided and governed by the certain rule of law, . . . and not by any uncertain and arbitrary form of government" — that is, government "not in accordance with received general laws."[19] Liberty, to the Whig mind, had a definite meaning: freedom from arbitrary (that is, "ruleless") coercion, whether emanating from the crown, the parliament, or the people. Such freedom was gained by strict adherence to the rule of law, that is, to "something permanent, uniform, and universal [and] . . . not a transient sudden order from a superior or concerning a particular person."[20] Note that the conception of liberty under law to which Hayek subscribed has nothing to do with what he regarded as the "French" conception of liberty — "political freedom" in the sense of participation in the determination of law or policy.[21] For Old Whigs such as Hayek, the only kind of freedom that can be secured by a political order is freedom under law in the sense of freedom from arbitrary coercion, and the chief means to secure this end is the rule of law. The rule of law, Hayek further explains, should be understood as a "meta-legal" doctrine or ideal regarding *what the law ought to be*. When our predecessors spoke of establishing "a government of laws, not of men," they understood law, implicitly or explicitly, in a definitive sense, that is, as a kind of rule with specific attributes, not mere legislation. Law and legislation are distinct entities that must be clearly differentiated if the rule of law is to serve its function of securing the framework of the free society. Hayek identifies two conceptually and functionally distinct types of legal rules that prevail in liberal society: the *nomos* (private law) and the *thesis* (public law). He regards only the former as true *law*—the evolved rules of conduct that define justice and secure spontaneous order. The latter consists of the rules that structure and are employed by organizations (including the organization of government)—directives and commands designed to realize particular concrete purposes determined by the directors of organizations, including legislation enacted to achieve various policy objectives of the government. The distinction between private and public law is one between standing general rules that all must obey and specific orders or policy measures to be executed by government officials. One cannot, of course, execute or carry out a rule of conduct.[22] There is, in short, a clear distinction between law and legislation, and as Hayek argues, the latter will serve to sustain the liberal order only if it is consciously modeled on the law, that is, crafted as a general standing rule and not as a specific directive or command.

The law, or *nomos*—the historically evolved rules of just conduct whose observance formed and maintains the liberal spontaneous order—generally takes the form of universally applicable negative prohibitions that delimit a private sphere within which individuals are guaranteed a free range of action protected from the arbitrary interference of others.[23] Hayek sometimes associates such "repressive or inhibitory" rules of conduct with the "thou shalt nots" of the Judeo-Christian tradition.[24] In *The Fatal Conceit* he accounts for the negativity of liberal rules by linking them to the progressive universalization of liberal morality: the gradual extension of a uniform legal code over an extended spatial area necessitated the gradual attenuation of specific positive obligations to others. It is impossible to fulfill a positive moral duty to assist someone (as is generally the rule in small, face-to-face communities) if one has no personal knowledge of the other's concrete needs or even of his existence. In any event, the function of the *law* is to create a secure and stable framework of expectations so that persons know which features of their environment they can count on when making their plans. It tends to reduce conflict, establish certainty, and allow the smoothest possible mutual coordination of activities. Significantly, it also allows the maximum utilization of knowledge in a society, and it is this, Hayek contends, that accounts for the tremendous success of the liberal order.

The Ordering Principle of the Market

For Hayek, the cultural achievements of Western civilization reflect not superior knowledge per se but the evolution of a method of coordinating human activity that encourages the generation and utilization of more knowledge than any other method yet discovered. No mind or group of minds could consciously assimilate or coordinate the vast knowledge and information that enters the social process on a daily basis via the market mechanism. Indeed, much of that knowledge *cannot* be consciously communicated or articulated. Knowledge, Hayek emphasizes, consists not merely of explicit, systematized theories and data. It also includes the inarticulate "know-how" embodied in habits, dispositions, mental techniques, and customs, as well as the fleeting local knowledge of specific time and place that is so essential to the functioning of a complex social order.

Every society exhibits an orderly pattern of activities; otherwise, no one would be able to engage in even the most ordinary daily pursuits. Hayek emphasizes that we pursue our aims within a comprehensive order of abstract social relations that most of us take more or less for granted (buyer and seller, lender and borrower, lessor and lessee, and so forth). Although we may not be consciously aware of the existence of this "background order," the realization of most of our plans depends on its smooth functioning. The order to which Hayekian theory refers manifests itself as the matching or coincidence of plans and expectations across individuals who are necessarily ignorant of most of the concrete circumstances prevailing throughout society and the concrete aims pursued by their (mostly unknown) fellows.[25] Why do strangers who have no explicit knowledge of our concrete needs and wants provide the means we require to realize both our transitory ends and our enduring values? How is the evident order we experience in our daily affairs generated and maintained even though most of us are only tacitly aware of its existence and do not deliberately aim to produce it? The answer lies in the existence of a framework of rules that secures general abstract conditions that allow the activities of millions of persons who do not and cannot know one another's concrete circumstances and intentions to fit together rather than come into conflict. In other words, such a condition arises from the observance of certain abstract inherited rules—perceptual, behavioral, moral, and legal—that structure the operation of the ordering mechanism we call the "market."

The market, of course, comprises a complex of social relations, institutions, and practices. According to Hayek, the market represents a historically evolved solution to the "central problem" all advanced societies must solve: how to generate, utilize, and coordinate knowledge that *only* and *always* exists fragmented and dispersed among the numerous members of a complex society. As he explains in *The Mirage of Social Justice* and elsewhere, the "price system" should be conceived as an evolved "medium of communication," a kind of language that allows people to bypass their constitutional ignorance of most of the facts that determine the success of their actions (the concrete circumstances prevailing throughout society) and integrate the actions of individuals and groups into a coherent overall order.[26] The ability to employ abstract thought and symbols such as prices, Hayek explains, enables humans to overcome their inability to master the infinite complexity of the environment. Prices serve as an indispensable guide to action. Without this guidance, individuals could not know how to employ their efforts in a manner compatible with the plans and actions of their fellows. Without the guidance of prices, human activity would have to be directed by command. This means, of course, that the only economic system compatible with human freedom is one structured by the price or market system grounded in the institution of private property. Moreover, in the absence of undistorted prices that reflect the reality of current circumstances ("demand" and "supply"), no one can know how resources "should" be employed. The economic irrationality and blatant failure of the various experiments in centrally planned economies of the twentieth century were the inevitable result of the elimination of a market-based pricing mechanism and the private property on which it depends.

In short, Hayek contends that certain epistemological facts render the "automatic" and impersonal coordination achieved via the market process far superior to any method of coordination based on conscious human direction. Nonmarket ordering devices, such as governmental planning or majoritarian decision making, must necessarily restrict the knowledge employed to that possessed by a relatively few limited minds, thereby preventing that flexible adaptation to ever-changing concrete circumstances by which the social order as a whole maintains itself. The market so conceived is dependent on the rule of law, the enforcement of general rules as previously discussed, for only such general rules permit the fullest use of essentially dispersed knowledge. Although each person must take the general rules into account in pursuing his own ends, he is free to act on his particular knowledge, bound only by general negative prohibitions that structure the means he may use to pursue his self-directed ends. He is thus free in the Hayekian sense, that is, he can "use his own knowledge for his own purposes." In this way, all the knowledge that exists within a society can enter the social process, and it is this, Hayek contends, that accounts for the complex growth and flourishing of the liberal order.

Law: The Grammar of Practice

Perhaps no aspect of Hayek's thought is as conservative as his insistence that members of liberal society are not free to choose or determine the laws (as distinct from legislative policy) under which they live if they also wish to preserve the freedom central to that kind of society. Hayek contends that members of liberal society are generally constrained to adhere to traditional rules insofar as these are presumed to embody the cumulative knowledge and experience of former generations and to serve the ongoing maintenance of the background order on which all depend for the realization of their purposes. Obviously, however, law is not and cannot be an utterly static institution and must continuously adapt itself to the changing circumstances of society. How does the body of law develop? And what are the implications for lawmakers and policy makers in the free society? I now turn to how, according to Hayek, the rules (or *nomos*) the government should enforce in liberal society are determined.

"The aim of jurisdiction," Hayek tells us, "is the maintenance of an ongoing order of actions."[27] He thus reminds us that all law tacitly presupposes the existence of and refers to an ongoing factual order of activities—the comprehensive background order discussed earlier. As Hayek explains in *Rules and Order*, law in the sense of enforced rules of conduct is coeval with society, for the de facto observance of common rules is what constitutes even the most primitive social group. Prevailing rules are not necessarily recognized or explicitly treated as rules but manifest themselves as habitual perceptions or behaviors, as customs and conventions. Those who practice certain inherited customs may not be aware that in so doing they are contributing to the maintenance of the social order; they may merely "know" that certain actions are taboo or are "just not done." Yet those who attempt to articulate the enforceable rules have a more or less conscious awareness that the rules "refer to certain presuppositions of an ongoing order which no one has made but which nevertheless is seen to exist."[28]

The rules that structure liberal society, then, refer to certain presuppositions about and requirements of that *kind* of social order—presuppositions and inchoate rules that are bound up with the prevailing sense of justice. An analogy drawn from language may clarify this relationship: One's "feeling for language" enables one to recognize the appropriateness or inappropriateness of a spoken or written word without explicit knowledge of the rule applicable to the case at hand. Likewise, one's "sense of justice" enables one to recognize an inappropriate (or unjust) rule or action without necessarily being able to articulate the rule of justice that has been violated. As the task of the grammarian is to articulate the general rule that governs a particular linguistic usage, so the task of the jurist is to "discover" the general rule that (implicitly or explicitly) governs the case at hand. The rules of both law and grammar belong to that abstract structure of rules "found" to be governing the operation of the mind.

The task of the jurist, then, is not to invent good law but to bring to conscious awareness the general principle or rule that, once expressed, will be recognized as just (or at least not unjust)—which means, more or less, a rule that conforms with the implicit rules that have customarily guided spontaneous interaction in a given society. The law that emerges from the law-finding efforts of jurists always emerges, in other words, as a result of "efforts to secure and improve a system of rules which are already observed."[29] The law that structures the spontaneous order of liberal society is, according to Hayek, of this nature. Evolved social phenomena such as law and language exhibit certain similarities. First, law, like grammar, refers to a factual overall order (or abstract pattern) of which actors and speakers are only tacitly aware. Second, the rules of justice are found, not made. The legal rules whose observance generated liberal society were no more the product of rational design or deliberate invention than were the rules of grammar. They emerged through the ongoing efforts of jurists to articulate, develop, and interpret the (implicit and explicit) rules that structured a preexisting order of actions. The development of law, in other words, always proceeds within a *given* framework of values, rules, and practices on which the integrity of the overall order depends.

The task of the jurist cannot be accomplished through engaged participation in public affairs, through more thoroughgoing democratization, or by legislative compromise among contending partisans. In resolving disputes, the judge is, in effect, asked to clarify which of the conflicting expectations will be treated as legitimate, a determination that depends on the requirements of the overall order and not on the judge's or anyone else's preferences. Justice is necessarily an impersonal virtue. For Hayek, the rules that structure liberal society arise not from achieving consensus or explicit agreement among rational men but from the structural requirements of the liberal order—from how society "works," or what earlier jurists referred to as the "nature of things." The lawmaker has a pointed intellectual task: to discover the rules that cohere with the overall body of accepted rules governing a working social order. This task must be undertaken by persons well versed in both jurisprudence and social theory, as well as intimately acquainted with the tacit dimensions of their society. According to Hayek, the correct rules are, in a sense, determined by the rationale and requirements of the existing order, not by a political process.

Hayek's legal philosophy, then, differs from that of both the traditional natural lawyers and the legal positivists. His legal philosophy resembles natural law doctrine to the extent that both share a belief in a source of law that is independent of human will and a belief in the objectivity of law. Nevertheless, the ultimate referent of law, for Hayek, is the existing mundane social order, not a transcendent one. It is obviously incompatible with legal positivism of any stripe.

Policy Implications: The Common Good

For policy makers, what conclusions follow from Hayekian theory? Perhaps the most important involves the nature of the common good, the realization of which has long been regarded as the fundamental task of government in liberal society. For Hayek, the common good in a "great society" such as modern liberal society—one characterized by individual liberty and an extensive division of labor and knowledge and inte-grated by common economic, legal, and moral practices—consists in the fulfillment of the fundamental value implicitly held by all its mem-bers: the preservation of the social order as a whole, the abstract, endur-ing structure within which all individual and organizational activities must occur. Such a good is realized, moreover, by securing the general conditions that ensure the smooth functioning of the automatic coordi-nation mechanism we call the market.

Government has a critical role to play in securing the common good, one that is primarily juridical in nature: to maintain and develop the legal framework indispensable to the operation of the ordering pro-cess itself. It does so by enforcing the rule of law as described, that is, enforcing certain general, universal, historically evolved "rules of just conduct." In this regard, the distinction between law and legislation is critical. In *The Political Order of a Free People*, Hayek emphasizes that contemporary governments are involved with two distinct yet often con-flated activities—lawmaking proper, the aim of which is to secure the rule of law, and "the direction of government" proper, the aim of which is to enact legislation to achieve various politically determined policy measures. His concern is that the conflation of these two activities in the same representative assembly (Congress), as well as the failure to distin-guish between law and legislation, is progressively undermining the rule of law and the limited government it aims to secure.[30] This is because legislative directives typically aim to realize certain concrete purposes, not to establish general and abstract rules of conduct (the law).

Such a process, if unchecked, must lead to the transformation of the spontaneous order of liberal society into a compulsory organization in which all are required to pursue politically determined concrete ends. This, of course, is precisely the character of socialism and other forms of collectivism. The free society, however, is not an organization ordered toward the realization of particular ends but an abstract, purpose-independent order within which individuals and voluntary associations pursue self-chosen objectives. Hayek's main warning to policy makers, then, is that legislation can undermine the free society if it is not distin-guished from, and consciously modeled on, the law—that is, crafted as a general standing rule and not as a specific directive or command. Such a distinction also establishes constraints on the legitimate activities of government.

According to Hayek, the confusion between law and legislation and the conflation of the two distinct activities of lawmaking and policy making in the same governing body prevent government from fulfilling its obligation to secure the common good. Again, the common good in an advanced liberal society is necessarily an *abstract* value—the preservation of a certain abstract pattern of social relations—not the fulfillment of particular concrete ends. Hayek contends that we can establish certain general conditions that "improve as much as possible the chances of any person chosen at random" to fulfill his or her goals and values, but we cannot simultaneously secure those abstract conditions and enact legislation designed to achieve concrete outcomes.[31] One of Hayek's main concerns is to repudiate any conception of the common good that entails the imposition of a preconceived *concrete* pattern of distribution on the social order. Although the intellectual poverty of socialism is now widely recognized, the moral and epistemological views that underlie socialist doctrines still inspire demands for social justice, economic justice, global justice, environmental justice, industrial policy, protectionism, and so on—demands for all sorts of piecemeal interventions in the market process. For Hayek, the fulfillment of such demands can never serve the common interest. If our world is one of scarcity, and if all persons benefit from the efficient use of scarce resources, then any attempt to override the results of spontaneous ordering processes or to impose a preconceived material distribution on the social order must work against the long-term common good. This applies to both "conservative" and "progressive" proposals.

Moreover, all plans to override the results of the spontaneous ordering processes in the name of an alleged common good must require persons to serve concrete ends determined by the government. Consequently, the indispensable incentive to discover and employ one's particular knowledge—for example, the necessity of integrating oneself into the overall order by choosing the direction of one's economic activity in line with price signals—is removed, so potentially valuable knowledge is lost to the social process. For Hayek, the decision to promote the common good by maintaining an abstract legal framework can be a conscious and rational decision—that is, we can understand the rationale and requirements of the liberal order and deliberately shape the legal framework in accordance with them. The common good itself, however, is not a product of intellectual design, reasoned debate, or extensive political participation but is generated, one might say, by the circumstances of human existence, the permanent limits of the human mind, and the nature of the liberal order.

Hayekian theory yields, then, certain strictures on democratic practice insofar as he denies that the liberal legal framework is, properly
speaking, an object of political determination. It is an outcome of a
transpersonal evolutionary process in which rules that secure the overall
order and best contribute to human flourishing are selected and transmitted over time. Members of liberal society must observe certain rules,
he argues, even though those rules have not been deliberately chosen by
engaged participants or anyone else, and even though their significance
may not be fully transparent to the reasoning mind. The realization of
the common good requires not greater participation in politics, as is often
recommended, but the willingness to honor the rule of law and forgo the
gratification of particular desires, including the desire for social justice
or material benefits for oneself or one's group. Government should not
be involved in the compulsory provision of concrete goods and services,
since there is no principle by which to objectively determine the relative
importance of conflicting concrete ends. No amount of deliberation or
discussion can produce agreement on the particular *concrete* manifestation our complex social order should assume if no such agreement exists
at the outset. To compel persons to serve some hierarchical scale of concrete ends (for instance, universal government-provided health care) in
the name of the common good can only mean that "common ends are
imposed upon all that cannot be . . . more than the [arbitrary] decisions
of particular wills."[32] Thus, for Hayek, the issue of an abstract versus a
concrete common good is also a moral one: whether persons have a
moral obligation to submit to political decisions concerning the pursuit
of substantive ends that can never be more than arbitrary commands of
the politically powerful.

Policy makers should remember that all we can truly have in common with our fellows in a great society, and thus the only basis for a genuine agreement regarding the common good, are certain shared *abstract*
values and opinions regarding the kind of society in which we would like
to live, as opposed to opinions about the particular concrete manifestations it should assume. Commitment to such shared general values, not
the pursuit of common concrete purposes, constitutes social cohesion
in modern liberal society. No one can possess the knowledge required
to justify a rational pursuit of common concrete ends. Most of the innu-
merable and ever-changing facts and circumstances that determine the
concrete shape of our fellows' lives in the spatially extensive contemporary liberal order are and must forever remain unknown to us. Regard-

less of how disinterested, just, intelligent, and altruistic we may be, we can never rationally design a nonarbitrary hierarchy of concrete ends that all persons should pursue, for those ends depend on concrete facts and circumstances that no human mind or group of minds can grasp.

Should one buy a Bible or a loaf of bread? It depends on one's needs, values, and desires; on the decisions of all the other persons in society (reflected in relative prices); and on prevailing concrete circumstances (relative scarcities). The most appropriate *concrete* pattern can only be continually rediscovered as persons employ their knowledge to adapt to the concrete circumstances encountered within their local environments. Such knowledge emerges only if persons are permitted to pursue self-chosen objectives in line with the information transmitted by prices. For Hayek, the "best" concrete pattern arises from the most comprehensive utilization of all the knowledge of particular conditions dispersed throughout a society, knowledge unavailable as a whole to anyone. Indeed, according to Hayek, abstract liberal rules prevail precisely because they bypass both the limits of the human mind and the need to reach consensus on concrete goals before taking action. By ignoring these epistemological considerations, one misunderstands the "whole rationale" of a liberal society, that is, a free society in which persons may choose the ends they will pursue.[33] Hayek's fundamental objection to any conception of the common good that seeks to employ the power of government to achieve particular concrete goals is that any such scheme must inhibit the generation and employment of knowledge, especially the knowledge of concrete circumstances known only and perhaps only tacitly to the countless individuals who compose a society of any degree of complexity. If the common good entails the effective functioning of the overall order and is meant to foster the long-term well-being of every person and the preservation and growth of civilization, then, Hayek argues, any scheme that inhibits the utilization of such knowledge cannot be in the general interest. "All institutions of freedom (law, markets, money, morals)," he contends in *The Constitution of Liberty*, "are adaptations to the fundamental fact of ignorance," to the irremediable limits of the human mind.[34] If we could somehow know the "best" concrete manifestation of the good society, the case for liberal institutions would collapse. If omniscient human beings could direct each person's activities toward his own and others' best fulfillment, we would not require the trial-and-error process whereby we *discover* the pursuits that fulfill our values (and what, in fact, those values are). Human fulfillment—the good of all—cannot be predetermined by democratic participation, legislative logrolling, or the rule of experts.

I conclude by noting that although Hayek insists that government must be limited by adherence to and enforcement of the rule of law, which severely constrains government's legitimate activities, he does allow for considerable governmental activity beyond the traditional protection of life, liberty, and property. Hayek makes a distinction between what he calls the coercive activities of government and its service functions. Only the former must be severely constrained. Contrary to the caricature of Hayek often sketched by his opponents, Hayek legitimizes governmental provision of a wide range of goods and services, so long as such provision meets certain qualifications.

First, governmental provision must not be compulsory or exclusive. For example, Hayek believes there are grounds for requiring the purchase of social or old-age insurance, and he does not object to a government-run program (such as Social Security) that provides this insurance, so long as the government does not claim a monopoly on its provision. People should be free to opt in or out of the government program, securing such compulsory insurance in whatever manner they deem best, and private insurance providers should be permitted to compete with the government-run program. Hayek's second stricture on governmental provision of goods and services follows from his social and economic theory. He argues that the chief issue is not what or how many services government provides but the *method* by which it does so. For instance, Hayek approves of the existence of a social "safety net," arguing that all prosperous societies have made provision for the weak, the sick, and others incapable of supporting themselves. Such services, however, must not interfere with the spontaneous ordering forces on which all depend for the fulfillment of their individual plans. That is, governmental provision must remain outside the market and, most important, must not involve the manipulation of market signals (relative prices), for this would throw sand into the ordering mechanism on which the flourishing of the society, the well-being of all, depends. This rules out, of course, price and wage controls and similar distortions of market signals.

In an age when the religious views that guided the development of the free society no longer inform the dominant worldview, an age enamored of progress and change and hostile to custom and convention, an age in which many look blindly to government as the fountain of material welfare, Hayek's appeal to rational comprehension of the function served by inherited rules of conduct, personal and political, may be indispensable to the preservation of civilized values and free government. Western society presently stands at a curious juncture. The authority of the moral and political traditions whose observance generated the liberal order has eroded in many quarters, and it has been suggested that we are living on the "moral capital" of an earlier era.

Hayek obviously hoped that rational insight into the function served by inherited moral and political traditions in the maintenance of civilized society might make up for the lack of traditional authority—religion and custom—that is increasingly characteristic of our time. His warning against the abuse of reason is equally pertinent. The modern mind has been profoundly shaped by Enlightenment doctrines; the more "modest and . . . humble creed" of Hayek and his Whig forebears has long been on the defensive.[35] The English ideal, the ideal of a "free government . . . that . . . temper[s] the . . . opposite elements of liberty and restraint in one consistent work," seems to many an anachronistic and indeed conservative chimera.[36] Perhaps, however, it is still possible to hope that Hayek's efforts to uphold the free society in the face of widespread misunderstanding of its nature and requirements may yet prove to be not in vain.

Notes

Portions of this chapter are reprinted from Linda C. Raeder, "Liberalism and the Common Good," *The Independent Review: A Journal of Political Economy* 2, no. 4 (spring 1998): 519–35, with permission from the publisher. Copyright 1998, The Independent Institute, 100 Swan Way, Oakland, CA 94621-1428; info@independent.org; www.independent.org.

I would like to thank Boyanna Jacobson and Cybele Seeds for their patient criticism and commentary throughout the development of this essay.

1. In "Why I Am Not a Conservative," Hayek explicitly disavows the "conservative" label. He prefers to be regarded as an "Old Whig." F. A. Hayek, *The Constitution of Liberty* (Chicago: University of Chicago Press, 1960), 397–411. Hayek was born in Vienna and earned advanced degrees in economics and law at the University of Vienna. In 1931 he moved to London, where he held a position at the London School of Economics for several decades. In 1950 he moved to Chicago to serve on the Committee on Social Thought at the University of Chicago, where he remained for twelve years. He then returned to Europe, teaching first at the University of Freiburg in Germany and later at the University of Salzburg in Austria. He is buried outside Vienna in Neustift am Wald.

2. Edmund Burke, "Reform of Representation in the House of Commons," speech given May 7, 1782.

3. F. A. Hayek, "Notes on the Evolution of Systems of Rules of Conduct," in *Studies in Philosophy, Politics, and Economics* (Chicago: University of Chicago Press, 1967), 77.

4. F. A. Hayek, *Political Order of a Free People*, vol. 3 of *Law, Legislation, and Liberty* (Chicago: University of Chicago Press, 1979), 167.

5. See Bruce Caldwell, *Hayek's Challenge: An Intellectual Biography of F. A. Hayek* (Chicago: University of Chicago Press, 2004), 232–60. Caldwell's is perhaps the best biography of Hayek to date.

6. F. A. Hayek, "Kinds of Rationalism," in *The Counter-Revolution of Science: Studies on the Abuse of Reason* (London: Free Press of Glencoe, 1955), 82–95.

7. F. A. Hayek, *Rules and Order*, vol. 1 of *Law, Legislation, and Liberty* (Chicago: University of Chicago Press, 1973), 8–34. Among the "constructivists" identified by Hayek are J. J. Rousseau, Voltaire, Condorcet, Jeremy Bentham, James Mill, J. S. Mill, Auguste Comte, G. F. W. Hegel, Karl Marx, and Thomas Jefferson.

8. Ibid. Representative thinkers within this tradition include Bernard Mandeville, David Hume, Adam Ferguson, Adam Smith, Edmund Burke, T. B. Macaulay, Lord Acton, William Gladstone, Alexis de Tocqueville, Immanuel Kant, Friedrich von Schiller, Wilhelm von Humboldt, and, in America, James Madison, John Marshall, and Daniel Webster.

9. F. A. Hayek, "The Principles of a Liberal Social Order," in *Studies in Philosophy*, 162.

10. Adam Ferguson quoted in F. A. Hayek, "The Results of Human Action But Not of Human Design," in *Studies in Philosophy*, 96.

11. Hayek, *Constitution of Liberty*, 33.

12. Ibid., 110, 61–63.

13. Hayek, *Rules and Order*, 9; F. A. Hayek, *The Fatal Conceit: The Errors of Socialism*, ed. W. W. Bartley III (Chicago: University of Chicago Press, 1988), 71.

14. Hayek, *Constitution of Liberty*, 61; F. A. Hayek, "The Legal and Political Philosophy of David Hume," in *Studies in Philosophy*, 114.

15. F. A. Hayek, *The Sensory Order: An Inquiry into the Foundations of Theoretical Psychology* (Chicago: University of Chicago Press, 1952).

16. Edmund Burke, *Reflections on the Revolution in France*, ed. J. G. A. Pocock (Indianapolis: Hackett Publishing, 1987), 218.

17. Hayek, *Constitution of Liberty*, 94.

18. According to Hayek, his conceptions of spontaneous order and organization are more or less equivalent to Michael Oakeshott's conceptions of the "nomocratic," purpose-independent "civil association" (*societas*) and the "teleocratic," end-dependent "enterprise association" (*universitas*).

19. "The Petition of Grievances of 1610" quoted in Hayek, *Constitution of Liberty*, 168, 163.

20. Blackstone's *Commentaries* quoted in ibid., 173.

21. Hayek, *Constitution of Liberty*, 55.

22. Hayek notes the existence in many Western languages of this traditional distinction between law and legislation: *jus* and *leges*, *Recht* and *Gesetz*, *droit* and *loi*, and so on.

23. More particularly, Hayek maintains that the law, or *nomos*, exhibits the following properties: each law is an abstract (general) rule intended to apply to unknown persons in an unforeseeable number of future circumstances; it is known, certain, and intended to be perpetual; it is the same for all persons (the ideal of "equality under the law"); it generally takes the form of a negative prohibition delimiting the protected domain ("property") of each person; it serves to regulate the relations between private persons or between such persons and the government; it is part of a system of "mutually modifying rules"; and it possesses no specific purpose except the "purpose" of the system of rules as a whole—that is, to maintain the overall social order.

24. Hayek, *Fatal Conceit*, 18.

25. Hayek defines the concept of order as a "state of affairs in which a multiplicity of elements of various kinds are so related to each other that we may learn from our acquaintance with some spatial or temporal part of the whole to form correct expectations concerning the rest, or at least expectations which have a good chance of proving correct" (*Rules and Order*, 36).

26. F. A. Hayek, *The Mirage of Social Justice*, vol. 2 of *Law, Legislation, and Liberty* (Chicago: University of Chicago Press, 1976), 125.

27. Hayek, *Rules and Order*, 98.

28. Ibid., 96.

29. Ibid.

30. Hayek, *Political Order of a Free People*, 105–27.

31. Hayek, *Rules and Order*, 114.

32. Hayek, *Mirage of Social Justice*, 32.

33. Ibid., 9.

34. Hayek, *Constitution of Liberty*, 30.

35. Ibid., 8.

36. Burke, *Reflections*, 216.

Bibliography

Burke, Edmund. 1987. *Reflections on the Revolution in France*. Edited by J. G. A. Pocock. Indianapolis: Hackett Publishing.

Caldwell, Bruce. 2004. *Hayek's Challenge: An Intellectual Biography of F. A. Hayek*. Chicago: University of Chicago Press.

Hayek, F. A. 1944. *The Road to Serfdom*. Chicago: University of Chicago Press.

———. 1948. *Individualism and Economic Order*. Chicago: University of Chicago Press.

———. 1952. *The Sensory Order: An Inquiry into the Foundations of Theoretical Psychology*. Chicago: University of Chicago Press.

———. 1954. *Capitalism and the Historians*. Chicago: University of Chicago Press.

———. 1955. *The Counter-Revolution of Science: Studies on the Abuse of Reason*. London: Free Press of Glencoe.

———. 1960. *The Constitution of Liberty*. Chicago: University of Chicago Press.

———. 1967. *Studies in Philosophy, Politics, and Economics*. Chicago: University of Chicago Press.

———. 1973. *Law, Legislation, and Liberty*. Vol. 1, *Rules and Order*. Chicago: University of Chicago Press.

———. 1976. *Law, Legislation, and Liberty*. Vol. 2, *The Mirage of Social Justice*. Chicago: University of Chicago Press.

———. 1978. *New Studies in Philosophy, Politics, Economics, and the History of Ideas*. Chicago: University of Chicago Press.

———. 1979. *Law, Legislation, and Liberty*. Vol. 3, *The Political Order of a Free People*. Chicago: University of Chicago Press.

——— 1988. *The Fatal Conceit: The Errors of Socialism*. Edited by W. W. Bartley III. Chicago: University of Chicago Press.

Willmoore Kendall, Man of the People

Daniel McCarthy

Few leading intellectuals of the early postwar conservative movement considered themselves majority-rule democrats. But Willmoore Kendall (1909–1967) was one who did. While James Burnham looked to a Machiavellian elite as the "defenders of freedom" and others of the Right defined themselves in opposition to what José Ortega y Gasset had called (in the title of his famous book) "the revolt of the masses," Kendall grounded his understanding of conservatism in the customs and attitudes of the American people.[1] This did not make him the father of right-wing populism: Senator Joseph R. McCarthy, for one, needed no help from Kendall in attracting a mass following, although Kendall was indeed "one of the great philosophical defenders of the Senator."[2] Rather, what this "wild Yale don"[3] achieved was to reconcile philosophical conservatism, particularly in its anticommunist and antiliberal modes, with the American political system, even at its most frankly democratic. His distinctive contribution to the postwar Right, historian George H. Nash has argued, was to Americanize and politicize the conservative intellectual movement.[4]

Kendall did this through brilliant readings of America's foundational documents, including not only the Constitution, the *Federalist*, and the Bill of Rights but also the Mayflower Compact, the Fundamental Orders of Connecticut, and the Virginia Declaration of Rights, among others. He sharply contrasted the tradition of these documents against modern liberalism's commitment to a totally open society. For Kendall, the American political system was properly "closed," and the keys to interpreting it were to be found not in theories of individual rights but in such concepts as deliberative assembly, constitutional morality, and public orthodoxy.

Today, no institute, foundation, or center bears Willmoore Kendall's name. Yet his contemporaries acknowledged him as one of the foremost, if not preeminent, conservative thinkers of his time. Jeffrey Hart called him "beyond any possibility of challenge, the most important political theorist to have emerged . . . since the end of World War II."[5] Leo Strauss considered Kendall "the best native [i.e., American] theorist of [his] generation."[6] Hart and Strauss were friends of Kendall's and philosophically sympathetic to him, but even critics, such as libertarian Murray Rothbard, recognized Kendall's gifts. Rothbard believed that Kendall's majoritarianism and hostility to theories of natural rights marked him as "the philosopher of the lynchmob," yet he credited him as "a very keen and stimulating thinker, incisive, and with a sharply radical spirit with a propensity to dig to the roots of issues without fear or favor."[7]

Why, then, has Kendall fallen into relative obscurity? Nash, the dean of conservative historiographers, has suggested three reasons. First, Kendall died at a comparatively young age (fifty-eight), before he could complete his projected oeuvre. Second, the corpus of his work in political philosophy is diffuse, consisting of just one original book (*John Locke and the Doctrine of Majority-Rule*); a volume of revised essays and reviews (*The Conservative Affirmation*); a posthumous anthology of other essays, talks, and unpublished fragments (*Willmoore Kendall Contra Mundum*); and another posthumous work completed by George W. Carey (*The Basic Symbols of the American Political Tradition*). "There is a tendency among intellectuals," Nash suggests, "to study and memorialize those who leave their thoughts behind in the form of finished books rather than scattered articles (however luminous)." Third, "the most important reason for Kendall's still somewhat shadowy place in the conservative pantheon" according to Nash, was "his own 'volatile' personality and intellect. . . . So colorful was he, and so fascinating, that there has been a tendency to remember him more as 'the most unforgettable character I've met' than as a deep and daring conservative thinker."[8]

"When writing about Willmoore Kendall," Carey concurs, "a strong temptation exists to deal with the man, not his teachings or theory."[9] Indeed, Kendall was such a remarkable man that, like Allan Bloom, he inspired a story by Saul Bellow ("Mosby's Memoirs," in Kendall's case).[10] However unfortunate it may be that Kendall's life and personality sometimes eclipsed interest in his work, his biography is important for understanding both the development of his thought and his impact on modern American conservatism. This is especially true in light of the powerful indirect influence Kendall exercised on the development of conservatism through his student William F. Buckley Jr.

Kendall was born on March 5, 1909, in Konawa, Oklahoma. His father, Willmoore Kendall Sr., a Methodist minister, was blind, and Kendall's later philosophical rigor evidently owed much to his extensive reading to and discussions with his father. The senior Kendall preached in small towns throughout Oklahoma, and Nash credits this "rural, Democratic" milieu with helping to inspire Kendall's "faith in the inarticulate common man and distrust of 'undemocratic' elites—a feature of his thought throughout his life."[11]

Young Willmoore was a prodigy. He learned to read at age two. He graduated from high school at twelve and from the University of Oklahoma at sixteen. His first book, *Baseball: How to Play It and How to Watch It,* was published (under the pseudonym Alan Monk) the year he turned eighteen. By 1932, he had completed course work for a Ph.D. in Romance languages at the University of Illinois. But before finishing his dissertation he accepted a Rhodes scholarship to Oxford, where he studied with philosopher R. G. Collingwood, who piqued Kendall's interest in political theory.[12] Kendall also became a fervent Marxist during his time at Oxford and conceived an ambition to become "a great socialist publicist."[13]

In pursuit of that dream, he worked for the United Press in Madrid between terms at Oxford, then returned to Spain as a full-time foreign correspondent after completing his studies. There he circulated among high-ranking Trotskyites; he seems to have had an aversion to Stalinism from the start. As the civil war approached, his sympathies lay firmly with the Republicans. What he saw in Spain, and later learned about the conflict after his return to the United States, cured Kendall of his youthful flirtation with communism. According to Nash: "The dictatorial, totalitarian, antidemocratic aspects of communism appalled him. He later told a friend that as Spain slid toward civil war he could tolerate the Communists' blowing up the plants of opposition newspapers. But when they deliberately killed opposition *newsboys*—this was too much. Exposure to the Spanish Republic 'really shook Willmoore up,' one friend recalled, and within a few months, 'his thought crystallized into fervent anti-communism.'"[14]

In 1936 Kendall returned to the University of Illinois, where he forfeited his credits in Romance languages and began work toward a Ph.D. in political science, which he received in 1940. His dissertation was published the following year as *John Locke and the Doctrine of Majority-Rule*. It was a work of startling originality, advancing a novel interpretation of Locke as a pure majoritarian and anticipating the later scholarly consensus that Locke's *Second Treatise* had been written before the Glorious Revolution of 1688–1689.[15] Kendall regretted, however, that the work did not receive more attention from the academic mainstream.[16]

He had a political as well as an academic interest in Locke. "The name of Locke, associated as it is in men's minds with such values as tolerance, freedom of inquiry, love of truth, *etc.*," he writes, "has become a *symbol* in the continuing struggle for power in the American constitution; and, as such has been extremely useful to those who prefer government by judiciary to majority-rule." Kendall knew which side he was on and recognized the practical consequences that might flow from his research. If, he observes, "Locke's natural rights are merely the rights vouchsafed by a legislature responsible to the majority, the opponents of judicial review can easily capture for themselves a symbol that might prove extremely useful."[17]

This is not to say that Kendall intended from the start to overturn the conventional understanding of Locke as a philosopher of natural rights. On the contrary, he expected his investigations to confirm "prevailing notions about Locke's political theory" and was surprised when his research led him to conclude instead that Locke was a defender of absolute majority rule.[18] But that was what his close study of the *Second Treatise* revealed. His reading was guided by methods he had learned from Collingwood. As Kendall described this approach years later: "Let's find out, above all, what *question* the book is asking, the problem to which it addresses itself first and foremost; let us try first to grasp that question, then to find out what the author's overall answer to the question actually is. Let us, in a word, not make the mistake of trying to get answers to the question of parts of the book that turn out to have no bearing either upon the question or upon the answer."[19]

Only after a painstaking reading that "accept[ed] no sentence or paragraph from the *Second Treatise* as Locke's 'teaching' without first laying it beside every other sentence in the treatise" did Kendall conceive his thesis: "that Locke did not *say* the things he is supposed to have said" about natural rights; instead, Locke's answers to the great permanent questions of political philosophy are *"at every point except one,* [those] *of the majority-rule democrats."*[20]

In *John Locke and the Doctrine of Majority-Rule,* Kendall argues that even in Locke's state of nature there are no truly individual rights. Rights, rather, are reciprocal with social duties and communal in character, community in the state of nature being the community of all humanity. Kendall illustrates this point with an analysis of Locke's account of the right to acquire property in the state of nature. "The right has its origin," Kendall writes, "in a need which Locke represents as a common (= community?) need," namely, the need for property as a means of ensuring humanity's survival and flourishing as a species. Locke "is thinking of the right of property simply as a function of one's *duty* to enrich mankind's common heritage," and what is more, "this same *functional* view of rights carries itself over into Locke's handling of the problem of rights *in* organized society." Kendall characterizes the presuppositions of Locke's theory of property as "collectivist in the extreme."[21]

He then proceeds to show that Locke's description of the law of nature is complex and seemingly contradictory, yet the apparent problems matter little, since "Locke's state of nature [is merely] an expository device," as is Locke's compact theory, "whose purpose," Kendall states, "is to lay bare the essential character of the rights and duties which belong to men as members of (legitimate) commonwealths."[22] Just as the community of the human race is the supreme authority in the state of nature, the people are sovereign in political society. And the relationship in a given commonwealth between the sovereign people and a particular government "is, quite simply, assimilable to that between principal and agent in Anglo-American law." The people as a whole remain sovereign and may cashier the government of the day, but the people may delegate to the government unlimited power over individuals, since "even the individual's right to life is valid only to the extent that it is compatible with the good (= preservation) of his community, and it is the people, not the individual, to whom Locke has clearly imputed the power to make the necessary judgments as to what is compatible with its [i.e., the people's] preservation."[23]

How is the will of the people to be expressed? Kendall reads Locke as assigning this power to the majority: "Wherever men live in community with one another, [Locke] is saying, the relations between them can be described in terms of an agreement which, in addition to assigning to the whole community that unlimited power which we have examined

. . . assigns to the numerical majority a *right* to make decisions (regarding the use of that power) which are binding upon the minority. The majority-principle is, in a word, implicit in the logic of community life."[24]

Kendall analyzes five arguments that Locke provides in support of majority rule, concluding that "what was really in Locke's mind" as the ultimate basis for majority rule was the belief that, "individual consents being . . . the only rightful title to the exercise of power," and consent being the only truly individual right for Locke, "the right of the majority flows as a matter of course from the fact that it can point to more consents than the minority." From this theory follows the idea that a legitimate commonwealth must have "an institutional context in which the people are as a matter of course invited, from time to time, to express (by majority-vote) their preferences regarding future government policy and personnel."[25]

Kendall makes one concession in *John Locke and the Doctrine of Majority-Rule* to the conventional interpretation of his subject. He accepts that "Locke could never have committed himself to the moral relativism implied in the proposition that majorities make right" because Locke "believed . . . not only in the moral law but also in the possibility of applying the moral law to the problems of politics!" To resolve the apparent contradiction between Locke's beliefs and the logic of his argument, Kendall proposes a "latent premise" within the *Second Treatise*: the idea that "a 'safe' majority of men (thus the 'average' man) are rational and just."[26] Thus majorities can be trusted to observe the moral law. (In 1966, after encountering Leo Strauss's scholarship on Locke, Kendall would reconsider this "latent premise" and conclude that Locke did indeed hold no law higher than the will of the people.)[27]

Many themes of Kendall's later work are present in *John Locke and the Doctrine of Majority-Rule*, among them Kendall's devotion to, and creative thinking about, majority rule itself; his concern for a reference in politics to a source of law higher than man; his rejection of individual rights; and his interest in the application of political philosophy to American political practice. Just as significantly, the book is a tour de force of Kendall's reading technique, what he calls the "universal confrontation of the text."[28]

By the time he wrote *John Locke and the Doctrine of Majority-Rule*, Kendall's personal politics had begun moving to the Right. He was outspokenly critical of Franklin Roosevelt's foreign and domestic policies (as he had been while on the Left) and supported Republican Wendell

Willkie in 1940. He also favored the Ludlow Amendment, which would have required a national referendum before the United States could go to war, and opposed U.S. intervention in World War II before the Japanese attack on Pearl Harbor.[29] After his father's death in 1942, however, Kendall resigned a post at the University of Richmond to work for U.S. intelligence in Latin America and later became chief of the CIA's Inter-American Division, Office of Reports and Estimates, after the war.[30]

He returned to the academy in 1947 as an associate professor of political science at Yale, where he quickly alienated colleagues by subjecting their left-wing prejudices to blistering criticism. Yet the qualities that his colleagues found appalling charmed many of the undergraduates who took Kendall's courses, perhaps none more so than two young men named William F. Buckley and L. Brent Bozell. "His pugnacity and panache attracted Bill and Brent," wrote Garry Wills, who later came to know all three men through National Review. "They made a formidable trio—all three bright, handsome, Catholic (in varying degrees), Spanish-speaking, war veterans, glib, argumentative."[31]

According to Wills, "we hear refracted in Bill Buckley's tone and language" Kendall's "extraordinary speaking and writing style, precise but also flamboyant. . . . I had thought everyone talked like Bill at National Review. But they were talking like Willmoore—like the Oklahoma boy whose diction had been sharpened by his years at Oxford and doctoral studies in Romance languages."[32] Kendall's influence on Buckley extended beyond his patterns of speech, however; he also channeled the course of Buckley's life and career. The younger man joined the CIA at Kendall's urging, and it was Kendall who introduced Buckley to the man who would become his "paramount associate at National Review," James Burnham. Kendall also provided, according to Buckley himself, "important editorial contributions" to Buckley's first two books, God and Man at Yale and McCarthy and His Enemies (the latter coauthored with Bozell).[33]

When Buckley launched National Review in 1955 he asked Kendall to become a senior editor, in which capacity he wrote a regular column, "The Liberal Line," and supervised the books department for a time. At the magazine Kendall soon discovered that his disagreements with other conservatives could be as bitter as his jousts with the Left. Reportedly, Kendall was never on speaking terms with more than one National Review colleague at any given moment. He may have made a permanent enemy of managing editor Suzanne La Follette by seducing a copy girl on her office couch—known thereafter as the Willmoore Kendall memorial couch.[34]

Ideas were certainly not Kendall's only passion. He married three times, with a series of extracurricular pursuits on the side. He was also prodigious in his cups. Jeffrey Hart spent a week at Oxford with Kendall in 1965 and recalls: "we consumed an ocean of booze, and after he left, for the only time in my life, I took up running. It was the only way to dry out." Hart provides a memorable taste of his friend's lacerating wit as well: "When a news report on an unsuccessful assassination attempt against Sukarno came over the pub TV, Kendall commented: 'This has all the earmarks of a CIA operation. Everyone died except Sukarno.'"[35]

Perhaps spurred by the launch of *National Review*, Kendall came into his own as an explicitly conservative theorist by the late 1950s. In several essays published between 1958 and 1960, he took aim at the ideology that stood in antithesis to his own principles, delimiting conservatism first in the negative. Liberalism, according to Kendall, was characterized by a desire to create an "open society" free from all public orthodoxy, a desire that Kendall traced to John Stuart Mill's *On Liberty*. The educated elite that wished to remake America into an open society did not understand, Kendall warned, that no society could exist without an orthodoxy. (This concern had been at the back of Kendall's mind since at least 1935, when he wrote to his father, "the greatest single problem . . . is this: how to get across, to a generation for which religion has lost its meaning, that minimum of morality without which life in a community is downright impossible.")[36]

As Kendall had earlier shown Locke to be something other than a natural law libertarian, so he now proceeded to examine other figures conventionally identified with minority freedoms. He began with one of the first and greatest martyrs to the mob: Socrates. In "The People versus Socrates Revisited" (1958), he argues that both the philosopher and the Athenian jury that condemned him had acted justly. Socrates, inspired by God and adhering to permanent truths, was not intimidated by his prosecution and refused to silence himself. Kendall notes, however, that Socrates did not claim in his defense anything like a right to free speech or freedom of thought. On the contrary, Socrates accepted his sentence of death and declined to escape from custody when given the chance. The texts of Plato's *Apology* and *Crito* make clear, Kendall argues, that Socrates endorsed the city's authority to punish dissent. The Athenians, for their part, were confronted with three alternatives: to condemn Socrates, to accept his philosophy and change their way of life, or to tolerate him. The second would have meant repudiating their own values, which they were not prepared to do. The third option also would have been a betrayal of their way of life, since it would have left Socrates free to preach a revolution that might have eventually succeeded. Kendall concludes that the best course for the Athenians would have been to adopt the ways of Socrates. But failing that, they chose the next best option by defending their way of life against a revolutionary agitator. "Perhaps," Kendall writes, "a second-best but eminently worthwhile task for political theory is to try to learn to build—and preserve—so good a city."[37] Kendall further develops his attack on the doctrines of the "open society" in "How to Read Milton's 'Areopagitica'" (1960), which argues that the poet was no more of a modern liberal than Socrates had been, and in "The Open Society and Its Fallacies" (1960). In what may be his most important scholarly article, "The Two Majorities" (1960), Kendall distinguishes between the plebiscitary majoritarianism favored by liberals and the carefully designed constitutional majoritarianism of James Madison. He identifies plebiscitary democracy as one of the tools by which liberals hoped to carry out their revolution, overthrowing the constitutional republic devised by the framers and substituting in its place the open society.[38]

The opponents of the open society, according to Kendall, are America's true conservatives. This would become the theme of his 1963 book, *The Conservative Affirmation in America*, in which he takes sharp exception to conservatives who define their philosophy otherwise. In a salvo evidently directed against traditionalist conservatives such as Russell Kirk, he writes: "I make no sense . . . of calling 'Conservative' the man who takes a dim view of his country's established institutions, feels something less than at home with its way of life as it actually lives it, finds it difficult to identify himself with the political and moral principles on which it has acted through its history, dislikes or views with contempt the generality of the kind of people his society produces, and—above all perhaps—dissociates himself from its Founders, or at least holds them at arms' length."[39]

Kendall's understanding of American conservatism has "no axe to grind for 'aristocracy,' no quarrel (any more than had the authors of the *Federalist*) with America's commitment to 'democracy' . . . . It views the pre-1789 John Adams with suspicion not reverence, shies off of vast reaches of the argument of Burke's *Reflections on the Revolution in*

France, and deplores the pre-*Federalist* writings of even Alexander Hamilton." He cites John C. Calhoun, Irving Babbitt, and Paul Elmer More as three figures with whom his conservatism could "do no business."[40]

Having thus disposed of the traditionalist brand of conservatism, Kendall turns his attention to the libertarians. In contrast to them, Kendall's conservatism "has sworn no vow of absolute fidelity either to free enterprise a la von Mises, or to a certain list of 'rights' a la John Chamberlain, or to a certain holy trinity of government functions a la . . . Frank Meyer, or to revolving-door mistrust of political authority as such a la Frank Chodorov."[41]

And again contra the traditionalists, Kendall proclaims that his book "treats the relation between American Conservatism and 'religion' as *problematic*" because "the United States is—has been up to now anyhow—a Christian society governed, or rather self-governed, under a secular Constitution. . . . Attempts to resolve the religious-society–secular-Constitution tension in the United States, in either the one direction or the other, are not only divisive, but contrary to the American tradition itself."[42]

Authentic American conservatism, according to Kendall, is nothing more or less than the defense of the constitutional order against the revolutionary attempt by liberals to transform the country into an open society. In practical politics, he argues, refining the case he made in "The Two Majorities," that means a defense of the traditions and prerogatives of Congress against attempts to remake the American system into a plebiscitary democracy led by the executive branch: "Nothing can be more certain than that the Founders of our Republic bequeathed to us a form of government that was *purely* representative—a form of government in which there was no room, in which moreover there is *to this day* no room, for policy decisions by the electorate—that is, for electoral 'mandates' emanating from popular majorities. Or rather there is one thing more certain: namely, that the Liberals intend to overthrow that traditional form of government. . . . Abolish the electoral college, the Liberals insist . . . and so make the President also the direct agent of the popular majority."[43]

The framers had indeed devised a majoritarian system, he contends, but of a special kind: one that depends on the "deliberative sense" of a virtuous people, who in turn choose virtuous representatives to deliberate in Congress. The people require only as much expertise as is necessary to elect virtuous representatives—moral expertise, rather than a minute understanding of political technicalities. The people do not give their representatives specific, binding mandates; rather, they expect representatives to deliberate thoughtfully within the legislature. As Kendall summarizes the process: "In the election of a member of Congress, a community faithful to the constitutional morality of *The Federalist* makes a decision about whom to send forward as its most virtuous man, a decision which is the more important, and which it accordingly takes more seriously, because the community knows that it [i.e., the community] can have little effect on a presidential election."[44]

What is crucial here is that congressional districts have much smaller constituencies than the nation as a whole, and this difference in scale translates into several qualitative differences that Kendall enumerates. Perhaps most important, the smaller constituency is more structured and hierarchical than the national community; reputation and social authority hold greater sway within its limits. The smaller size of the constituency allows better opportunities for constituents to deliberate among themselves in choosing the most virtuous person to represent them. They are more likely to know the candidates, or at least to have a better sense of the candidates' moral qualities, because of the relatively close proximity between the voters and the candidates. Moreover, the interests represented in small constituencies are more concrete than those in a national race, where candidates speak not to well-defined groups but to the nation at large using abstract, ideological rhetoric.[45]

Perhaps surprisingly, Kendall draws on Jean-Jacques Rousseau, a bête noire to many conservatives, for some of these insights, pointing to the admiration Rousseau expresses in *The Social Contract* for "small bands of Swiss peasants gathered around oak trees to conduct their affairs." Rousseau trusts these small groups above "all the governments of Europe."[46] Kendall understands the Constitution as providing representation for "structured communities," like those of the Swiss peasants gathered around oak trees, through congressional elections. Elections for the executive branch, in contrast, embody the momentary impulses of a national, unstructured community and thus bear a closer resemblance to the homogeneous, egalitarian plebiscitary elections in which liberals prefer to rest authority. In presidential races, "there are no issues, because both candidates for the most part merely repeat, as they swing from whistle-stop to whistle-stop and television studio to television studio, the policy platitudes that constitute the table-talk in our faculty clubs . . . what you get out of the presidential election is what amounts to a *unanimous* mandate for the principles *both* candidates have been enunciating, which is to say: the presidential election not only permits the electorate, but virtually obliges it, to overestimate its dedication to the pleasant-sounding maxims that have been poured into its ears."[47] The presidential electorate, Kendall fears, is vulnerable to manipulation by demagogues and ideologues and permits no leeway for reasoned deliberation between representatives of different perspectives. He therefore cautions that there must be "no room in the American system for a presidential office so aggrandized as to be able to itself determine how much farther the aggrandizement shall go."[48]

One of Congress's virtues, Kendall argues in *The Conservative Affirmation*, is that it is more sensitive than the executive branch to subversion and other threats to the public orthodoxy. Joseph McCarthy's anticommunist investigations illustrate this sensitivity. Kendall found great significance in the white-hot anger the McCarthy hearings and other Red Scare episodes of the 1950s elicited from partisans of each side. For Kendall, McCarthyism was about much more than McCarthy or subversion; it was a struggle over public orthodoxy itself, a test of whether the American tradition or the doctrines of the open society would prevail in political practice. Each side of the clash "understood the other perfectly, and each was quite right in venting upon the other the fury reserved for heretics because each was, in the eyes of the other, *heretical.*" Alas, Kendall notes, a decisive confrontation was averted when liberals retreated to the "clear and present danger" doctrine as the test for whether subversion could be suppressed. The actual heart of the dispute, according to Kendall, was not whether real danger could be suppressed but whether anything like absolute freedom of speech or thought existed—whether the American body politic could, at will, punish elements it considered "wrong and immoral" quite apart from whether they were dangerous.[49]

Behind the clash over public orthodoxy lay an even greater question that Kendall called "the ultimate issue between conservatism and liberalism": the acceptance or rejection of a higher authority than individual consent in politics and society. In formulating his thoughts on this subject, Kendall drew on his reading of Leo Strauss, whom he called "*the* great teacher of political philosophy, not of our time alone, but of any time since Machiavelli."[50] From Strauss, Kendall had learned to construe the conflict between liberals and conservatives as ultimately a war between the "great tradition" (the absolute truths of Western philosophy and religion) and a revolutionary moral relativism promulgated first by

Machiavelli and later by Hobbes, Locke, Rousseau, and other modern philosophers. Locke's role in this struggle, Kendall came to believe, had been to camouflage relativism in the language of natural rights and contractual consent.

There is a critical difference, Kendall argues, between a contract such as the Old Testament covenant, which merely articulates rights and duties in an existing relationship (between God and his people, in this case), and a contract that actually creates a society out of nothing but human will. "We must distinguish between contracts understood as *creating* society, justice, law, and principles of right and wrong," he cautions, "and contracts understood as merely *specifying* society, justice, law, and principles of right and wrong in particular situations."[51] Classical philosophers such as Plato and Aristotle predicated society on ideas of what was natural for man, and for them, "justice, the principles of right and wrong, and the law are not artificial and man-made, but rather are discovered by man through the exercise of reason." For modern philosophers such as Hobbles, Locke, and Rousseau, in contrast, "agreement . . . is the sole creator of society, of justice, of right and wrong."[52] In the American context, the followers of Locke and the other social-contract philosophers were necessarily liberals, while the conservatives placed their faith "in the growing Great Tradition."[53] Conservatives must be anti-Lockeans, Kendall now believed.

He once confided to a friend that he wished to become American conservatism's answer to Edmund Burke.[54] *The Conservative Affirmation* was his bid to lay down, once and for all time, the definition of the American Right. But much as the widely hailed *John Locke and the Doctrine of Majority-Rule* did not revolutionize the study of Locke, *The Conservative Affirmation* failed to reorient the American Right's self-conception. In sales terms, the book "was only moderately successful," according to publisher Henry Regnery, who recalled in his memoirs, "we printed 6,000 copies and sold during the first year or two about 3,800."[55]

Kendall had originally proposed a different book — tentatively titled *What Is Conservatism Anyway?* — to Regnery.[56] Three chapters of that unfinished work, whose title later became *Sages of Conservatism*, were published in the posthumous collection *Willmoore Kendall Contra Mundum*. They suggest how far Kendall was willing to go in criticizing the errors of other conservatives. Although the chapter on John Courtney Murray, "The True Sage of Woodstock," is appreciative of its subject, the others, on Russell Kirk and Clinton Rossiter, are scathing.

Kendall argues, for example, that "Mr. Kirk's teaching on tradition is, on the face of it, an assertion of the very relativism and positivism that, in other contexts, he abhors."[57] Kendall had once written to Francis Graham Wilson, his dissertation adviser at the University of Illinois, that he considered The Conservative Affirmation a "declaration of war" against Kirk. As Nash suggests, Sages of Conservatism would have made the war explicit.[58] The book probably would have shown many of conservatism's other "sages"—among them James Burnham, William F. Buckley Jr., Frank Meyer, and M. Stanton Evans—in a similarly unflattering light.

"Within the conservative movement, as well as the political science profession," Nash writes, Kendall "remained to the end the Great Dissenter."[59] Through students, colleagues, and friends such as John Alvis, Jeffrey Hart, and George Carey, Kendall continues to shape the intellectual Right's understanding of the American political tradition. But his influence has been limited by his exacting definition of conservatism. Kendall cannot be placed in any of the intellectual Right's factional camps, and he had a propensity to alienate each of them in turn (and on occasion, as in the preface to The Conservative Affirmation, all of them at once). Certainly as an avowed opponent of individual rights, Kendall could not expect to find many allies among libertarians. But he was a poor fit for traditionalists as well: he thought them too attached to European traditions, too preoccupied with literature, and insufficiently confident in the American people and the U.S. constitutional system. As a great admirer of Leo Strauss, Kendall might have gained a following among Strauss's disciples, and to some extent he has.[60] But Kendall's interests diverged from those of Strauss and his students on several points, particularly regarding the concept of equality in the American tradition. Harry Jaffa, the preeminent West Coast "Straussian," has objected vehemently to Kendall's criticisms of Abraham Lincoln and the equality clause of the Declaration of Independence, going so far as to claim that Kendall's conservatism in practice amounts to "a distinctive American fascism, or national socialism."[61]

The personal qualities that made Kendall a memorable individual could cost him friends, and jobs as well. He "never lost a polemic, but could not keep a friend," recalls Reid Buckley, who, like his brother Bill, studied with Kendall at Yale.[62] Such was the animus toward him among his colleagues at the university that in nineteen years Kendall never received a promotion. He was encouraged to take sabbaticals. Finally, in 1961, he offered the university an opportunity to buy out his tenure, a deal that was quickly accepted. He received $42,500, paid out over five years, "to teach, not at Yale."[63] In 1963 he resigned from *National Review* after Buckley, noting that Kendall had not written for the magazine in two years, suggested that he step down as senior editor and accept the title of contributing editor instead. Kendall wrote back that it would be "too great an honor" to remain on the masthead. Later, after the magazine refused to run a free advertisement for the University of Dallas, where Kendall had become chairman of the Department of Politics and Economics, he wrote to Buckley that he now thought about *National Review* "much as I would about an ex-wife of mine who'd become a call-girl." Buckley replied that he could "only welcome the news that you have finally learned to distinguish between the two."[64]

His feuds with other conservatives may create the impression that Kendall could not appreciate anyone else who stepped on his philosophical turf, but that was far from the case. He was profoundly respectful, even deferential, toward Leo Strauss and Eric Voegelin, and he nominated Richard Weaver "for the captaincy of the anti-Liberal team" in a review of *Ideas Have Consequences.*[65] He also suggested that Weaver's later *Visions of Order* belonged alongside *The Federalist* on any conservative's bookshelf.[66] To be sure, Kendall's affection for Strauss, Voegelin, and Weaver may have endured, in part, because he had only limited interaction with them, chiefly by correspondence. But in any event, his strained relations with other conservatives were not a product of professional jealousy. He may have aspired to be the American Burke, but he was not above apprenticing himself, even in middle age and at the height of his reputation, to other scholars he esteemed.

After *The Conservative Affirmation*, Kendall turned his attention with renewed vigor to the American tradition. Having shown that neither Socrates nor Milton had advocated an open society, he now sought to demonstrate that the American founding fathers had not done so either. He found confirmation for this belief in Leonard Levy's books *The Legacy of Suppression* and *Jefferson and Civil Liberties: The Darker Side.* In 1964 Kendall wrote an essay-length review of the latter for the *Stanford Law Review.* Among the founders, Thomas Jefferson might have been expected to be a proponent of the open society, if anyone was. But as Levy showed, despite his libertarian rhetoric when out of power, as president, Jefferson did not govern as an open society liberal. Moreover, Kendall argued on the basis of Levy's work that even Jefferson understood freedom of the press (the keystone of the open society) to mean only freedom from prior restraint, not freedom from prosecution for seditious libel. None of the founders had subscribed to doctrines with any resemblance to modern notions of freedom of speech.[67]

In his 1964 essay "The Bill of Rights and American Freedom," Kendall's contribution to the Frank Meyer–edited volume *What Is Conservatism?* he contends that "the major provisions of the First Amendment are conspicuous precisely for the *absence* of overtones to the effect that the 'freedoms' involved are 'rights' and so, in [Justice Hugo] Black's favorite phrase, 'absolute.'" Madison had carefully phrased the First Amendment so as not to embed the language of inviolable individual rights in the Constitution. He did so in part, Kendall argues, because he knew that such rights would have been unenforceable against Congress and could only have led to a disruptive showdown between the legislative and judicial branches. The true bulwark for natural rights, according to Kendall, is found not in the "parchment barriers" Madison derided but in "the deliberate sense of the American community" as expressed within Congress.[68]

This, it must be said, seems to imply something very similar to the "latent premise" Kendall once detected in Locke's *Second Treatise*. In Kendall's account of Madison's thinking, natural or minority rights are better protected by a virtuous majority than by abstract guarantees; the majority, properly constituted, is simply too good to jeopardize the minority. In his 1965 introduction to *The Federalist* coauthored with George Carey, Kendall elaborated on how majority rule can protect rights. In the American system, the answer could be found in the "constitutional morality" taught by *The Federalist*. In Kendall's reading, the Philadelphia Constitution established legislative supremacy; the genius of *The Federalist*, however, was to teach legislators to use the Constitution wisely, to respect moral limits on their own power and thereby preserve legitimate rights and avert confrontations that could only humiliate the Supreme Court. *The Federalist*, in short, transformed the Philadelphia Constitution into something more than a charter for majority rule; it became a charter for a special kind of majority-rule government that would emphasize reasoned deliberation within Congress over intragovernmental confrontation.[69]

Kendall had lost none of his interest in majority rule by the mid-1960s, but he had developed a more supple understanding of the concept. In light of his reading of Strauss, he reexamined his earlier work on Locke, finding now a moral void in place of the "latent premise" he had once perceived. The influence of Strauss is also evident in Kendall's 1966 introduction to Rousseau's *Government of Poland*, a work that Kendall translated. (He had earlier produced a translation of *The Social Contract* for Regnery's Gateway Editions.) Kendall supplies not one but two incisive interpretations of *The Government of Poland* in his introduction. The first takes the text at face value, "as a book dealing centrally with Poland, and saying pretty much what it seems to say." In this reading, Kendall finds Rousseau's surprising support for the inefficiencies of the traditional Polish constitution to be indicative of a rejection of the modern, centralized nation-state. For Rousseau, Kendall argues, "the alleged 'vices' of the Polish Constitution represent a clearheaded and intelligent choice on the part of the rank-and-file Poles, against the centralized authority that their intellectual betters are urging upon them, and are, therefore, not vices but *virtues*."[70]

Kendall's second reading of *Government of Poland* treats it as an exercise in "secret writing" that "is apparently addressed to the Poles but is actually intended for a much wider audience, encompassing all those who find themselves unwilling participants in the modern, territorially extensive political regime." On this telling, Rousseau is attempting to show modern states how they might supply the public-spirited ethos that allowed classical regimes to flourish, an ethos above "those selfish and private attachments of modern man that cause division in society." Rousseau's answer, Kendall reveals, is to devise a "radically new," gentle but totalistic society permeated by the power of the state. "It is the business of the state, or, more properly, it is the business of the founder of the state," Kendall explains, "to see to it that the citizen passes every waking moment within institutions that will insure his constant attention to public affairs."[71] Control of the state educational apparatus is the means by which this revolution can be realized. Rousseau is not, it must be noted, attempting to abolish political liberty; rather, he is looking for a foundation for political liberty other than natural law.

The contrasts Kendall highlights between *Government of Poland* and *The Federalist* illuminate both works. Whereas Publius advocates a national constitution that draws moral strength from heterogeneous local communities, Rousseau has devised a genuinely federal system for "a people who have been made more or less homogeneous through the inculcation of a national *ethos*." Rousseau "seems to feel that the only sure means of providing against the despotism of the large nation-state is to decentralize the deliberative process so that the general wills of the

192 ★ Daniel McCarthy

local assemblies may assert themselves, when the occasion demands, against the incursions of the national legislature." Kendall concludes that *Government of Poland* "provides us with a model for representative government which, because it is in many ways opposed to the prevailing Publian version, enables us to better understand both the virtue and the limitations of our current practices."[72] The *Government of Poland* is the anti-*Federalist*.

In 1963 Kendall accepted what would be his final academic post, as chairman of the Department of Politics and Economics at the University of Dallas in Irving, Texas. Returning to the Southwest, he told Francis Wilson, made him feel like Moses reaching the promised land. He was leaving "the world of the Buckleys" for "the warmth and affection of *home*."[73] By all accounts, his four years at Dallas were happy ones. After two annulments, he was married for a third and final time in 1965, to Nellie Cooper. In the final year of his life, he created a unique Ph.D. program at Dallas, which he described in a letter to Voegelin: "We are launching, this Autumn, a Ph.D. program—built, as nearly as I have known how, in the image of you and Strauss—in Politics and Literature."[74] He hoped that Strauss and Voegelin would teach at Dallas as visiting professors. But before that could happen, Kendall died of a heart attack in his sleep on June 30, 1967.[75]

At the time of his death, Kendall was working on a volume expanding on lectures he had delivered at Vanderbilt University in 1964. Those lectures, and the book posthumously published as *The Basic Symbols of the American Political Tradition*, attest to the impact of Voegelin's thought on Kendall. Voegelin, Kendall wrote, "has set us off, as political scientists, on a new kind of task, specifically, the identification and understanding of the symbols and myths that 'represent' the American people in their experience as a political society.'" Through Voegelin, Kendall now understood political tradition as "a matter . . . of a people's own understanding of its place in the *constitution of being* and of its *role in history*, of what it calls itself to be and do as it lives its life as a political society—a matter, in short, of the *symbols* by which it represents or interprets itself to itself."[76]

In *Basic Symbols* Kendall applied the insights he had acquired from Voegelin to the interpretation of four of the American political tradition's foundational (or prefoundational) documents: the Mayflower Compact, the Fundamental Orders of Connecticut, the Massachusetts Body of Liberties, and the Virginia Declaration of Rights. (George Carey, with whom Kendall had discussed his ideas at length, completed the book after Kendall's death, contributing chapters on the Declaration of Independence, *The Federalist*, and the Bill of Rights.) Kendall called attention to the similarities in the four documents he examined: the texts of the Mayflower Compact and Massachusetts Body of Liberties attested to their composition through a deliberative process and demonstrated that minority views had been subsumed into the final consensus; the documents' wording leaves no unreconciled minority. All four documents assume the existence of a virtuous people united in self-government under a higher law. And in all four, Kendall finds, "a man's legal rights are, in general, the rights vouchsafed to him by the representative assembly—which, like the Lord of the Scriptures, giveth and taketh away."[77]

The documents do possess significant differences, however. Indeed, they demonstrate over time what Voegelin called the process of symbolic "differentiation." The status of religion, in particular, undergoes several changes. The Mayflower Compact refers to the "advancement of the faith" as one of the purposes of political community. The Connecticut Orders denote, in greater detail ("ominously, some might say," Kendall remarks), a mission "to maintain and preserve the liberty and purity of the gospel of our Lord Jesus which we now profess, as also the discipline of the Churches, which according to the truth of said gospel is now practiced amongst us."[78] The Massachusetts Body of Liberties, yet again, assumes a Christian society but invokes a less doctrinally specific kind of Christianity than the Connecticut Orders. Finally, the Virginia Declaration of Rights sounds faintly deist in its formulation of religion as "the duty which we owe to our Creator" that "can be directed only by reason and conviction, not by force or violence," although it also cites "Christian forbearance" among the "mutual duties" of citizens. Kendall, however, contends that the authors of the Declaration of Rights did not see themselves as any less Christian than their Massachusetts and Connecticut counterparts. Rather, with the Declaration of Rights, "we are on the threshold of the idea, which in due course will become explicit in *The Federalist*, of a Christian *society* with a secular, that is precisely *not* religious, form of government."[79]

Basic Symbols serves as a capstone to Kendall's political philosophy. To the end of his life, he defended majority rule and legislative supremacy, doctrines that he found embodied in the foundational documents of the American tradition no less than in Locke's *Second Treatise*. Even in the Massachusetts Body of Liberties and Virginia Declaration of Rights,

Kendall found no support for absolute individual rights of the kind advocated by modern liberals. In the earlier documents, as in *The Federalist*, reasoned deliberation and recognition of a higher source of law temper the legislative assembly's awesome power. The tension between a secular Constitution and a Christian society that Kendall noted in *The Conservative Affirmation* he saw developing in the process of symbolic differentiation throughout America's colonial experience. Kendall's own philosophy, it can fairly be said, also underwent a process of development and differentiation over the course of his career, but it never changed tracks entirely. He incorporated what he learned from Strauss and Voegelin into what remained a remarkably consistent outlook.

Kendall championed legislative supremacy at a time when many other conservatives, such as James Burnham, also considered Congress the proper institutional focus for conservatism. In the four decades since his death, however, American conservatives have moved decisively in a presidentialist direction. This transformation of the American Right may have as much to do with Kendall's neglect as a theorist as his difficult personality. What place can Kendall have in an intellectual movement that, for forty years now, has largely seen its role as defending the presidential prerogatives of Richard Nixon, Ronald Reagan, and George W. Bush?[80]

Even Kendall's admirers have struggled with this question. Writing in 1985, Gregory Wolfe mused that "Ronald Reagan may signify the reversal of the system as Kendall saw it."[81] A year later, in an appreciative essay titled "Prophet of the Heartland," Samuel Francis similarly contended that, "since 1968 . . . the American presidency has displayed conservative inclinations that are well to the right of what most members of Congress are willing to support. This development appears to contradict Kendall's understanding of how the electorate and its representatives manifest the political aspects of the traditional public orthodoxy." Francis noted that "congressional investigating committees were abolished in the 1970s, and it seems unlikely that they will be restored to perform their traditional functions."[82]

In 1988 John Alvis undertook a close examination of how well Congress lives up to Kendall's theories. Alvis, a professor of literature at the University of Dallas, is in many respects sympathetic to Kendall. But there are indications throughout his essay that he takes a more sanguine view of executive power than did Kendall. He speculates, for example, that the president may indeed, at times, possess a national mandate.

"One has to wonder," Alvis writes, "whether Kendall gave due weight to those three or four presidential elections that did seem to set the course of national policy for generations and which did so by elevating one political party decisively over the others precisely because that party recaptured the founding principles of equality and liberty." That aside, however, Alvis holds that "Kendall could hardly be pleased with the present Congress," not only because "it is certainly true that Congress is now more liberal than the president" but also for several institutional reasons: Congress no longer deliberates openly about controversial issues such as abortion and affirmative action, preferring to leave them to the courts; the proliferation of congressional staffers and executive agencies has given representatives a more administrative, and less deliberative, role than in the past; and congressional districts may now be so large as to make the small-scale electoral deliberation that Kendall described impossible.[83]

Alvis suggests the solution to these problems in the form of a question: "Can these changes be offset by a President more determined than Reagan has been to restore deliberative virtue to Congress?" His conclusion leaves no doubt about his answer: "If Kendall's ideal of democratic responsibility can still guide us, it must guide us in electing presidents who will force congressmen to govern by lawmaking rather than by inquisition, private pressure, or *ex parte* negotiation" with executive agencies.[84]

Kendall's faith in the legislative branch may have derived from a latent premise: namely, the Congress would continue to be more conservative, or more in line with Kendall's own views, than the executive branch. As the remarks of Wolfe, Francis, and Alvis suggest, a case can be made that Kendall, confronted with Congress's drift to the Left during the Nixon, Carter, and Reagan years (and again since 2006), might have felt compelled to reassess his belief in legislative supremacy. But at least as strong a case can be made that Kendall's constitutional theory is fundamentally correct regardless of whether Congress or the president is more "conservative" at a particular time.

The degradation or absence of legislative deliberation to which Alvis called attention surely would have dismayed Kendall. Yet it is hard to imagine him embracing Alvis's solution. Kendall, after all, not only argued in favor of the virtues of Congress but also was alert to the dangers of executive aggrandizement carried out in the name of high moral purpose. He warned of "a future made up of an endless series of Abraham Lincolns, each persuaded that he is superior in wisdom and virtue to the Fathers, each prepared to insist that those who oppose this or that new application of the equality standard are denying the possibility of self-government.[85]

In the closing chapter of *Basic Symbols*, "Derailment and the Modern Crisis"—a chapter revised by Carey but based on Kendall's fifth, supplemental Vanderbilt lecture—Kendall describes presidentialism as a species of utopianism, a manifestation of the belief that "God does not exist, but the American people are still the chosen people who must . . . build the Promised Land on earth."

> According to this myth, our national genius expresses itself not so much in the Constitution and *The Federalist*, but in an apostolic succession of great leaders: George Washington, Thomas Jefferson, Abraham Lincoln, Roosevelts I and II, and John Kennedy, each of whom sees more deeply than the preceding leader into the specifically American problem, which is posed by the "all men are created equal" clause of the Declaration of Independence. America will build a New Jerusalem which will be a commonwealth of free and equal men. If all of this requires remaking human nature, making the unequal to be equal— well, no job is too big for the self-chosen people if it knows its destiny and is determined to achieve it.[86]

Nor is the hubris of this vision mitigated by adding a religious component. In fact, for Kendall, a divinized sense of an American mission in the world represents an even "more important derailment" of the founders' tradition. In this scenario, "God has appointed America, not as the suffering servant of mankind, but as the arbiter of mankind, the supreme judge of all people, with a special insight into Divine Providence that no other people can match. . . . In due course . . . we, God's own people, can get down to our proper business, which is building the New Jerusalem and spreading it over the face of the entire earth."[87]

Kendall was not only an advocate of legislative supremacy but also a keen critic of executive power. However disillusioned he might be, if he were alive today and saw the present condition of Congress, there is every reason to believe he would continue to admonish conservatives against aligning themselves with presidential power. Indeed, he was inclined to support the legislature even at its least "conservative"—for example, in its pork-barrel spending and trade protectionism—against the executive's claims to represent a more enlightened, unselfish conception of the national interest.[88] Kendall would not have looked with favor on conservatives' newfound commitment to presidents with "the vision thing," who seek to lead the country and the world into a more open and liberated future.

Notes

1. According to Burnham, "Political freedom is the resultant of unresolved conflicts among various sections of the élite. . . . The future of liberty will, therefore, depend upon the extent to which, whether by necessary accident or conscious design, society is kept from freezing." See James Burnham, *The Machiavellians: Defenders of Freedom* (Chicago: Henry Regnery, 1970), 287. For postwar conservatism as "A Revolt against the Masses," see George H. Nash, *The Conservative Intellectual Movement in America: Since 1945* (Wilmington, Del.: ISI Books, 2006), 51–83.

2. Francis G. Wilson, "The Political Science of Willmoore Kendall," *Modern Age* (winter 1972): 38.

3. Dwight Macdonald, reviewing the first issue of *National Review*, characterized Kendall as "a wild Yale don of extreme, eccentric and very abstract views who can get a discussion into the shouting stage faster than anybody I have ever known." Dwight Macdonald, *Memoirs of a Revolutionist* (New York: Farrar, Straus and Cudahy, 1957), 333.

4. George H. Nash, "The Place of Willmoore Kendall in American Conservatism," in *Willmoore Kendall: Maverick of American Conservatives*, ed. John E. Alvis and John A. Murley (Lanham, Md.: Lexington Books, 2002), 12.

5. Jeffrey Hart, "Willmoore Kendall: American," in *Willmoore Kendall Contra Mundum*, ed. Nellie D. Kendall (New Rochelle, N.Y.: Arlington House, 1971), 9.

6. Letter from Leo Strauss to Willmoore Kendall, May 14, 1961, in *Willmoore Kendall: Maverick*, 237.

7. Murray Rothbard, "Report to Volcker Fund, Sept. 1956." 6. I am indebted to David Gordon of the Ludwig von Mises Institute for providing me with a copy of the unpublished manuscript.

8. Nash, "Place of Willmoore Kendall," 3–15.

9. George Carey, "How to Read Willmoore Kendall," *Intercollegiate Review* (winter–spring 1972): 63.

10. The story was published most recently in Saul Bellow, *Collected Stories* (New York: Penguin Books, 2001), 355–73.

11. For Kendall's background, see George H. Nash, "Willmoore Kendall: Conservative Iconoclast (I)," *Modern Age* (spring 1975): 127–35, and George

H. Nash, "Willmoore Kendall: Conservative Iconoclast (II)," *Modern Age* (summer 1975): 236–48.

12. Letter from Willmoore Kendall to Leo Strauss, August 29, 1960, in *Willmoore Kendall: Maverick*, 228.

13. George Carey, "Prologue," in *Oxford Years: The Letters of Willmoore Kendall to His Father*, ed. Yvona Kendall Mason (Bryn Mawr, Pa.: Intercollegiate Studies Institute, 1993), xx.

14. Nash, *Conservative Intellectual Movement*, 353.

15. For the dating of the *Second Treatise*, see Peter Laslett, "Introduction," in *Two Treatises of Government* by John Locke (Cambridge: Cambridge University Press, 2004), 123–26.

16. For Kendall's reflections on the reception of *John Locke and the Doctrine of Majority-Rule*, see Willmoore Kendall, "John Locke Revisited," in *Willmoore Kendall Contra Mundum*, 418–48.

17. Willmoore Kendall, *John Locke and the Doctrine of Majority-Rule* (Urbana: University of Illinois Press, 1965), 57–58.

18. Ibid., 53.

19. Kendall, "John Locke Revisited," 423.

20. Kendall, *John Locke and the Doctrine*, 58, 67 (emphasis in original).

21. Ibid., 70–72.

22. Ibid., 90.

23. Ibid., 106.

24. Ibid., 113.

25. Ibid., 117, 131.

26. Ibid., 133, 134.

27. Kendall, "John Locke Revisited," 418–48.

28. Ibid., 422.

29. Nash, "Willmoore Kendall: Conservative Iconoclast (I)," 128.

30. George Carey, "Epilogue," in *Oxford Years*, 513.

31. Garry Wills, *Confessions of a Conservative* (Garden City, NY: Doubleday, 1979), 21. Kendall had taken an interest in Catholicism during his time in Spain and would convert in 1956. See Nash, "Willmoore Kendall: Conservative Iconoclast (I)," 132.

32. Wills, *Confessions*, 22.

33. William F. Buckley Jr., "Foreword," in *Willmoore Kendall: Maverick*, ix.

34. For Kendall's relations with his colleagues at *National Review*, see Hart, "Willmoore Kendall: American," 10, and Jeffrey Hart, "Willmoore Kendall: The Unassimilable Man," *National Review*, December 31, 1985, http://findarticles.com/p/articles/mi_m1282/is_v37/ai_4074623.

35. Hart, "Willmoore Kendall: The Unassimilable Man."

36. Mason, ed., *Oxford Years*, 451.

37. Willmoore Kendall, "The People versus Socrates Revisited," in *Willmoore Kendall Contra Mundum*, 149–67.

38. Willmoore Kendall, "The Two Majorities," in *Willmoore Kendall Contra Mundum*, 202–27.

39. Willmoore Kendall, *The Conservative Affirmation in America* (Chicago: Gateway Editions, 1985), xxv.

40. Ibid., xxv–xxvi.

41. Ibid., xxvii.

42. Ibid., xxviii.

43. Ibid., 16–17.

44. Ibid., 44.

45. Ibid., 44–45.

46. Ibid., 45.

47. Ibid., 47.

48. Ibid., 27.

49. Ibid., 76.

50. Nash, "Willmoore Kendall: Conservative Iconoclast (I)," 132.

51. Kendall, *Conservative Affirmation*, 88.

52. Ibid., 98.

53. Ibid., 99.

54. Nash, "Place of Willmoore Kendall," 3.

55. Henry Regnery, *Memoirs of a Dissident Publisher* (New York: Harcourt Brace Jovanovich, 1979), 188.

56. Ibid, 185–86. In a letter that Regnery reproduces, Kendall writes that his book will cover "the Old Sage of Mecosta, the Pseudo-Sage of Ithaca, the Rubbed Sage of Woodstock, the Young Sage of Stamford, the Muscleminded Sage of Kent, and the Nascent Sage of Indianapolis." These sages correspond, respectively, to Russell Kirk, Clinton Rossiter, Frank Meyer, William F. Buckley Jr., James Burnham, and M. Stanton Evans.

57. Willmoore Kendall, "The Benevolent Sage of Mecosta," in *Willmoore Kendall Contra Mundum*, 29–57.

58. Nash, "Place of Willmoore Kendall," 9.

59. Ibid., 7.

60. *Willmoore Kendall: Maverick of American Conservatives*, for example, contains several scholarly essays on Kendall by "Straussians," including contributions from George Anastaplo and Leo Paul de Alvarez. The volume also contains the collected Kendall-Strauss correspondence.

61. Harry V. Jaffa, "Willmoore Kendall: Philosopher of Consensus?" in *American Conservatism and the American Founding* (Durham, N.C.: Carolina Academic Press, 1984), 198.

62. Reid Buckley, *The Future of American Culture* (Camden, S.C.: Peor Es Nada Press, 2006), 21.

63. Carey, "Epilogue," 514.

64. John B. Judis, *William F. Buckley, Jr.: Patron Saint of the Conservatives* (New York: Simon and Schuster, 1988), 212.

65. The review is reproduced in Kendall, *Conservative Affirmation*, 184–87.

66. Willmoore Kendall, "How to Read Richard Weaver: Philosopher of 'We the (Virtuous) People,'" in *Willmoore Kendall Contra Mundum*, 386–402.

67. Willmoore Kendall, "Jefferson and Civil Liberties: The Darker Side," in *Willmoore Kendall Contra Mundum*, 290–302.

68. Willmoore Kendall, "The Bill of Rights and American Freedom," in *Willmoore Kendall Contra Mundum*, 303–25.

69. Willmoore Kendall and George W. Carey, "How to Read *The Federalist*," in *Willmoore Kendall Contra Mundum*, 403–17.

70. Willmoore Kendall, "Introduction: How to Read Rousseau's *Government of Poland*," in *The Government of Poland* by Jean-Jacques Rousseau, trans. Willmoore Kendall (Indianapolis: Hackett Publishing, 1985), xix, xxvi.

71. Ibid., xxvi, xxxi, xxxii.

72. Ibid., xxxix.

73. Nash, "Willmoore Kendall: Conservative Iconoclast (II)," 244.

74. Letter from Willmoore Kendall to Eric Voegelin, July 24, 1966, in "The Eric Voegelin–Willmoore Kendall Correspondence," ed. Steven D. Ealy and Gordon Lloyd, *Political Science Reviewer* (fall 2004): 401.

75. Hart, "Willmoore Kendall: American," 26.

76. George W. Carey and Willmoore Kendall, *The Basic Symbols of the American Political Tradition* (Baton Rouge: Louisiana State University Press, 1970), 18, 22.

77. Ibid., 71.

78. Ibid., 44.

79. Ibid., 73.

80. For an account of the American Right's turn toward presidentialism, see Gene Healy, *The Cult of the Presidency: America's Dangerous Devotion to Executive Power* (Washington, D.C.: Cato Institute, 2008), 118–22.

81. Gregory Wolfe, "Introduction," in Kendall, *Conservative Affirmation*, xviii.

82. Samuel Francis, "Prophet of the Heartland," in *Beautiful Losers: Essays on the Failure of American Conservatism* (Columbia: University of Missouri Press, 1993), 85.

83. John Alvis, "Willmoore Kendall and the Demise of Congressional Deliberation," *Intercollegiate Review* (spring 1988): 59–63.

84. Ibid., 65.

85. Kendall, *Conservative Affirmation*, 252.

86. Carey and Kendall, *Basic Symbols*, 153.

87. Ibid., 153–54.

88. Kendall, *Conservative Affirmation*, 22–23.

Bibliography

Alvis, John. 1988. "Willmoore Kendall and the Demise of Congressional Deliberation." *Intercollegiate Review* (spring): 57–66.

Alvis, John E., and John A. Murley, eds. 2002. *Willmoore Kendall: Maverick of American Conservatives*. Lanham, Md.: Lexington Books.

Bellow, Saul. 2001. "Mosby's Memoirs." In *Collected Stories*, 355–73. New York: Penguin Books.

Buckley, Reid. 2006. *The Future of American Culture*. Camden, S.C.: Peor Es Nada Press.

Buckley, William F. Jr. 2002. "Foreword." In *Willmoore Kendall: Maverick of American Conservatives*. Edited by John E. Alvis and John A. Murley, ix–xxii. Lanham, Md.: Lexington Books.

Burnham, James. 1970. *The Machiavellians: Defenders of Freedom*. 2nd ed. Chicago: Henry Regnery.

Carey, George. 1972. "How to Read Willmoore Kendall." *Intercollegiate Review* (winter–spring): 63–65.

———. 1993. "Epilogue." In *Oxford Years: The Letters of Willmoore Kendall to His Father*. Edited by Yvona Kendall Mason, 510–19. Bryn Mawr, Pa.: Intercollegiate Studies Institute.

———. 1993. "Prologue." In *Oxford Years: The Letters of Willmoore Kendall to His Father*. Edited by Yvona Kendall Mason, xi–xxiv. Bryn Mawr, Pa.: Intercollegiate Studies Institute.

Carey, George W., and Willmoore Kendall. 1970. *The Basic Symbols of the American Political Tradition*. Baton Rouge: Louisiana State University Press.

Ealy, Steven D., and Gordon Lloyd, eds. 2004. "The Eric Voegelin–Willmoore Kendall Correspondence." *Political Science Reviewer* (fall): 357–412.

Francis, Samuel. 1993. *Beautiful Losers: Essays on the Failure of American Conservatism*. Columbia: University of Missouri Press.

Hart, Jeffrey. 1971. "Willmoore Kendall, American." In *Willmoore Kendall Contra Mundum*. Edited by Nellie D. Kendall, 9–26. New Rochelle, N.Y.: Arlington House.

———. 1985. "Willmoore Kendall: The Unassimilable Man." *National Review*, December 31. http://findarticles.com/p/articles/mi_m1282/is_v37/ai_4074623.

Healy, Gene. 2008. *The Cult of the Presidency: America's Dangerous Devotion to Executive Power*. Washington, D.C.: Cato Institute.

Jaffa, Harry V. 1984. "Willmoore Kendall: Philosopher of Consensus?" In *American Conservatism and the American Founding*, 192–201. Durham, N.C.: Carolina Academic Press.

Judis, John B. 1988. *William F. Buckley, Jr.: Patron Saint of the Conservatives*. New York: Simon and Schuster.

Kendall, Willmoore. 1965. *John Locke and the Doctrine of Majority-Rule.* Urbana: University of Illinois Press.

_____. 1971. *Willmoore Kendall Contra Mundum.* Edited by Nellie D. Kendall. New Rochelle, N.Y.: Arlington House.

_____. 1985. *The Conservative Affirmation in America.* Chicago: Gateway Editions.

_____. 1985. "Introduction: How to Read Rousseau's *Government of Poland.*" In *The Government of Poland,* by Jean-Jacques Rousseau. 2nd ed.. Translated by Willmoore Kendall. Indianapolis: Hackett Publishing.

_____. 2002. Willmoore Kendall–Leo Strauss Correspondence. In *Willmoore Kendall: Maverick of American Conservatives.* Edited by John E. Alvis and John A. Murley, 191–261. Lanham, Md.: Lexington Books.

Laslett, Peter. 2004. "Introduction." In *Two Treatises of Government,* by John Locke. Edited by Peter Laslett, 3–133. 16th printing. Cambridge: Cambridge University Press.

Macdonald, Dwight. 1957. *Memoirs of a Revolutionist.* New York: Farrar, Straus and Cudahy.

Mason, Yvona Kendall, ed. 1993. *Oxford Years: The Letters of Willmoore Kendall to His Father.* Bryn Mawr, Pa.: Intercollegiate Studies Institute.

Nash, George H. 1975. "Willmoore Kendall: Conservative Iconoclast (I)." *Modern Age* (spring): 127–35.

_____. 1975. "Willmoore Kendall: Conservative Iconoclast (II)." *Modern Age* (summer): 236–48.

_____. 2002. "The Place of Willmoore Kendall in American Conservatism." In *Willmoore Kendall: Maverick of American Conservatives.* Edited by John E. Alvis and John A. Murley, 3–15. Lanham, Md.: Lexington Books.

_____. 2006. *The Conservative Intellectual Movement in America: Since 1945.* 30th anniversary ed. Wilmington, Del.: ISI Books.

Regnery, Henry. 1979. *Memoirs of a Dissident Publisher.* New York: Harcourt Brace Jovanovich.

Rothbard, Murray. 1956. "Report to Volcker Fund, Sept. 1956." Unpublished manuscript in author's possession.

Wills, Garry. 1979. *Confessions of a Conservative.* Garden City, N.Y.: Doubleday.

Wilson, Francis G. 1972. "The Political Science of Willmoore Kendall." *Modern Age* (winter): 38–47.

Wolfe, Gregory. 1985. "Introduction." In *The Conservative Affirmation in America,* by Willmoore Kendall. Chicago: Gateway Editions.

Contributors

KENNETH L. DEUTSCH is professor of political science at SUNY Geneseo. In 2003 he was the recipient of the State University of New York Award for Scholarship and Research. He has published five books on political theory, the most recent a textbook entitled *An Invitation to Political Thought* (Cengage, 2008).

ETHAN FISHMAN is professor of political science at the University of South Alabama. Among his publications are *Likely Stories: Essays on Political Philosophy and Contemporary American Literature* (University of Florida Press, 1989) and *The Prudential Presidency: An Aristotelian Approach to Presidential Leadership* (Praeger, 2001). His essay "Not Compassionate, Not Conservative," which originally appeared in *The American Scholar*, was reprinted in *The Best American Political Writing of 2007* (Thunder's Mouth Press, 2007).

PETER AUGUSTINE LAWLER is Dana professor of government at Berry College. He was a member of President Bush's Council on Bioethics and is executive editor of *Perspectives on Political Science*. He has written or edited a dozen books, including *The Restless Mind: Alexis de Tocqueville on the Origin and Perpetuation of Liberty* (Rowman and Littlefield, 1993), *Postmodernism Rightly Understood* (Rowman and Littlefield, 1999), *Stuck with Virtue* (ISI Books, 2005), and *Homeless and at Home in America* (St. Augustine's Press, 2007). He was a recipient of the Richard M. Weaver Prize in Scholarly Letters.

DANIEL MCCARTHY is senior editor of *The American Conservative*.

ROBERT A. PRESTON was president of Belmont Abbey College from 1995 to 2001. After his retirement, he served as executive director of the Bradley Institute for the Study of Christian Culture, which he founded in 1996. He also served as executive director of the Ingersoll Prizes and oversaw the awarding of the Richard M. Weaver Prize for Scholarly Letters. His essay "Ideas Have Consequences Fifty Years Later" appeared in *Steps toward Restoration: The Consequences of Richard Weaver's Ideas* (ISI Books, 1998).

LINDA C. RAEDER is associate professor of political science at Palm Beach Atlantic University. She has been associate editor of *Humanitas*, published by the National Humanities Institute, since 1994. Her publications include *John Stuart Mill and the Religion of Humanity* (University of Missouri Press, 2002), as well as various book chapters and articles on the nature and development of the Anglo-American liberal tradition.

GERALD J. RUSSELLO is a fellow at the Chesterton Institute at Seton Hall University and editor of *The University Bookman*. He is the author of *The Postmodern Imagination of Russell Kirk* (University of Missouri Press, 2007) and editor of *Christianity and European Culture: Selections from the Work of Christopher Dawson* (Catholic University of America Press, 1998).

BRAD LOWELL STONE is professor of sociology and director of American studies at Oglethorpe University. He authored *Robert Nisbet: Communitarian Traditionalist* (ISI Publishers, 2001) and wrote the introduction to Nisbet's *Conservatism: Dream and Reality* (Transaction Publishers, 2002).

JAMES L. WISER is provost of the University of San Francisco. His scholarship focuses on classical Greek political philosophy and contemporary German political thought. He is the author of *Political Philosophy: A History of the Search for Order* (Prentice-Hall, 1983) and *Political Theory: A Thematic Inquiry* (Wadsworth, 1986) and the editor of *Eric Voegelin, History of Political Ideas*, volume 5, *Religion and the Rise of Modernity* (University of Missouri Press, 1998).

Index

CPSIA information can be obtained at www.ICGtesting.com
Printed in the USA
LVOW060259281211

261286LV00002B/7/P